# The Goc
# and Philosophy

# Pop Culture and Philosophy®

General Editor: George A. Reisch

**For full details of all Pop Culture and Philosophy® books, and all Open Universe® books, visit www.carusbooks.com**

Pop Culture and Philosophy®

# The Godfather and Philosophy

*An Argument You Can't Refute*

Edited by

JOSHUA HETER AND RICHARD GREENE

OPEN UNIVERSE
Chicago

Volume 11 in the series, Pop Culture and Philosophy®, Series Editor George A. Reisch

To find out more about Open Universe and Carus Books, visit our website at www.carusbooks.com.

*The Godfather and Philosophy: An Argument You Can't Refute*

ISBN: 978-1-63770-037-2

This book is also available as an e-book (978-1-63770-038-9).

Library of Congress Control Number: 2022945083

# Contents

# Thanks

Working on this project has been a pleasure, in no small part because of the many fine folks who have assisted us along the way. In particular, a debt of gratitude is owed to David Ramsay Steele at Carus Books, the contributors to this volume, the School of Humanities at Jefferson College and the Department of Political Science and Philosophy at Weber State University. Finally, we'd like to thank those family members, students, friends, and colleagues with whom we've had fruitful and rewarding conversations on various aspects of all things *Godfather* as it relates to philosophical themes.

# Words of Wisdom from *The Godfather*

*The* Godfather (the 1969 novel) was born out of a piece of advice so well known that it has long since been branded a cliché: *write what you know!*

As legend has it, sometime during the late 1960s, Mario Puzo was brainstorming his next big project. Though the struggling author had been published in a number of different venues, he was deeply in debt and hadn't yet penned a work that would allow him to truly break through. It was at this point that his agent gave him that simple but fateful advice: write what you know.

Having grown up in Hell's Kitchen just after World War II among a number of figures who weren't entirely dissimilar from characters who would appear in *The Godfather*, Puzo set out to write the great American organized crime novel. What he created would not only be one of the bestselling books of all time but would lead to three beloved and acclaimed films as well as a handful of subsequent novels and even a few video games. And, as fans of popular culture know, Puzo's creation has been the object of parody and homage as much as any other work of modern storytelling.

Indeed, the Corleone family and the universe they inhabit have captured the attention of fans the world over for the better part of two generations. And of course, this is due in large part to the fact that the *Godfather* franchise isn't *really* (or at least isn't primarily) a story about the Mafia. It's a story about America, capitalism, and the immigrant experience. And ultimately, it's a story about family.

It was that same, simple advice which led Puzo to write *The Godfather* that led to the creation of this book. If they know anything, the talented collection of authors whose work comprises this book (and the all too fortunate editors who were able to bring them together) know philosophy and they know *The Godfather*. As you might imagine, when they haven't been studying, teaching, or composing philosophy, they've spent *at least* their fair share of time poring over *The Godfather* in all its forms.

It should then be of little surprise that the depths of Puzo's storytelling raise a number of interesting philosophical questions addressed by these philosophically minded *Godfather* fans here in these pages. What is the difference between an organized crime family and traditional governmental authorities? Does Michael deserve forgiveness for his sins? Is it worse to kill your brother than another person? How would an expert in political maneuvering like Machiavelli grade the Don's leadership? Is Vito Corleone a just man? What (in the underworld or anywhere else) *is* justice? With these and a number of other fascinating questions in mind, the marriage between *The Godfather* and philosophy, one could argue, is worthy of the most elaborate Sicilian wedding.

As Puzo was writing his soon to be cherished novel at his Long Island home, it's alleged that he'd occasionally scold his children when they got a little too noisy and disruptive. "Quiet!" he would shout from the basement, "I'm writing a bestseller!" Is it reasonable to expect that the book you're now reading will have a similar cultural impact, one akin to that of *The Godfather*?

That's a pretty tall order. However, if you continue on and read even a handful of chapters, at the very least we're confident that you'll be led to think deeply, to appreciate Puzo's world more fully, and to understand the story on a newly profound level. Hopefully, that's an offer you can't refuse.

# I

---

## "Yeah, let's talk business."

# 1
# Michael the Hegedon

COLIN J. LEWIS

Michael Corleone: son, war hero, husband, father and, most notably, Mafia don—but what sort of crime boss *is* Michael? This isn't just a question about whether he's talented (of that, there's no doubt), but about his character and style as a leader.

It's a question that Michael even asks himself, pondering why it was that his father, Vito, was beloved and respected while he is feared and reviled, despite serving in the same role. The same question could very well be posed to leaders in general: why is it that some folks have an obvious knack for being in charge, while others either have to force their way or simply fall apart at the seams?

In seeking answers to this question, we find a peculiar parallel between the leadership styles of Vito and Michael, and the three kinds of ruler described by an early Confucian scholar called Xunzi: the sage, the hegemon, and the tyrant. The sage rules benevolently—they care for the masses. The tyrant rules brutally (if they rule at all)—they care about personal gain. In between, though, is the hegemon. The hegemon might, unlike the tyrant, have the best interests of the realm at heart but lacks the ease and attunement of the sage.

It's Xunzi's hegemon that best describes Michael Corleone, and thinking about Michael as a hegemon helps to explain both his successes and failures as don of the Corleone family. The saga of Michael the hegemon also shows us how such pragmatic 'wartime' leadership lacks perpetual stability: it's great in certain circumstances, but it can't serve as an ideal model of governance.

## Xunzi's Three Kings

Among the different qualities of ruler, Xunzi describes three types—the sage, the tyrant, and the hegemon. Ideally, you want a sagely ruler for obvious reasons: the sage sees their state like a family, and every member of the family is deserving of compassion and respect. Consequently, as the sage establishes their government, they do so with eyes and ears toward what's going to facilitate, maintain, and enhance that compassion and respect, spreading it throughout the realm and helping the people to harmonize with one another.

This also means that the sage has to a. be attuned to things like the cultural and creedal norms and practices that hold societies together, or b. establish these norms and practices for just such purposes. These are like rules of the house and family traditions: they aren't really laws, and they aren't inflexible, but they do help to cultivate a sense of stability and belonging, as well as help members of the family identify as such and even forge their own, individual identities. It's why folks like Peter Clemenza don't just relate to Vito as employees or subjects, but as genuine friends and family (or at least family-adjacent). With that, you get loyalty, kindness, and all that jazz. More importantly, you're also building a community of like-minded (or at least like-valuing) people, and it's this sense of community, and not merely any singular personality or outlook on rules, that binds the people together. When things are run this way, the community tends to hold together, even in the face of adversity (be it mass flooding in ancient China or an assassination attempt on your family's don).

In stark contrast to the sage, there's the tyrant. These guys are nasty pieces of work: at best, they're incompetent rubes; at worst, they're malicious mongers of power and wealth. An infamous tyrant from China's history was the last ruler of the Shang Dynasty, a guy called Zhou. Zhou was known for taxing his subjects into poverty while hoarding mass wealth for himself. Rather than attend court, he'd spend his time cavorting around his many palaces, some of which were said to be filled with lakes of wine and forests of meat, all while enjoying orgies with beautiful young folks. Oh, and then there was the torture: Zhou was so fond of torturing those who displeased him that he even supposedly invented some new methods, the most famous being the "burning pillar," where the victim was forced to walk on a burning hot beam covered with oil until they, inevitably, fell into the fires below. Real stand-up guy, right?

Don Fanuci, while not as bad as Tyrant Zhou, is still a great example of tyrannical rule in the context of the Corleone saga:

he runs his protection racket throughout the borough, exploiting and harming his own community in the process, all while maintaining the illusion of being an influential and respected member of the community. This is apt, if you understand "influential" to mean "oppressive" and "respected" to mean "feared." Perhaps unsurprisingly, tyrants (and their domains) tend to meet rather horrible ends: Zhou is deposed and Fanuci is assassinated (by none other than Vito himself), and their clans are effectively disassembled in the aftermath.

Finally, there is the hegemon. The hegemon is in a weird space between the sage and the tyrant. Presumably, like the sage, the hegemon actually wants what's best for the realm: they *want* things to go well, and they *want* the people to have nice, orderly lives. Unfortunately, the hegemon isn't as talented or attuned as the sage, lacking the character, charisma, or general cultural knack that the sage has to build and maintain a realm or family; the hegemon can't rely on their own virtuosity. What's a guy to do?

Well, according to Xunzi, it's for this reason that the hegemon has to rely more on things like laws and punishments, and strategies and logistics, to both clarify their authority and establish some form of trust within the community. Here's where things start to get shaky: while having the people trust you might sound like a solid plan, Xunzi warns that this approach to governance isn't without its shortcomings, since a. that trust has to be constantly maintained, and b. you have to rely on those in your employ to be equally trustworthy. All well and good if the members of your family are as loyal as Luca Brasi, but if their faith in your leadership can be shaken, as with a Sal Tessio type, then you'll have to go back to the drawing board and refine your tactics for holding things together.

This is why the hegemon just can't match up to the sage: the sage, with their cultivation and attunement, creates a community that inculcates and self-maintains certain perspectives and values that are shared and appreciated among its members; the hegemon relies more on a combination of cult of personality and carefully designed stratagems to either win people to their side by impressing them or keep them in line by efficient, if legalistic, methods.

## Michael the Hegemon

It's arguable that it is in this last category in which our dear Michael Corleone falls. Over the course of *The Godfather* movie trilogy, we're treated to the myriad rises and falls, triumphs and betrayals, marriages and assassinations of the Corleone family under Michael's leadership. Beginning with his acts of vengeance against the other Five Families of New York and expansion of his own family (including snuffing out Moe Greene), Michael is often faced with the predicament of maintaining the reputation and practices of his father, while also adapting the projects and methods of the family so as to maintain power in a rapidly changing world.

Michael's predicament is made clear in the second movie, when he questions why it is that his father was beloved and respected while he is feared and reviled, despite serving in the same role and, presumably, acting in the best interests of the family.

What Michael seems to not understand is that keeping a family together isn't just about *what* you do or *why* you do it, but also *how*. It's the *how* that influences whether you end up with a harmonious family or a merely orderly one. Consider how Michael's ascent to donhood differs from Vito's: in flashbacks, we see that Vito's high standing sprang from his family-oriented sensibilities that extended into his general community. Vito was not a crime boss seeking power, but rather a member of the community willing to do his best to help solve its problems. For his services (and they are genuine services, not mere virtue signaling like Fanuci), we often see Vito asking nothing in return but, nonetheless, being gifted material goods and garnering the respect and friendship of his neighbors. Vito's power is homegrown: it is both earned and expressed by his actions and commitments—he is *made* a don in the public eye, and the ethos that he adopts himself spreads among his constituents.

Michael, by contrast, inherits his position and power (albeit reluctantly), and against his father's initial intentions. In many ways, and despite Vito's attempts to rectify his own shortcomings as a mentor, Michael enters this role unprepared, only partially initiated into the family business and without the respect and friendships his father had garnered over many years. Consequently, Michael must often rely on blunter means of maintaining order even within his own family, lacking Vito's harmonious ease. Beginning with the roughly curated assassination of Virgil Sollozzo and Mark McCluskey to initiate war among the Five Families, and followed some years after by his reorganization of the Corleone family's business structure (both criminal and legitimate), Michael works to not only resecure power for the Corleone's, but also to maintain the faith of their allies.

This is by no means an easy transition of power: Michael's ability is questioned by Clemenza, and he is betrayed by multiple members and allies of his organization, notably Tessio, Pentangeli, and Don Altobello; even Fredo betrays the family under Michael's (admittedly imperfect) eye! All of this, of course, occurs during Michael's bid to modernize the Corleone family's methods and, ultimately, turn it into a legitimate business enterprise. This bid only partly succeeds: while Michael is able to convert the Corleone family's business interests into (largely) legitimate ones over a period of many years, he is never able to *fully* relinquish his status as a crime boss, despite accumulating extraordinary wealth and influence for both himself and his allies.

Michael remains the target of multiple attempts against his life and his businesses, and his (often lethal) responses to such attempts serve to alienate him from his actual family: his surviving siblings resent him, his spouse and children leave him, and he is ultimately left isolated aside from his professional associations. Granted, these associates often come to respect (or at least fear) Michael's ability, and increasingly place their trust in his cunning leadership, but Michael eventually does lose his core, his family. Alas! Such is the potential fate of Xunzi's hegemon.

## Pros and Cons

Before you take this as a blanket condemnation of Michael's leadership, understand that the hegemon, for all their shortcomings, is by no means an inept leader, and there might even be situations where the way of the hegemon is (at least practically) preferable to the way of the sage . . . well, at least when the sage isn't available, which is probably most of the time. See, it's really hard to find someone who's actually culturally attuned and a brilliant, sagelike leader all the time—Vito, for all his skill, had his pitfalls and blind spots. Even if you could become a sage, it's not as if it's an instantaneous or overnight process: if Xunzi's right, it takes loads and loads of training and, while anyone could *potentially* reach sagehood, it's unlikely that most will get there. Given this pragmatic reality, it's reasonable to turn to the hegemon for leadership and guidance when there's no sage around to bring the world to order. Why? Three reasons: strategy, unity, and trustworthiness.

First, the hegemon, while not necessarily the most benevolent of rulers, is at least a canny one when it comes to things like warfare and geopolitics: they understand and value keep-

ing their community intact, and they know how to read both
their own people as well as others when it comes to determining state policy. In particular, Xunzi suggests that the hegemon
is a solid wartime leader, since they're able to recognize things
like when troops are exhausted or rallied, when an enemy is
preparing to strike, and how to counteract attacks accordingly.
As a result, even when the hegemon cannot transform the
realm with their virtuosity, they can still preserve their state
because they understand strategy.

In this aspect, Michael is largely successful as don of the
Corleone family both financially and in terms of maintaining
influence. Over the years, he bolsters the Corleone family's cof-
fers while also eliminating both actual and potential threats to
the family: he takes revenge on the Five Families of New York
and relocates to Lake Tahoe; he eliminates the treacherous
Hyman Roth while securing the family's business interests
against congressional investigations; he counters the machina-
tions of Altobello and Lucchesi and (more or less) secures
the Corleone legacy. Michael's tactics are imperfect, but he
gets the job done—he protects his family and maintains the
order within.

Maintaining the internal structure of the family brings us
to the second desirable aspect of the hegemon: they provide
unity, order. For all of his transgressions, Michael always puts
(some form of) family first in his decision making. Sure, the
assassination of Carlo Rizzi upends any possibility for Connie
to provide her children with at least the illusion of a stable,
two-parent home, but eliminating Carlo was also arguably necessary for Michael to enact vengeance on behalf of his brother,
Santino, to free Connie from an abusive spouse, and to preserve
the business. Connie is quite reasonably upset by Michael's
decision, cursing him and even attempting to reveal the extent
of his criminal activity to Michael's wife, Kay, but Connie and
Michael ultimately reconcile during the events of the second
movie:

> Michael, I hated you for so many years. I think that I did things to
> myself, to hurt myself so that you'd know—that I could hurt you. You
> were just being strong for all of us the way Papa was. And I forgive
> you . . . You need me, Michael. I want to take care of you now.
> (2:54:30–2:55:20)

Connie keeps coming back because Michael, like Vito before
him, is foremost a provider for his family. His decisions may not
always be to everyone's pleasure, and they might not always be
the best calculated, but he always strives to act in the interest

of the family. That alone makes him consistent, makes him a unifying and stabilizing force in a world fraught with chaos. It's why Tom Hagen, even when offered an out during the congressional investigation of the Corleone family, affirms his loyalty and continues to support Michael as *consigliere*: Michael might not be the greatest leader in the history of organized crime, but he is a dedicated one, and that dedication's something to rally around.

This leads us to the final feature of the hegemon: a leader who is first and foremost trustworthy, and aims to employ trustworthy vassals (or, in Michael's case, *capos*). In working to unify the Corleone family, Michael consistently makes good on his word to his allies, in no small part as a means of establishing and maintaining their fealty. Michael's relationship with Tom is exemplary of this reciprocal loyalty: although Tom started under Vito, and despite not being Sicilian himself, he was one of the few members of Vito's old regime who didn't hesitate to embrace Michael as new head of the family and serve him faithfully over the course of his life. Michael, in turn, both worked to protect Tom from liability and entrusted him with authority and influence in the family when he could not provide direct leadership himself. Similar loyalties develop between Michael and his *caporegimes* Al Neri and Rocco Lampone (the former eventually becoming underboss and the latter sacrificing himself to assassinate Hyman Roth).

Perhaps more interesting than the successful displays of loyalty, however, is one of the more complicated ones: Frank Pentangeli. Pentangeli, who served first under Vito, is introduced to theatrical audiences as being in conflict with Michael (despite Michael having previously entrusted him with family operations in New York). Although Michael indicates that he has plans to secure Pentangeli's position in New York following his dealings with Roth, Pentangeli is effectively duped into turning state's evidence against Michael following an assassination attempt misattributed to Michael. Although Pentangeli ultimately recants his testimony, leaving Michael's accusers with insufficient evidence to convict him of any crimes, Pentangeli was aware that his initial betrayal could not go unpunished. It's here that Pentangeli's loyalty shines: with Tom (as Michael's proxy) promising that Pentangeli's family would remain protected, Pentangeli subtly assents to, and follows through on, committing suicide in recompense for his transgressions and to ensure the Corleone family's continued protection. In the end, Frankie Five Angels' commitment really

does come through, in no small part from trusting that Michael
will hold up his end of the bargain. Trust is foundational to
these sorts of relationships, business practices, and modes of
governance. This is the way of the hegemon.

Again, none of this is to say that Michael's leadership style
is ideal. He *does* deal with inter- and intra-organizational complications time and time again, and his actual family life functionally dissolves over the course of the saga. We could also
ponder whether, had Michael been less impulsive and vengeful
over the course of his reign, he might have been able to cultivate the same levels of friendship, respect, and communality
that were hallmarks of (at least the early years of) Vito's time
as don. Had Michael been more attuned to the community (and
family) within which he was operating, had he been more sensitive to that ethos, perhaps he could have avoided some of the
bloodshed and retained the affection and stability of his siblings, spouse, and children.

This we cannot do—the variables here are too many, and so
it's better to focus on the story we receive from Puzo and
Coppola. Thinking too much about the 'what-ifs' also risks
ignoring just how successful the hegemonic style of leadership
employed by Michael *can* be, especially in times of conflict and
when genuine sages are absent. It parallels our own political
realities: given the choice between tyrants and hegemons,
given the relative lack of political sages, how much better off
we are when we endorse the hegemon over the tyrant!

The hegemon is by no means a genius, but they do a. value
the interests of the state, b. strive to lead in a trustworthy manner, and c. demonstrate genuine competence when it comes to
actually running the state/community/family/organized crime
syndicate. Contrast this with the way in which contemporary
politics are often conducted: when you have political authorities who are willing to sacrifice the interest of the state for personal interest, then only the authorities and their favored few
will benefit, and all at the expense of those who are under their
protection. When this happens, the authorities risk either losing their position (by being voted out or by coup, depending on
the nature of the state), or outright destabilizing the state (losing their family). It's for these reasons that hegemony cannot
be easily dismissed as a path to success: the road may be long
and violent, as it is for Michael, but it is a road we can travel
with a clear destination. The remaining question for us is the
one that Michael must consider throughout his tenure as don:
what exactly are we willing to sacrifice for the sake of family,
and might that include family itself?

## Faltering Families

While watching Michael's reign, we come to see how such pragmatic, 'wartime' leadership lacks perpetual stability across all circumstances: approaching our relationships (be they personal, professional, or geopolitical) as matters of competition or conquest, rather than as cooperation or camaraderie, we place ourselves in circumstances that promote tenuous alliances or loyalties of convenience *at best*. Such leadership styles fail to promote a sociopolitical culture of mutual benevolence among the governors and governed. Consequently, faith in the leadership, and loyalty of the followers, are all predicated solely on power dynamics: when the hegemon is strong and capable of preserving the state, the constituents may be placated and go along with their ruler. The second that stability fizzles out, though, the people are much more likely to turn on them.

The same problems apply to modern states as much as they do mafiosos. Need an example from recent history? Look no further than when a GOP-dominated US, including both its state military *and* private contractors, engaged in an unjustified war in Iraq. This collection of military and paramilitary operations, while financially and politically lucrative to select economic and political elites, was wildly destructive not only to human life and infrastructure on all sides, but also woefully weakened the US's reputation and set the stage for even more infighting and insurrection that we experience to this day. Far from bringing about peace and stability, the pursuit of war and hegemony weakened not only the US, but possibly the entire human community.

Now, as we see in the contrast between Vito and Michael, a crime family cannot sustain itself solely on constant conflict with others, no matter how materially beneficial—a sociopolitical culture is also necessary to ensure stability and harmony among members of the family. Criminal or otherwise, every country is made up of families, and if hegemony can't sustain a single family, then it sure as hell won't work for an entire country.

# 2
# Betrayal and Forgiveness in *The Godfather*

Timothy M. Kwiatek

The *Godfather* movies are a study of loyalty and betrayal, of revenge and forgiveness. It's easy to watch them and suppose that this whole system is just an arbitrary exercise of power. But is there a principled practice in the background here? What makes for a betrayal? What is the power of betrayal? Who is implicated in betrayal and what can be done to them? And what is it to forgive a betrayal?

At least in the world of *The Godfather*, betrayal, snitching, or otherwise being a rat seems to have its own nature and set of norms. You have to be in a particular position to betray someone. And there seems to be a difference between betrayals that involve cooperating with the law, and betrayals among members of the Mafia. These betrayals can be more or less forgivable. They can implicate only the betrayer, or their whole family. And they can be more or less sensitive to considerations which might reduce the harshness of the retaliation. We can see in the movies that there is an understanding—sometimes spoken, sometimes unspoken—that there will be adverse consequences for betrayals of any kind.

## Fredo and Frankie

Betrayal has the power to changes relationship dynamics. If I remain loyal to you, my fellow mobster, you would be unjustified in harming me. And further, I have grounds for complaint if you harm me or threaten to harm me. Recall when Michael threatens to report Tom's extramarital affair to his wife, Tom asks, "Why do you hurt me, Michael? I've always been loyal to you." However, if I betray you, whatever that means, you have a new permission that you didn't have before.

Where it would have been impermissible for you to retaliate, now you're permitted, maybe even required, to retaliate. In
some ways these aren't all that different from the norms
around blame. If you knowingly blab my secrets to my enemies,
I'm now permitted to be upset with you in a way that would
have been inappropriate had you kept mum. Maybe I can get
angry at you, or stop talking to you. It's the same in *The
Godfather*, except if I blab your secrets, you might be able to
kill me in response.

Consider two contrasting cases: Fredo Corleone and
Frankie Pentangeli. Fredo relays information about Michael
to his enemies. This results in an attempt on Michael's life.
Michael discovers it was Fredo, but still offers to help him get
out of Cuba as the government is being overthrown and chaos
abounds. Fredo declines. In one last conversation, Fredo explains that he didn't know it was going to result in the attempt
on Michael's life. Michael asks him once more if there is anything he can do to help, and to his credit, Fredo supplies information. Fredo is then completely cut out of Michael's life and
ultimately Michael has him killed. Michael exercises a certain
restraint, not wanting their mother to suffer. So, he doesn't
have Fredo killed until after she dies. Even then, he has it done
secretly so it looks like he wasn't involved.

Frankie Pentangeli talks to the FBI. He gives them information about the Corleone family, implicating Michael in particular. He does this after being led to believe Michael
attempted to have him killed. Later, at the trial where he is to
testify and faced with the distraught look of his brother from
the old country, Frankie recants his testimony and perjures
himself, thus protecting Michael. This helps him regain a certain standing and retain the Pentangeli family's honor. While
he is still expected to kill himself after his betrayal, doing so
redeemed him enough that his family is protected.

Looking at these two instances as examples of the same
kind of thing raises some questions. If Pentangeli's family
would have been implicated, why weren't all the Corleone's
implicated in Fredo's betrayal? Why was there no threat to the
Corleone's honor? The answer, I suggest, is because Fredo and
Frankie performed importantly different actions. Let's distinguish *betrayal* from *snitching*.

## Betrayal

Michael concisely explains one aspect of betrayal: "Never take
sides with anyone against the family. Ever." It's a punchy and

quotable line, but it's worth thinking about what it means. Families are full of dissenting opinions. You can take sides with one member of a family but not another. I could side with a cool cousin against a bad uncle. Maybe that's taking sides against the family. Or maybe it's siding with any non-family member against any family member. If we think any individual member of the family is what you can't take sides against, then Michael too is guilty of this. In this respect, we could say that Michael betrays Fredo just as surely as Fredo betrayed Michael.

So what does it mean to not take sides against the family as a whole? A more democratic family might be divided about a great many things, making this hard to answer. But the Corleone family is officially a patriarchy, and the patriarch is Michael. So here the answer is clear. Don't take sides against the family means don't cross Michael. His word is final, just as Vito's was previously. Nobody cares what Tom or Connie thinks. This is not just because Michael is the most powerful, but because he is the official leader. He is the one people answer to. He is the one people ask for money or help or permission. Maybe in a different family, betrayal would look different, but for the Corleones, it's clear enough.

This isn't the whole story about betrayal. Obviously, it has to be possible for other family members—Luca Brasi or Johnny Ola—to betray one another. Betrayal seems more subjective. Betrayal is based on individual expectations and a relationship of trust. These seem to be set by the person who would be betrayed. It's harder to imagine a case where I think I've betrayed you and you insist that I have not.

There aren't any requirements about power differences when it comes to betrayal. In principle, anyone could betray anyone. Sometimes power dynamics can make a betrayal particularly egregious, like when someone in a powerful and trusted position betrays someone in a more vulnerable position. But it's still betrayal when the roles are reversed. So, we could say that Michael betrays Fredo by having him killed or that Michael betrays Kay by excluding her from the family and cutting her out of his life. But this has less dramatic consequences because neither of them is in a position to retaliate the way Michael can. But they can be betrayed just the same.

## Snitching

Beyond betrayal there is a nearby concept of snitching. What exactly is snitching? At first glance, snitching is when you turn in one of your peers to some authority. The difference between snitching and betrayal also tracks a difference in power and establishment. You can only snitch on someone of a comparable standing, and you can only snitch to someone with more power. These dynamics don't just happen in the mob. In school, your friend could betray you by siding with the class bully or by sitting with other kids at lunch. But they could also snitch on you to the teacher. Snitching involves failing to exercise a kind of solidarity that is expected among people who are trying to operate outside of some established set of rules. That could be running an elaborate criminal network, or just trying to copy your friend's homework before class starts.

Once somebody snitches, they become a snitch. Being a snitch is a special status that seems to change your standing in at least two ways. First, when you snitch, you seem to forfeit your status as someone who is protected from snitching. You aren't one of us anymore, whoever "us" was. It could be mafiosi, dissenting political factions or schoolkids. Second, and relatedly, when you snitch, you are liable to sanctions and punishments from which members of your community are otherwise protected. In the mob, these seem to include attempts on your life. This tacit threat may even extend to your family and associates.

The terminology surrounding this is interesting and it's important to get it right. Note that a snitch is not the same as a stool pigeon. A snitch is a member of the group who turns on their own kind. The mobster who talks to the FBI, for example. A stool pigeon was never really a member of the group and was ultimately a member of the more powerful class the whole time. So, what's bad about them is different. The snitch is a traitor, not a spy.

So, you can betray someone without snitching, but it's harder to snitch without betraying anyone. When you snitch, you might not be betraying the person you snitched on, because you might not have had the right kind of connection in the first place. But when you snitch, you probably are betraying someone. You might think that by snitching on Michael, Frankie betrayed his whole family (his personal family, not his criminal family) by exposing them to the threat of retaliation.

## Nature and Norms

Betrayal and snitching seem to have distinct natures and norms governing them. These norms help us determine whom we can trust and deal with the people we cannot. Consider some of the differences.

Betrayal is individual and snitching is large scale. When you betray someone, you do wrong by that specific person. If your betrayal was bad enough, you might incur the ire of people particularly loyal to them, but it's not usually the case. When you snitch on someone, you do wrong by a whole community.

You have to be personally close to someone in order to betray them, but you do not have to be close to snitch. Again, think to the classroom example. The student who snitches on you to the teacher could be anyone. They don't need to be a friend or a confidant. It could be someone who just watched you copying your homework before your second period class.

Snitches also have a certain contagion about them. Once one is a snitch, anyone who knowingly continues to associate with the snitch is suspect. At worst, they might be liable to sanctions and punishments of their own. This is true even if the snitches snitching had nothing to do with you. Snitching tarnishes your reputation permanently. Betrayal isn't like that. You might not be able to fix your relationship with the person you've betrayed, but that betrayal doesn't necessarily follow you in all your other relationships the way snitching does. Maybe a serial betrayer could develop such a reputation, but with snitching it only takes one.

Snitching is public in a way that betrayal is not. Frankie's case took it to an extreme with a public spectacle and testimony before congress. Not all snitching has to be at a public hearing, of course. It can take place behind closed doors, as Frankie's snitching initially did. But, word gets around. People can come to know about any given betrayal as it might make for interesting gossip. But they *must* know who the snitch is. Everyone in the community needs to know that. Only Michael had to learn who betrayed him. He needed to know for his own safety and for the security of his organization. But anyone in the community needs to know who the snitch is because they need to know whom they can trust in the future. Again, this is true even if the snitch didn't snitch on you in particular.

Another difference is that betrayal permits a response, while snitching demands a response. Again, in different contexts, these responses can admit of different degrees. Snitching in school might just mean you don't get invited to the fun parties anymore. Certain considerations once extended to you might be withdrawn. But if you are in the mob and you snitch, it seems that the rule is you must die. But again, a betrayal, even among the mob, just means that you can be killed, not that you have to be.

A brief comparison to blame is helpful since that's something in the background to all this. I might blame someone less if they wrong me by mistake, or due to a misunderstanding. When I'm deciding who to blame, consciously or unconsciously, I care about what they meant to do. So, if you maliciously smash the nib of my beloved fountain pen because you hate me and want me to suffer, I'll blame you as much as I blame anybody. But if you smash the nib on my beloved fountain pen because you've never heard of a fountain pen before and you thought it was a ballpoint pen, I might understand. This is because my blame is somewhat responsive to the knowledge you had in doing whatever you did that wronged me. We often think you can't be responsible, and thus shouldn't be punished, for things you didn't know about and couldn't have known about. Accordingly, it does seem that we treat people less harshly if we discover a big misunderstanding.

Surprisingly, it looks like these considerations about intention apply to snitching but not to general betrayal, at least in *The Godfather*. Frankie makes a mistake in talking to the FBI. But it's not because he suddenly, maliciously doesn't care about loyalty or honor anymore. It's because he thinks he has nowhere else to go and Michael wants him dead. When he learns this isn't the case, he is loyal once more. This serves to redeem him.

Fredo gets no such consideration. While he explains that he didn't know anyone would try to assassinate Michael, this seems to make no difference. Intentions seem to carry no weight here. Even Michael says earlier that Fredo's "got a good heart, but he's weak and he's stupid." It's important that Fredo has a good heart, a heart just as loyal as Frankie's. Reconsider the point about my fountain pen. If my stupid friend with a good heart smashed it, I would react differently than I would to a clever friend with a mean streak. But not so for Michael. For him at least, betrayal seems insensitive to considerations about intentions.

Finally (and perhaps obviously), snitching is not an honorable activity. Ever. We could dream up certain circumstances in which betrayal might be the more honorable thing to do. It seems like snitching is never like that. Even the side you snitch to might not respect you. Snitching is so dishonorable that it can implicate your associates or your family. This explains why Frankie's brother would have been on the hook for Frankie's snitching, and why he looked so concerned at the prospect of Frankie's testimony. It's hard to tell what he's more frightened by, the prospect that his brother is a snitch, or the retribution he can expect because of it.

## Forgiveness

So Fredo betrayed Michael and Frankie snitched on him. How can each be forgiven? Or can they? Bishop Butler characterized forgiveness as "foreswearing resentment." Though in this context we might also be concerned with foreswearing revenge. Vito Corleone knew how to forgive. Anyone would have understood if Vito chose to retaliate for Sonny's murder, but he asks, "will that bring my son back?" and instead he makes peace. Michael makes a public gesture of forgiving Fredo when he hugs him at their mother's funeral. Perhaps he gave up his resentment; we have no way of knowing. But he clearly had not given up his desire for revenge for Fredo's betrayal. He chillingly gives the signal for Fredo to be killed while hugging him.

In contrast, Frankie snitched on Michael. Sure, he recanted his testimony, but snitching isn't a success term. We wouldn't say that Frankie snitched on Michael only if it succeeded in getting him punished. It seems to consist in just the attempt. Michael was entitled to retaliate against Frankie and Frankie's whole family. But since Frankie agrees to kill himself, Michael foreswears the revenge to which he is entitled. In that respect, he forgives Frankie. The deal is even sealed with handshake from Tom on Michael's behalf.

Now it might not look very forgiving to insist that Frankie kill himself, but since Michael was now allowed to kill Frankie's whole family, he did choose the more lenient option. It was just enough to show that you cannot cross Michael with impunity. Remember, snitching is public. But in special, rare circumstances, you can get some leniency for snitching. This seems as close to foreswearing resentment as Michael Corleone gets.

## The Death of Fredo Corleone

Some things can never be forgiven. Some things should be forgiven but are not. Frankie had to pay for his snitching because, as I have argued, snitching not only allows a strong response, but requires one. Since Frankie was acting on bad information and he confessed, he was able to redeem himself. So, his punishment was minimized.

Betrayal, in contrast, allows a strong response but does not require one. Michael was free to have truly forgiven Fredo instead of the mere performance we saw in the film. Clearly, Fredo was a security risk. But rather than punish him, Michael could have found a way to quarantine him. Fredo should have been kept in a position where it would be impossible for him to betray Michael, even by accident. This wouldn't even have to mean exclusion from the actual Corleone family. Indeed, this is what Michael did prior to having Fredo killed.

There was no reason to kill Fredo, at least none that comes from the norms surrounding snitching or betrayal. Isolation was enough and it solved the problem. Killing Fredo didn't restore honor, order, or balance to the universe. Michael did not need to signal his willingness to uphold the set of norms surrounding trust and betrayal because Fredo's betrayal was private. Very few people within the story knew about it. And even if it was his intention to signal this, Michael did not signal any such willingness since he had Fredo killed only after making a public display of pretending to forgive him. If you give sensitive information to someone whom you know you cannot trust, and they inadvertently betray you, they are not the one to blame.

# 3
# Does Vito Corleone Live a Good Life?

TIM DUNN

$V$ito Corleone's life is a classic American immigrant success story. He immigrates to New York from Sicily at the age of twelve with little money and no knowledge of English. Through hard work, determination, and intelligence, he starts his own business, raises a family, and acquires substantial wealth and power. As he expands his business interests, he outwits competitors, and with some luck, survives an especially hostile takeover bid. He eventually retires, passing the family business on to his son. He dies peacefully in his garden, surrounded by family.

Okay, so maybe it's not a classic story. He is, after all, not just Vito, but Don Corleone, the head of one of New York's most notorious fictional Mafia families. He doesn't merely outwit rivals, he murders them if necessary. His wealth comes not from importing Italian olive oil but from racketeering, gambling, loan sharking, and other illegal, predatory activities. How could such a man live a good life?

This is a troubling question. It's unsettling to think that a person who is vicious, ruthless, violent, and corrupt—a man like Don Corleone—could live a good life. We want to think that bad people live bad lives. And yet Vito does not seem to regret the life he has chosen, and in many respects, he does seem to live a good life. What's the connection between the good life and the ethical life?

## Aristotle on the Good Life

The ancient Greek philosopher Aristotle thought a lot about this question. In his most famous ethical work, *Nicomachean Ethics*, Aristotle argued that a virtuous character is a necessary but insufficient condition for a happy life. In other words, Aristotle thought that if a person were not virtuous, they could not truly be happy, regardless of how contented they might be with their lives. Such a person might not recognize that they are living a defective life, but they are.

To show why this is so, Aristotle begins by noting that human beings do things for a reason—we go to work in order to earn money, we exercise in order to stay healthy, and so on. Typically, working and exercise are things we do for the sake of other things, in this case money and health. He reasons that there must be something we do, or seek, for its own sake, and not merely for the sake of other things. This, he says, is *eudaimonia*, which is commonly translated as "happiness" or "human flourishing."

In her book *Aristotle's Way*, classicist Edith Hall distinguishes three different conceptions of happiness (pp. 3–7). One conception is psychological—to be happy is to be in a good mood, to have a positive attitude or "upbeat" mental state. Happiness in this sense is contrasted with depression—both are psychological descriptions of our mental state.

A second, highly influential definition of happiness can be found in the ethical theory known as utilitarianism. John Stuart Mill, a nineteenth-century expositor of utilitarianism, defines "happiness" as "pleasure and the absence of pain." Both of these definitions have some merit, but for Aristotle, they are insufficient to describe accurately a good life. According to Aristotle, happiness is not just passive enjoyment of a pleasant mental state, it requires rational activity—forming plans and goals, developing our talents, pursuing projects, and forming lasting and meaningful relationships, among other things.

It is this third conception of happiness that is most relevant to the question whether Vito Corleone lives a good life. At first glance, it seems clear that Vito does engage in a great deal of rational activity, often quite successfully. Does this mean he lives a happy life? Not necessarily. For Aristotle, not just any rational activity will do. Only rational activity "in accordance with virtue" will lead to genuine happiness. Planning to rob a bank or execute a rival may require a great deal of rational activity—detailed planning, elaborate deceptions, self-discipline, good decision making, and the like—but insofar as these are vicious, unethical actions, they are incompatible with happiness. In other words, in Aristotle's view, virtue is necessary for happiness. For this reason, it appears that Aristotle would deny that Vito lives a good life.

It's important to clarify what Aristotle means by "virtue." Virtues are stable aspects of our character or personality that enable us to live well, accomplish our goals, and promote our ends. Aristotle distinguishes two types of virtues: intellectual virtues and virtues of character. Intellectual virtues include such things as prudence, understanding, being able to deliberate well and make good decisions, and wisdom. Virtues of character are numerous and include bravery, generosity, temperance, calmness, friendliness, truthfulness, and justice.

It might seem strange to include intellectual virtues in the list of virtues. Being good at solving puzzles, for instance, or being good at deductive logic or science seem more like talents than virtues. The term "virtue" seems applicable only to ethical aspects of character, and being prudent, or making good decisions, may seem to be rather different qualities—desirable, yes, but not really *ethical* qualities. But in many situations, to act in an ethically virtuous way may require at least some intellectual virtues. A courageous person will need to be able to assess risks accurately, deliberate about the likely prospects for success, and prudently avoid unnecessary or futile actions. Moreover, Aristotle is talking about intellectual activities, and not merely capacities or talents. Being naturally good at math or learning languages are not virtues, but talents; using one's math or language skills effectively to make wise decisions is a virtue.

Aristotle did not merely assert that virtue is necessary for happiness, he argued for it. In Book II of the *Nicomachean Ethics*, Aristotle lays out what philosophers now call the Function Argument. Aristotle argues that the good for anything is dependent on that thing's nature or function. The good life for a pig, for example, is whatever best promotes the things that pigs naturally or characteristically do, such as playing with other pigs, or rolling around in mud. One of the things that humans characteristically do, that sets us apart from other creatures, is engage in rational activity. To engage in rational activity well, we must do so in accordance with virtue. Therefore, he concludes, the good life for human beings is to engage in rational activity in accordance with virtue.

Aristotle's argument assumes that to do something well, we must do it virtuously. To be a good accountant, for example, means not just being good at adding numbers or knowing the tax law, it means not defrauding your customers, not lying to the IRS, and so on. But as Edith Hall points out (p. 27), the classical Greek term 'well' is ambiguous. It could be used in a practical sense or a moral sense. The practical sense is roughly equivalent to saying that someone does something competently or accurately. But someone can live well in this practical sense, yet not live well in an ethical sense. A mob accountant who knows how to deceive the IRS is a good *mob* accountant, but he is not acting ethically.

This ambiguity in Aristotle's argument is the source of our question: can mobsters like Vito or Michael Corleone live good lives?

## Is Vito Virtuous?

If we think that Vito lives a good life, does that mean we must reject Aristotle's claim that virtue is necessary for a good life? Not necessarily. We could argue that Vito is virtuous, or at least virtuous enough to be capable of living a good life. This is not as absurd a suggestion as it might seem. Consider first the intellectual virtues of prudence, understanding, and deliberative skill. Both Vito and Michael certainly seem to possess these virtues in abundance.

For instance, consider Vito's plan to bring Michael back from exile in Sicily. After Sonny is killed, he calls a meeting of the heads of the five families, negotiating a truce and assuring the other dons that he will never be the one to break the truce. After Michael's safe return, he prepares Michael for his eventual succession as don, laying the groundwork for a masterful stroke of vengeance without literally violating his promise. After Vito's death, some of the other dons, sensing weakness, plot to lure Michael to his death under the guise of friendship. But Michael is well prepared for this, and just hours before the meeting is to take place, Michael's assassins successfully eliminate all of the family's enemies, clearing the way for Michael to move the family business to Las Vegas.

Michael and Vito consistently outwit and outmaneuver the other families. After Sollozzo's assassination attempt on Vito leaves Vito alive but incapacitated, it is Michael who devises the retaliatory strike. Taking advantage of his status as a civilian and Sollozzo's underestimation of his cunning, Michael agrees to meet Sollozzo and the corrupt Captain McCluskey in a Bronx restaurant, ostensibly to negotiate a truce. Instead, he waits until they let their guard down, then shoots them.

Admittedly, both Vito and Michael sometimes benefit from luck—it was bad luck for Sollozzo that the assassination attempt on Vito failed, and further bad luck for him that Michael was able to foil the second planned attempt on Vito's life at the hospital. Michael, too, through luck narrowly avoids execution in Sicily. They are not invincible. But over time, in an extremely risky and dangerous business, they surpass all rivals and competitors.

The mafia generally, and the Corelone family in particular with its extensive network of police informants and political connections, operates an intricate and highly organized family 'business'. Important decisions are made at the top and orders are passed on to underbosses or *caporegimes*, who in turn pass them on to further underlings. This structure helps to insulate the bosses from risk of criminal prosecution, as does the code of *omertà* (silence and refusal to cooperate with police), which is strictly observed and enforced. Though Vito survives two assassination attempts, he is never at serious risk of arrest. Michael also avoids detection for most of his career. In *The Godfather, Part II*, when he is finally brought before a Congressional Investigatory Panel, he avoids criminal conviction by threatening to kill a key witness's father.

Both Vito and Michael are also able to run legitimate businesses, whether it's importing olive oil or running a casino. Admittedly, the tactics they use to establish and expand their businesses are not always legitimate. In the book, Mario Puzo describes how Vito expanded the olive oil importing business by threatening competitors or destroying their inventory. Nevertheless, they are fully capable of engaging in rational activity and making smart decisions, much like any other businessperson.

What about the virtues of character? How do Vito and Michael fare in this department? On a charitable read, not too badly. For instance, consider the virtue of generosity. Vito is frequently generous, not only to his family and friends, but also to other members of the community. Early in his career, Vito assisted a distraught old woman he did not previously know who was being forced by her landlord to vacate her apartment, eventually persuading the landlord to relent. Granted, he was successful in part because of an implied threat of violence, but he acted on behalf of a defenseless poor woman against a corrupt landlord, siding with the weak against the powerful. His actions were not only generous, but also just.

Additional examples of the Don's generosity abound. On his daughter's wedding day, he promises to help an old childhood friend, the baker Nazorine, whose future son-in-law faces deportation. The Don promises to use his connections to help him remain in the country and eventually become a citizen. When his godson Johnny Fontane comes to him for help, the Don promises to help him revive his stalled career. In some cases, of course, he makes it clear that he might one day ask for a favor in return for his generosity, but reciprocal generosity is still generosity.

Both Vito and Michael possess great courage as well. In *The Godfather Part II*, we see how Vito stood up against the corrupt local boss Fanucci, refusing to pay him a percentage of his illegal earnings, something his friends and eventual lifetime partners Clemenza and Tessio were willing to do. Vito murders Fanucci and takes his place. He eventually became Don Corleone because he had the courage to do what others would not. And when Vito was left helpless and alone in the hospital, Michael, aided only by a baker's apprentice who had come to pay respects to Vito, scared off Sollozzo's men and stood up to McCluskey until help could arrive. He then overcame his obvious fear to successfully execute McCluskey and Sollozzo, thereby avenging his father. Some of these actions may be reprehensible, but they do require courage.

Indeed, Michael and Vito are successful dons in large part because they possess these virtues. To be a don requires some degree of magnanimity and generosity, a lot of courage, and many other virtues. Contrast Michael and Vito with Sonny, whose fatal character and intellectual flaws render him unfit to be a don and impair his chances for a good life, especially by shortening it. Sonny is notoriously hotheaded, and his decision-making skills are suspect. Growing increasingly anxious as they wait for Sollozzo to call with the location of the meeting place, Sonny suggests just sending someone out to blast everyone in the car. The family *consiglieri* Tom Hagen angrily reminds him that Sollozzo might not even be in the car. Sonny's predilection for brute force stands in contrast to the cold calculation of Michael and Vito. Even his courage is not the Aristotelian mean but rather impetuousness or rashness. The rival families exploit his weaknesses to snare him in a deadly trap.

## Vito and Michael: A Defense

There are at least three other reasons why someone might be inclined to view Vito's and Michael's actions, if not favorably, then at least in a more sympathetic light. The first is that many of their victims are themselves mobsters. As such, they are hardly innocent victims. They are "in the game," and are therefore fair targets. Does anyone shed a tear for Sollozzo, Barzini, or Philip Tattaglia? They plotted to kill both Vito and Michael and they got what they deserved. To quote the memorable line of Cormac McCarthy's sheriff Ed Tom Bell from *No*

*Country For Old Men*, describing the brutal murders of Mexican drug runners, "They died of natural causes—natural to the line of work they are in."

Other victims, while not themselves members of the mafia, nevertheless behave like gangsters. Jack Woltz, the movie producer who refuses Don Corleone's request to offer the starring role in his new picture to the Godfather's godson Johnny Fontane, mocks the don openly, insisting that if the don tries anything, Woltz has the muscle and the moxie to make him regret it. Woltz, of course, is in over his head, as is his horse Khartoum, whose gruesome death serves to force Woltz to grant the don's request. Woltz is, if not a gangster, then at best an unscrupulous Hollywood mogul, leveraging his fame and power to take advantage of others. In the novel, Puzo describes him as a Harvey Weinstein-esque sexual predator—worse, in fact, since many of his victims were very young girls. Woltz got what he deserved even if his horse did not.

A second reason has to do with contextual factors in the story. As mafia historian Selwyn Raab points out in *Five Families*, both Puzo's novel and the movies include "an underlying subtext" that "appears to rationalize the virtues of Mafia or 'family' loyalty" (p. 196). Vito emigrates to the United States to avoid certain death at the hands of the Sicilian mafia. As he rises to power, he uses his cunning and the threat of violence to protect Italian immigrants from a "hostile American culture and environment" (p. 196). He dispenses justice to those who have been disappointed or exploited by the system. Michael, too, seeks justice against his father's enemies, a justice not possible in the corrupt American legal system (for one thing, the police are in on it). Michael is compelled to resort to violence, and if we despise the person he eventually becomes, we might at least understand his motives.

As Robert J. Thompson observes in the afterword to the fiftieth anniversary edition of *The Godfather*, at an emotional level, there is something compelling about the godfather. Vito and Michael satisfy an almost primitive wish to "mete out swift and effective justice to those over whom we have no power." (p. 434). If something should happen to our loved ones, we wish that we had a Godfather to take care of it.

Finally, narrative conventions make it easier for us to identify with the Corleone family. We see things through their perspective, and so it is natural for us to root for them, at least at first. Their enemies are our enemies. If the story had been told from Sollozzo's perspective or that of the Tattaglia family, we might judge the Corleone family much more harshly.

## The Virtuous Gangster: A Reconsideration

Our analysis so far suggests that Vito and Michael have at least some worthwhile qualities. Yet a closer read of Aristotle reveals that their "virtues" might not be genuine virtues after all. In his explanatory notes on the *Nicomachean Ethics*, Terence Irwin argues that for Aristotle, in order to possess the intellectual virtues of prudence, understanding, and good deliberation, you have to employ these skills to good ends. If your aims or ends are themselves bad, then your use of prudential reason to achieve those ends is not a virtue. Aristotle calls prudence in pursuit of bad ends "cleverness" to distinguish it from the virtue of prudence. If we follow Aristotle's more nuanced definition of prudence, then at least some of the actions we have been calling prudent turn out to be merely clever. Michael's grand plot to assassinate the heads of the five families nearly simultaneously, for example, is quite clever and brilliantly executed, but it would not count as prudential or an example of good deliberative judgment.

Aristotle's insistence that prudence and other intellectual virtues require not merely sound instrumental reasoning, but also a worthwhile end accords at least somewhat with contemporary linguistic usage. We would call someone prudent who lives a frugal lifestyle in order to save for retirement. But if instead they saved all their money in order to purchase a custom-made golden commode, we would probably regard their actions as imprudent, no matter how wisely they managed their money along the way. On the other hand, since reasonable people may disagree about what counts as a good or worthwhile end, it might be better to use prudence as a synonym for instrumental rationality only.

Aristotle also believes that one of the most important elements of a good life is friendship. He devotes two of the ten chapters of the *Nicomachean Ethics* to a discussion of friendship, distinguishing three different kinds of friendship. Some friendships exist primarily or exclusively for mutual pleasure (think friends with benefits). Others are based primarily on utility or usefulness. Aristotle recognized that these are legitimate forms of friendship, and they each have a place in a good life. But they are incomplete, in part because they are unstable. Friendships based on utility fall away once either friend is no longer of use to the other. If I am friends with someone only because they are in a position to help me with my career, the friendship likely won't last if I change careers. Likewise for friendships of pleasure.

The highest form of friendship is one that is based on promotion of each other's welfare for its own sake. If I value your success and happiness, regardless of its impact on my happiness (indeed—your happiness might even come at the expense of my own), then you are my friend in this highest, most complete sense.

Aristotle regards relationships between spouses, or those between parents and children, as friendships also, though he understands that relationships between different kinds of people might require different elements to flourish. A healthy friendship between a husband and wife will obviously involve different elements from those required for a healthy friendship between a child and a parent.

From an Aristotelian point of view, one of the most glaring defects of both Vito's and Michael's lives is its lack of complete friendships. Vito has many friendships of utility—people with whom he has a transactional relationship based on mutual advantage. But he has few, if any, true friends. Perhaps his closest friends are Peter Clemenza and Tom Hagen, his *consiglieri*, though even these friendships are limited by the roles they play in the family business. Tessio, one of his lifelong friends, betrays him by aligning with Barzini and attempting to set up Michael. Though Vito is not alive to witness this act of betrayal, he foresees it, warning Michael that whoever betrays him will approach him as a friend. Even good people are sometimes betrayed by lifelong friends. But it's telling that Michael is not surprised that Tessio betrayed him. "It's the smart move," he says. Only someone who expects a friend to betray them when circumstances change would say such a thing.

Michael, likewise, has few true friends. Before he makes his fateful decision to become a gangster, his relationship with Kay is in many ways a model one, based on mutual love and respect and a commitment to each other's welfare. But once he takes over the family business, his relationship with Kay is permanently and irreparably damaged. In the memorable scene at the end of *The Godfather*, when Michael's sister Connie accuses him of having her husband Carlo killed, Kay demands to know whether the accusation is true. Michael denies it, and in the film, it seems that Kay might actually believe him. But as she leaves the room, she looks back in horror as Clemenza kisses Michael's hand, acknowledging his status as Godfather. Her look suggests she knows it's a lie. In the novel, this is stated explicitly. We know where this marriage is headed, and our suspicions are borne out in *The Godfather Part II*.

One of the most commonly uttered phrases in *The Godfather* is "It's just business." While trying to persuade Tom Hagen to accept a deal, Sollozzo assures him there will be no more violence. "It's good business," he says. "Blood is a big expense." In their deliberations regarding how to respond to Sollozzo, Hagen says that if Don Corleone dies, they should take the deal. "It's just business," he says. After Tessio realizes that Tom and Michael are on to his scheme, he tells Tom that he always liked Michael. "Tell him it was just business," he says. In many contexts, the ability to put aside personal feelings would be considered a strength, a virtue. But Vito and Michael reduce all relationships to business transactions, making it difficult to value others for their own sake.

## No Regrets?

When Vito calls a meeting of the five families to negotiate a truce, he contemplates his life choices. In the novel, he attempts to justify his life, arguing that he and the other dons "refused to be fools, . . . puppets dancing on a string pulled by the men on high." But he also acknowledges that "None of us here want to see our children follow in our footsteps, it's too hard a life" (Puzo, p. 278). In the film he tells Michael that he never wanted this life for him, and in the scene where he is told by Tom Hagen that it was Michael who killed Sollozzo and McCluskey, Vito is visibly upset. If he truly had no regrets about his life choices, why would he not want Michael to follow in his footsteps? Is it merely because such a life is "too hard," or is it because the moral ruthlessness required of a mafioso exacts too great a toll on a person's happiness?

As for Michael, by the end of the *Godfather Part II*, he has defeated all his enemies once again, but has crossed almost every moral boundary imaginable, even killing his own brother. The camera lingers on his solitary figure, sitting in forlorn silence. We can only imagine what he is thinking, but as viewers, we pity him, for he has brought this horrible misery upon himself. Whatever virtues Michael has, or had, by the end of the *Godfather* saga, he has lost most of what constitutes a good life on Aristotelian terms.

Throughout his life, Vito relied heavily on the counsel of his *consiglieri*, Tom Hagen. Perhaps he would have done well to take advice from Aristotle instead, who could have warned him not to pursue wealth, power, and honor at the expense of happiness, and that without virtue, he has no chance of being happy.

# 4
# Loyalty as *Omertà*

ALEXANDER E. HOOKE

He has to be taught a lesson: that mercy comes only from the Family, that the Family is more loyal and more to be trusted than society.

—MARIO PUZO

A human conundrum. Why does one act of disloyalty destroy all previous acts of loyalty? After all, one bad beam does not bring down a structure. A team can still win with an inept player.

*Godfather* fans know the scene well. Salvatore Tessio plans to facilitate peace talks to prevent a war among the five families. Michael Corleone initially accepts the offer. Then he remembers his father's caution: The first one who comes to you for a peace talk is the traitor. As Tessio prepares for the meeting, the plans suddenly change and he immediately realizes that he has been discovered. He looks to Tom Hagen and pleads, "Tom, can you get me off the hook? For old times' sake?"

In his novel, *The Godfather*, Mario Puzo introduces Tessio as a "man of unquestioned loyalty to the Don." To the very end this was true, but the Don had just died. His son Michael had not yet earned the respect for his authority as the new patriarch of the Family. Until then "Tessio had been the best soldier in the Corleone Family." But he sensed that he was being cut out of the Family's move to the Las Vegas gambling venues and he would lose all his financial dealings to the other four Families.

American philosopher Josiah Royce contends that loyalty is a foundation for the good life. Loyalty takes us out of the citadel of individualism to commit to something greater. Conflicting loyalties or fealty to a harmful or destructive cause presents a central concern for Royce, as he has observed numerous cases where mindless dedication leads to massive ruination of humanity, from war and fanaticism to religious and political zealotry. Genuine loyalty, in his view, embraces a respect for the loyalty of others. Blind loyalty is more than worshipping one's own ideal or cause— it neglects the ideals or causes that propel other human beings to embrace meaningful or worthy lives.

In Royce's words, "If loyalty is a supreme good, the mutually destructive conflict of loyalties is in general a supreme evil." Much of the *Godfather* enterprise challenges these words. Looking at various scenes from the movies while interweaving insights from the novel, we can see how loyalty is a fundamental source for harmony and disharmony in both the outlaw family governed by Don Corleone and social organizations in general.

This source is best exemplified by the idea of *Omertà—the law of silence,* which in Puzo's novel is described as an integral element in Sicilian life. The concept and practice of *Omertà* illuminates a tense relation between political power of the state and the informal mechanisms of control found in small towns and villages. As seen in the *Godfather* novel and the movies, the law of silence is difficult to pinpoint even though it underlies so many decisions and illuminates the suspense when the characters work with or betray one another.

## Loyalty To?

Royce posits that humans can be loyal to any number of causes and ideals. Teams, clubs, fraternities and sororities, institutions, countries, heritage, among so many others are familiar examples. He is troubled by the emphasis on enlightened egoism that permeates modern society. He does not deny the importance of individuals finding their own meaning or purpose in life, as long as they connect to something that unites them with a general principle or ideal that guides their everyday actions and duties.

Though Royce is usually associated with the absolute idealist tradition founded by Georg Hegel, he often presents an existentialist perspective on the significance of embodiment that was described by Jean-Paul Sartre and Maurice Merleau-Ponty. According to Royce, "I cannot be loyal to barren abstractions. I can only be loyal to what my life can interpret in bodily deeds. Loyalty has its elemental appeal to my whole organism."

This point underscores much of the drama and suspense in *The Godfather*. Indeed, part of the drama is the test of loyalty. When Sonny is riddled with bullets from a rival, Don Corleone calls the undertaker in middle of the night to request that they immediately meet at the coroner's office. No one wants to check on a corpse at such a late hour, but the undertaker remembers his gratitude to the Don and directly goes to see how he can make Sonny's bloody and disfigured body look presentable at the funeral. Then there is the notorious Luca Brasi. His loyalty to the Don has no limits—quite willing to torture, dismember and savage anyone who threatens the Corleone family. He even tries to infiltrate an adversary's organization only to be discovered and cruelly strangled to death.

In *The Godfather* there are several entities that demand loyalty: friendship  the business, and the Family—both as a biological unit and as an organization that functions outside ordinary laws. Many of the ruptures in these devotions stem from shifting demands. Friendship gives way to business; business betrays Family; Family drives the harmony heralded by Josiah Royce but also disrupts any ordinary sense of daily life. After all, the closer you are to the Corleone family, the closer you live in the Corleone mall and ultimately become involved in the everyday lives of all those related to the Don's wife, children, guards, and agents.

This priority of loyalty is addressed by Royce, but insufficiently in my view. He assumes the ideals and causes that provoke devotion are clearly recognized. The *Godfather* movies and novel highlight the shortcomings of Royce's optimistic approach. When Sonny is tricked into driving to his sister's home on the spur of the moment because he is enraged that her husband Carlo beat her up again, the Corleone family is confused how anyone knew where Sonny would be. Eventually, Michael and confidantes learn the brother-in-law Carlo arranged it. They bribed a telephone agent to provide a record of Carlo's calls and discovered that he was in contact with one of the rival families.

It's not obvious to viewers and readers whether Carlo had any sense of loyalty or simply functioned in his self-interest. His fate is part of the famous closing scenes in which viewers see Carlo's departure while Michael swears to his wife that he would never make his sister Connie a widow. Viewers can speculate but never be sure since Carlo and other renegades live by *omertà*—the law of silence.

## *Omertà*, the Law of Silence

In many entertainment venues the implicit obedience to silence is ever present. This point does not apply only to mafia types in fictional venues. The obedience to silence can and has been found among clergy, Hollywood stars, royal and commoner families, sports, academics (despite the invariable promise of transparency), among so many others. There is also the silence that an actual oath or promise is rarely uttered or formalized. When the baker comes to Don Corleone to help his daughter obtain a legal visa for her beloved, the Don uses his contacts in the court system to circumvent the ban on this visa application. He cheerfully notes that he might need a favor from the baker in the near future. Soon the baker is nervously standing next to Michael on the hospital steps to scare off a rival gang that wants to enter the hospital in order to ensure the death of the Don. In a sense, the movie shows how the law that connects loyalty to silence is implicit or tacit. Mario Puzo's *The Godfather* novel is more explicit.

Puzo traces *omertà* to the early days of Sicily, when the Italian government (national and local) became so corrupt and violent that local residents needed their own form of resistance. They formed area groups to fend off the government tyrants. But this resistance could only succeed if every resident refused to snitch when captured by the tyrants. Eventually forms of resistance evolved into competing gangs or outlaw organizations, what will eventually be called Families, with their names associated with the leaders, such as the Tatagllia or Sollozzo Family.

The Corleone Family got its start in Sicily (as vividly portrayed in *Godfather II*). Upon immigration to America, the Corleones gradually developed one of the most powerful niches among syndicates. Just as religions or military groups place tests upon their members to check on their commitment and trust, the crime Family has to be thorough and cautious when deciding who can be "the button," a key figure who knows how to push the button on an enemy or traitor with secrecy and without reservation. When the Button emerges as a traitor, as when Paulie Gatto helped arrange the attempted assassination of the Don, the ruination of the Family is probable. As with democracies, autocracies and institutions, interregnum can be a messy affair—especially for an outlaw Family.

In Puzo's words, the Button "had to be tough and he had to be smart. He had to be safe, not a person who would talk to the police if he got in trouble, one well saturated in the Sicilians' law of *omertà,* the law of silence." The Button was not an exception but rather the exemplar of *omertà*. When injured, he did not seek the help of the police or local judge. To tell them of the harm done to him would only increase the likelihood of more harm, given the sordid reputations held by those who are elected or assigned the duty to protect the laws of the land.

Here *The Godfather* enterprise contributes to the genre of writing and movie making that illuminates not the harmony of society as imagined by Plato and his adherents in the history of social/political thought. It instead dramatizes the inherent disharmony of society. The law does not outline a peaceful resolution in adjudicating disputes. It becomes a weapon itself insofar as everyone imposes a law they themselves violate.

Consider classic Westerns like *The Outlaw Josey Wales*, where victorious Union renegades massacre Rebel soldiers after they peacefully resign their military duties, where the old Indian witnesses how every agreement between the United States and native tribes is violated time and again by the government's forces. A novella and prison movie *The Shawshank Redemption* portrays a warden and his staff uninterested in any reform or redemption of the convicts but rather brutalizing them while stuffing their own pockets with government money. *The Twilight Zone* often did thought experiments where the notion of law and justice were absent in a dystopia of complete authority, as presented in the episode "Obsolete Man." Such presentations compel viewers to consider whether the law is more of a clever weapon than a worthy ideal.

One reason the Corleone family is so powerful is its all-too-close influence on numerous politicians and police when it comes to enforcing or ignoring the law when it benefits the Don and his allies. There is one scene when the heads of the five Families in New York meet to discuss an emerging illegal market—drugs. Don Corleone is reluctant to shift from his "olive oil import" business to the trafficking of drugs. Gambling, bookies, prostitution, and graft suffice for profitable ventures. The other Families want to engage in the growing drug market in light of huge profits, yet they would need more cooperation of police officials who are under control of the Corleone Family.

Puzo's account of police chief McCluskey, soon murdered by Michael, is typical. He had four children who were attending college and extra income always helped. For the most part he benefited from "clean graft," which meant taking bribes from bookies and unions. True, he did make an exception when receiving $10,000 for helping with the attempted assassination of Don Corleone. While politicians might make the laws, they also are no paragons of virtue. When Michael meets with a Senator in Lake Tahoe as the Corleone family tries to extend its business into legalized gambling and casino entertainment in Nevada, the Senator berates Michael and his "slimy family" for trying to force his way into the casino business, Michael responds, "Senator, we are all part of the same hypocrisy, but don't ever think it applies to my family." This loyalty to a corrupt system, though, is not formalized in a pledge or oath. It is sealed in the law of silence.

## Irrational Loyalty and Lost Causes

One of the functions of rationality involves proving a justification or an account of one's beliefs and actions. We justify beliefs and actions that are grounded in verifiable claims, recognizable consequences and sincere intentions. Yet Royce acknowledges that "Loyalty may be sometimes dumb." Dumb in two senses: First, dumb as in not verbally expressed; and second, dumb as in being oblivious to devotion to a lost cause.

In the first sense Royce cautions against suspecting others of lacking loyalty because they cannot find the right words to justify themselves. Loyalty can arise in "obscure and humble" individuals who can't formulate the words to support their commitment. "They express their loyalty clearly enough in deeds." Viewers sense this silent aspect of loyalty when someone new is introduced to the Family. For example, Kay Adams is in love with Michael and first meets the family at Connie's wedding. She peppers Michael with numerous questions about the various individuals coming and going. She then spots several individuals who seem unhappy, including the baker, Luca Brasi, and Bonasera. Michael assents and briefly explains, "They're waiting to see my father in private." The oath of loyalty is conveyed in a silent chamber.

In the second sense, loyalty to a lost cause, Royce presents an inner debate with pragmatists (such as his friend William James) by addressing the argument that the truth of a belief or perspective partly depends on the effects of such belief or perspective. It would seem that loyalty to an illusion or lost cause presents a pragmatic refutation of your cause or devotion. To the contrary, contends Royce, there have been many cases where what seems to be a lost cause in your own life eventually triumphs as an enduring movement of a custom, ideal or even a new religion. He cites Judaism and Christianity as worthy examples of the "lost cause" legitimatizing an individual's loyalty. Perhaps, but a posthumous victory eludes the loyal person's own vision and belief.

At what point do characters in *The Godfather* decide to jump ship and betray the family? Is it naked self-interest which Royce deplores, or have they discovered a more worthy target of their loyalty that brings a more intense unity into their lives? The most notable cases of treachery seem locked into narrow egoism and the improvement of the person's own life. The phrase in the *Godfather* movies is "it's not personal, but business" is overshadowed in the novel when Michael admits that many decisions are indeed personal, particularly ones anchored to revenge. As Michael confides to the Family's consigliere, "Tom, don't let anybody kid you. It's all personal, every bit of business. Every piece of shit every man has to eat every day of his life is personal. They call it business. Okay. But it's personal as hell. You know where I learned that from? The Don. My old man."

Brother-in-law Carlo wants to be part of the inner circle and have richer ventures in the Family business, and his betrayal of Sonny shows his selfish ambition. Brother Fredo resents how the younger Michael has assumed central power in the Family, so he coddles up with members of enemy Families. Tessio, long-time friend and virtual member of the Family, might present the most hurtful treachery. Their subsequent executions raise uncertain aspects of Royce's principle about how loyalty to loyalty is central to the good life.

Indeed, Michael Corleone embodies the most intense paradox in Royce's ideal. In *The Godfather*, he abruptly becomes the most loyal son following the attempt on his father's life, taking over the business and protecting all those living in the mall. Yet the more loyal he becomes the more he lives amid disloyalty. In *The Godfather Part II,* he has his brother executed after the death of their mother, his marriage to Kay crumbles, and he knows that old Hyman Roth—a former ally of Don Corleone—pretends to confide in Michael while actually planning to kill him. In a word, the more loyal we become to our icon or cause, the less we respect the loyalty of others to their icon or cause.

Royce is aware of this problem and proposes that the practice of loyalty begin at an early age. For example, team sports is one venue in which a child learns loyalty to both teammates and the spirit of the game. The participant grasps the relation between physical effort and mental agility, the hard work that goes to improving one's skills as well as understanding and contributing to the dynamics of team play. However, these efforts can be undermined by excessive emphasis on victory and publicity. In Royce's words, "It is the extravagant publicity of our intercollegiate sports which is responsible for their principal evils. Leave wholesome youth to their natural life, not irritated and not aroused to unwise emotions

by the exaggerated comments of the press . . ." Remarkable
how that was written in 1907, a century before today's obsession with parents bullying referees in little leagues, col-
leges paying football coaches five million dollars a year, and
cities building stadiums to host professional teams.

## Are We True Believers or Zealots?

The distinction is not so simple. Each accuses the other of delu-
sion, blindness, madness. Recall Pascal's memorable epigraph,
"Men are so necessarily mad, that not to be mad is another
form of madness." Perhaps we could shift this quote to the perspective of Royce and fans of *The Godfather*: Humans so need
a sense of loyalty, that to be disloyal is another kind of loyalty.
We shift the direction of our loyalty rather than resign ourselves to a life without it.

In Chapter 25 of Puzo's novel there is a conversation between Michael and Kay about whether and why they should
get married. This is after Michael returns from Italy and Kay
knew nothing about him during the extended absence. Michael
envisions a future that, for Kay, is a recurrence of the marriage
of The Don and his wife. Kay is startled, amused, and incredulous. He even wishes, as the Don did, that their own children
will grow up to be model citizens, elected officials or esteemed
lawyers and doctors.

Finally flabbergasted, Kay asks how Michael can marry her
when he does not seem to trust her. To the contrary, the Don
trusted his wife—she raised their children and protected him
when trouble arose—but he did not tell her everything. Yet he
adds, "She believed in him. He was always her first loyalty
for forty years." In other words, until death do them part. As
witnessed in *Godfather II*, the marriage of Kay and Michael
Corleone, the new Don, was not as enduring. For those within
a circle of believers, zealotry is little more than the proper attitude to devote to the cause, even if it demands the risk of your
own life. For those outside the circle true belief is corrupted by
zealotry, because the true believer holds onto the possibility
that more evidence, testing, and debate are needed.

## Tomorrow Never Knows

Royce approaches loyalty as a candidate for the seven cardinal virtues. It embraces faith in the cause, love for the ideal,
courage to risk one's life, justice in terms of respecting the
loyalty of others. As seen in so many moments in *The*

*Godfather* novel and the movies, loyalty (and treachery) is central to grasping the dynamics of friendship, business and the Family.

Yet despite his eloquence and insight, Royce overlooks two aspects. First is the virtue of reciprocity in which loyalty goes both ways. Second is what we might call the Nietzsche "ascetic ideal" subterfuge—loyalty is a trick in which the servants do the dirty work for the Don, or the State, or the Church, or the Institution.

Loyalty is not simply tied to the present. It is conveyed as a promise or duty for some future issue. The baker does not know that in the future he will be called to stand on the hospital steps, pissing his pants, staring at potential assassins of Don Corleone. Johnny Fontane accepts the help of the Family for his movie role but does not know that he will be eventually asked to perform at Las Vegas casinos to draw larger audiences. Tom Hagen visits a tycoon on the West Coast and must order the murder of the tycoon's beautiful and valuable horse, leaving the bloody head next to the tycoon who refused the Don's first offer.

The law of silence, *omertà,* complicates rather than clarifies many of the aspects of loyalty addressed by Royce. For such a law is made in the present whereas it can only be upheld in an uncertain future—tomorrow never knows. *The Godfather* project highlights and entertains such complications.

# 5

# *The Godfather Coda* and Conspiracy Theories

MARK HUSTON

Francis Ford Coppola's *The Godfather Coda: The Death of Michael Corleone* (2020), the re-edited version of *The Godfather Part III* (1990), is the least appreciated of the three (or four?) *Godfather* movies. In fact, *Coda* was the title that Coppola always wanted for the third movie. Whereas the first two were meant to be understood as part of an extended whole, *Coda* was meant to be just that—the conclusion of the life of Michael Corleone.

If you have not watched *Coda*, you ought to. Even though the newer version is not tremendously different from the original, it's different enough that it's a better movie. Recognizing the conspiracy theory genre elements adds a further layer of appreciation.

At its most basic, *Coda* is the story of Michael, as an older man, trying to atone for his various sins, most notably the murder of his brother Fredo. As part of that atonement, Michael is attempting to legitimatize his various business interests via a deal with the Vatican Bank. Michael and Kay are divorced but they are still on reasonable terms, especially about their children. Their daughter, Mary, is very close to Michael, while their son, Anthony, is closer to Kay who is helping break the news to Michael that he is leaving law school to become an opera singer.

Michael's sister, Connie, is also still in the mix and is quite strong in her own right, acting even more ruthlessly than Michael in many instances. Most of the other main characters from the previous films are no longer around; however, the most important new entry is Sonny's bastard son Vincent. Vincent ends up becoming a surrogate son to Michael and has the goal of taking over and continuing the family business. The end of *Coda* has Michael's daughter Mary being killed by a bullet meant for

Michael, with the final shot showing Michael alone as an old man with nothing left but his own internal demons.

## *Coda* as a Genre

None of the *Godfather* movies would typically be considered conspiracy theory films in any traditional sense. However, there is a unique and interesting way in which *Coda* can at least, in part, be understood through the lens of the conspiracy theory movie genre. The family elements of *Coda* that drive at least half of the movie are more in line with drama, or maybe better even melodrama given the heightened nature of the emotions at play throughout the movie. The other half of the movie, with its political, business, and religious intrigue, is fruitfully understood by considering it as a conspiracy theory movie; contrary to the typical analysis of the movie as a straightforward crime drama combined with family tragedy. As a result of the reasonable focus on the family and personal elements, which are fantastic, the other elements get short shrift. Yet in *Coda* those additional elements add layers and depth to the movie.

## The Definition of 'Conspiracy Theory'

As I reported (in "The Greatest Conspiracy Theory movies") there has been a tremendous amount of academic work done on conspiracy theories in the last twenty-five years or so. Within philosophy, most of that work relates to epistemological and conceptual issues. Much of the conceptual work is an attempt to provide a proper definition of 'conspiracy theory'.

Philosophers such as Brian Keeley, M R.X. Dentith, Charles Pigden, Quassim Cassam and many others have provided definitions that they deem correct. I believe these attempts fall into one of two problematic areas: either the definition is too broad (the definition categorizes too many instances of theorizing as "conspiracy" theorizing) or the definition is too narrow (the definition automatically categorizes all instances of conspiracy theorizing as problematic and false; thus, definitionally ruling out even the possibility of a true conspiracy theory). So, a definition that would categorize any old crime collusion, assuming that collusion was done in secret, would be too broad. Two or more people planning to rob a bank, even though they are in fact engaging in a conspiracy to bank rob, should not count as a 'conspiracy theory' given any reasonable understanding of the concept. However, a definition that rules out Watergate or MK Ultra as conspiracy theories merely because they are well established as true is surely too narrow. To conceptually stipulate the impossibility of true conspiracy theories runs counter to traditional modes of academic reasoning. That is why my own preferred view is to avoid the traditional trap that results from attempting a classic definition in terms of necessary and sufficient conditions, and instead to provide a Wittgensteinian account of 'conspiracy theory'.

According to the great twentieth-century philosopher Ludwig Wittgenstein most social concepts (as opposed to natural kind concepts) cannot be defined according to necessary and sufficient conditions. Instead, to properly analyze a concept, one must first look at paradigmatic instances and paradigmatic criteria of the concept in question. Then, when deciding whether or not something new falls under the concept, one looks at the overlapping similarities between the new instance and the paradigmatic instances. If the new instance is similar enough, then it will correctly fall under that concept. The virtue of this account is that allows for our ordinary language understanding of 'conspiracy theory' while neither counting all instances of collusion as automatically falling into that category (read: too broad) nor automatically ruling all conspiracy theories to be false (read: too narrow).

Classic paradigmatic examples of conspiracy theories would include the assassination conspiracy theories of, for example, JFK, MLK, RFK, and including clearly true events such as Watergate, MK Ultra, Iran-Contra and others. Also, 9/11 conspiracy theories, CIA conspiracy theories, and newer ones such as Pizzagate and Q-anon. Some of the criteria that are typically, but never essentially, associated with conspiracy theorizing include: the theory runs counter to the received or expert analysis of an historical event or events, the theory proposes a malevolent explanation, the theory typically suggests a small group of conspirators are in charge, they often refer to secret societies of some sort or a group within the government and/or a corporation (such as the pharmaceutical industry) using undue influence, and the conspiracy theory usually provides a narrative that links events that otherwise seem disconnected.

In addition, the political philosopher Michael Barkun offers "three principles" of conspiracy theories: nothing happens by accident, nothing is as it seems, and everything is connected. Again, Wittgenstein helps us make sense of how understanding this wide range of criteria allows us to properly conceptualize new instances of theorizing as conspiracy theorizing (or not). If a new theory has a lot of overlap with these instances and properties, then it is properly best understood as a conspiracy

theory. If it has very little overlap, then it is most likely a different type of theory, such as a scientific theory or an ordinary
instance of criminal collusion. These distinctions also apply
equally well when trying to make sense of conspiracy theory
movies.

In the case of *Coda*, there is constant deception and a variety of connections that these principles help decode. Especially
upon a second viewing, there are a variety of moments where
these principles come into play. Apart from the obvious situations, such as the dealings between Michael and The Vatican
banker, there are also the nefarious dealings of Don Altobello
(played by Eli Wallach) who ends up attempting to assassinate
Michael. Michael's warning to Vincent that it will be someone
close to him that will commit an act of betrayal embodies "nothing is as it seems" in particular. Michael in turn also acts in a
similar manner by sending Vincent "undercover," under the
pretense that he is betraying Michael, in order to gain information on Michael's enemies.

Another set of useful distinctions discussed by Michael
Butter include internal/external and bottom-up/top-down conspiracies. A bottom-up conspiracy is a conspiracy by a group or
secret society (such as Freemasons) not currently in power to
try and take power, whereas a top-down conspiracy is when a
subset of those already in power, for example a secret group
working within the government, attempt to institute malevolent control beyond that which they already maintain.

Internal conspiracies would be groups working within a system of which they are already a part, while external would be
an outside group trying to gain control over another entity—
such as the worries in the 1800s that the Freemasons or elements within the Vatican were attempting to gain control of
the United States government. *Coda* interestingly blends these
various distinctions. For example, Vatican as the seat of power
plays the role of a top-down conspiracy with the head of
the Vatican Bank, Archbishop Gilday, as the primary, internal
conspirator.

A final set of conceptual tools is the distinction between
event, systemic and super conspiracy theories. An event conspiracy theory is merely a conspiracy theory about a single
event, such as JFK or 9/11 conspiracy theories. Systemic conspiracy theories attempt to link several event conspiracies by
appealing to a group to explain the occurrence of the seemingly
disconnected events. For example, the idea that the CIA assassinated JFK, RFK and MLK via MK Ultra mind control of the
assassins. Finally, a super-conspiracy links various group con-

spiracies via an even grander narrative, such as the idea that shape-shifting lizard aliens are behind the Freemasons, Illuminati, Knights of Malta and so on. The line between systemic and super conspiracies is not always completely clear, but super-conspiracies tend to be everything-but-the-kitchen-sink conspiracies. Keep these various categories and distinctions in mind as we move to a discussion of conspiracy theory films.

## Conspiracy Theory Film Genre

Much like in the real world, movies contain many instances of conspiracies—pretty much every single crime movie or murder mystery. For a film to be categorized as a conspiracy film, it needs to filmically meet many of the same overlapping criteria that must be met of a real-world conspiracy theory. In other words, the film must portray a conspiracy explanation that runs counter to the mainstream view, proposes a small group intentionally trying to produce a malevolent outcome, or some other subset of the overlapping criteria. I argued in "The Greatest Conspiracy Theory Movies" that those conspiracy theory movies that work best, in terms of conveying complicated emotions such as paranoia, work at the systemic level.

*JFK* (1991) is a classic example of a conspiracy theory movie, but one that walks the line between working at the systemic and super conspiracy level. *National Treasure* (2004) and *The Da Vinci Code* (2006) are both examples of super-conspiracy movies that propose overarching conspiracies that bring together a range of other conspiracies. They also play into classic real-world conspiracies in the broadest, and goofiest, sense. Finally, two of the greatest conspiracy theory movies are both directed by Alan J. Pakula and both operate at the systemic level: *The Parallax View* (1974) and *All the President's Men* (1976).

Given that Watergate meets most of the overlapping criteria of a conspiracy theory, the only reason to rule it out as a conspiracy theory is via an unreasonable stipulation that there is no such thing as a true conspiracy theory. That is an arbitrary and unfounded view that is very difficult to defend. Hence, since I think Watergate was clearly a conspiracy theory, then the filmic representation of Watergate (*All the President's Men*) is clearly a conspiracy theory movie—an incredibly effective one at that. *The Parallax View*, for those unfamiliar, is a political assassination film that proposes that a global corporation is the driver of political assassinations. I believe it is a much more emotionally powerful reworking of the assassinations, in terms of conspiracies, of people like JFK and RFK than the movie *JFK*. In part because it hews to the systemic level and does not slip into the potential absurdity of the super-conspiracy level as *JFK* does at times. Also, then, given that *All the President's Men* is a conspiracy theory movie, similar reasoning would apply to *Coda*.

## *Coda* as a Conspiracy Theory Film

Thinking of *Coda* as being basically split into two core genres, the family melodrama and conspiracy theory genre, heightens the aesthetic experience. I believe some of the unwarranted dislike of this film is based upon trying to read it as fundamentally part of the same genre as the first two *Godfather* films: an elevated version of the gangster/crime genre. However, when reading it in the way I propose, the emotional experience is much richer. The tragic family circumstances are not merely related to battling other groups of gangsters, as in the first two, but are better understood against the backdrop of much grander (though not super) conspiracies. Thus, providing the operatic counterpoint to the operatic tragic family ending.

The conspiracy theory elements of *Coda* are reflected in Michael's dealings with the Vatican. In the movie, Michael is attempting to go fully legitimate by effectively laundering his money by buying up shares of a massive, global company called Internazionale Immobiliare. To do so he needs approval of the Vatican bank which owns twenty-five percent of the shares of Immobiliare. In a very impressive shakedown, the head of the Vatican Bank, Archbishop Gilday, insists that Michael give $600 million to the bank for the Vatican's approval of the deal. Through various plot points Michael, with the help of Vincent, comes to understand that the head of Immobiliare, Licio Lucchesi, has been orchestrating a deal to exclude Michael while keeping his money. In addition, a new Pope has just been elected and he has reportedly claimed that he is going to "clean house." These two elements set up the series of killings that consolidate Michael's and Vincent's power. However, the collateral damage of the deal includes the new Pope, who is poisoned, and Michael's daughter who is gunned down on the steps of the opera house.

These elements of the film are based upon the 1970s and 1980s Vatican Bank scandal and the death, after only thirty-three days, of Pope John Paul I. According to conspiracy theorists such as Robert Anton Wilson these events, much like Watergate, provide clear examples of true conspiracy theories. Without going into deep detail, the Vatican Bank scandal, much like in the film, has to do with the head of the Vatican bank, Archbishop Paul Marcinkus, working with the chairman of Banco Ambrosiano (a privately held banking group) Roberto Calvi, dubbed God's banker, and the network of shell companies that they set up in the Seventies and Eighties.

Much of the initial information that established the criminality of Calvi came because of a raid of an illegal, shadowy masonic lodge called Propaganda Due (P2) headed for many years by Licio Gelli. P2, and Gelli, has been linked to many crimes, murders, and political assassinations. One of those is the death of Roberto Calvi. Calvi, a member of P2, was initially arrested and then released on bail. Soon after his release he was found hanging from Blackfriars Bridge with bricks in his pockets. While initially ruled a suicide, Robert Anton Wilson and many others have argued that the death is reflective of ritual masonic killings. This death is also in the movie, but in the movie it is the Vatican accountant murdered in that way. Even in official circles the death of Calvi continued with the most recent trial, of several mafia/P2 members, occurring in 2007. However, due to lack of evidence, there were no convictions.

In addition to Calvi's mysterious death, the recently elected Pope John Paul I somewhat mysteriously died after only thirty-three days in office. The journalist David Yallop in his 1984 book *In God's Name* argues that John Paul I was murdered because he was planning to clean up the corruption in the Vatican bank. However, most others who have looked at his death believe the official story that he died of a heart attack. The movie clearly reflects the conspiratorial understanding of his death.

## Conspiracy Analysis

*Coda*, similarly to *All the President's Men*, is based on elements that are now clearly understood to be true. But also, in similar fashion to Watergate, the Vatican Bank scandal is only excluded from being considered a conspiracy theory via an unwarranted stipulation. In fact, it encompasses even more conspiratorial elements than Watergate given the role not only of the Vatican and a global company, but also a rogue masonic lodge. Adding the more traditional conspiracy theoretical element that John Paul I was murdered provides even further reason to read a significant part of *Coda* as a conspiracy theory film.

In keeping with the better conspiracy films, the conspiracy elements of *Coda* occur at the systemic level by focusing on various international groups such as the Vatican bank and Immobiliare. The film creates a sense of unease and paranoia, like other conspiracy films, due to the recognition that the various groups not only have immense power and money but are illegally working to increase both and willing to do virtually anything to do so. Adding to the unease is the veil of religiosity due to the Vatican bank and, if you do know the true backdrop, the even more hidden freemasonic influence. Given that Michael is also part of a somewhat secret group, the mafia, and given that he has significant money and power, the behind-the-scenes illegal battle between the competing groups lends itself to classic conspiracy theorizing.

Thinking of our earlier distinctions, Michael's attempting to take over can be seen as a bottom-up/external conspiracy. Bottom-up because, even though he is quite powerful, he is attempting to take over a more powerful grouping. External because he is not a part of the group already since he is from the United States. The fact that Michael is already powerful does provide a clear point of departure from most other conspiracy theory movies. Typically, in conspiracy theory movies the protagonist is a lone person, often a journalist (or two), that recognizes a conspiracy that others do not. However, due to his powerlessness, the revelation of the conspiracy is an uphill battle that the protagonist may not even survive. In addition, the goal is to bring the conspiracy out into the light of day to try and stop it.

In *Coda* the goal is not to stop the conspiracy so much as to co-opt it. Since we primarily follow Michael's perspective, it is easy to forget just how powerful he has become. Yet it is his, and subsequently the viewer's, recognition of the wider conspiracy that provides the narrative threat resulting in the carnage of the final scenes. The death of the relatively innocent daughter and the death of an honest Pope reflect the more typical elements of conspiracy theory films, where innocent folks are sacrificed when they get too close to the conspiracy.

These various components, when combined with the family melodrama, work together to create a much more unique film than previously reflected in critical analysis. I believe that the conspiracy elements have either been underplayed, or outright dismissed, when the film has been evaluated. Yet it is these various elements in *Coda*, especially when placed against the background knowledge of how much is based in truth, that give rise to a fuller emotional experience than we derive from an ordinary tragic melodrama.

# 6

# This Is Business, Not Personal!

ABIGAIL LEVIN

The *Godfather* trilogy is the story of the Corleone Family, the business enterprise, as much as it is the story of the Corleone family, the blood relations. Indeed, the two are so enmeshed that they cause confusion and deep suffering for Vito, Michael, and Kay as they struggle to navigate both The Family and the family; or, to paraphrase Tom Hagen, the business and the personal.

This divide is what liberal political philosophers call 'the public-private distinction'—business and government constitute the public sphere; family and household life the private sphere. For the Corleones, nothing is ever that simple, and when we look at the central theme of the movies—leadership and success at a precarious time, in a precarious business—struggles with how to navigate the public-private distinction drives the drama that unfolds for Vito, Michael, and Kay.

## Michael's Liberal World

*Part I* opens in 1945 as Michael returns home for Connie's wedding as a war hero; he is the embodiment of post-war American liberalism, triumphant after the defeat of fascism. By wearing his uniform to the wedding, he chooses to distinguish himself from his family, Sicilian immigrants who were living under quite a different political paradigm, which I will liken to the Aristotelian conception of public and private. Indeed, he says pointedly to Kay, his college-educated American girlfriend: "That's my family, Kay. It's not me." As events unfold, Michael is unable to draw this tight distinction between himself and his family, which is an endless source of tension for the marriage and a major cause of dissatisfaction with his life.

That said, the tidy division between oneself and others, between business and personal, is a distinctly liberal conception of the public-private distinction, befitting this post-war moment. Liberalism is the overarching political philosophy of the post-Enlightenment West, and its central concern is the freedom of the individual from unnecessary state regulation. This makes sense: the Enlightenment emphasized personal autonomy. It's the role of the state, according to liberalism, to provide the theoretical and political infrastructure necessary to facilitate each citizen's maximal liberty consistent with liberty for others. This is achieved through state apparatus: laws which enshrine rights to personal liberties and property, free from incursions by the state or by other individuals; and a justice system to adjudicate rights claims. In liberal philosophy, we limit state power and protect these central freedoms for individual citizens by insisting that the public and private spheres warrant different degrees of state incursion.

The private sphere consists, paradigmatically, of family life within the household, and concerns such intimate matters as the decision whether or not to have children (which Kay, importantly, makes), the manner in which we rear them if we have them, our sexual life and preferences, and our religious practices, if any. State regulation of these areas of life is considered a noxious intrusion into individual autonomy over what one of liberalism's founders, John Stuart Mill, famously called "self-regarding" conduct in his foundational liberal work *On Liberty*. Catherine MacKinnon puts the classical liberal position this way: "The liberal ideal of the private holds that, so long as the public does not interfere, autonomous individuals interact freely and equally. Privacy is the ultimate value of the negative state." In other words, all the state needs to do in order to protect its citizens' liberty rights is refrain (the "negative" part) from interference in the private sphere—a hands-off approach by the state allows for free actors to flourish in their private lives.

The presumption of privacy is assumed in the absence of a compelling state interest to the contrary, and the onus is on the state to establish such an interest. Writing after the overturning of *Roe v Wade* in the United States—and the threat to such private issues as birth-control and same-sex marriage rights that the Court's reasoning portends—it seems fair to observe that liberal societies have struggled to live up to these ideals.

In contrast, the public sphere—which is constituted by the government itself and by the business world—is a legitimate venue for state regulation, as long as it is achieved through properly promulgated, transparent, laws, which are themselves understood as in the service of allowing citizens the freedom to express their political views and autonomous bodily and religious choices. According to Ian Shapiro, "This view . . . of a private sphere surrounding an individual that cannot be entered (first by other individuals and eventually by the state) without his consent, became the standard view of freedom in the liberal tradition" (p. 277). This strict separation causes suffering for Michael, as he tries to do three things at once: embody these liberal ideals by strictly separating public and private: "Don't ask me about my business, Kay!" while also retaining the best of his father's paradigm, which involves quite a different, more merged, understanding of public and private; and, finally, while trying to be Kay's husband, which brings problems of its own, if we understand Kay's behavior as anticipating the feminist critique of the liberal public-private distinction.

From the 1960s to the 1980s, second-wave feminist philosophers critiqued the liberal public-private distinction—a time-period that both encompasses when *Parts I* and *II* were released, and also when Michael and Kay's marriage dissolves. As Susan Moller Okin, one of the central figures in second-wave feminism puts it: "'The personal is political' is the central message of feminist critiques of the public-private dichotomy. It is the core idea of most contemporary feminism" (p. 124).

Second-wave feminist critiques of the liberal distinction give the lie to the liberal conceit that the private realm is the privileged site of freedom, and instead argue that the liberal state functions to enshrine male privilege in the private sphere at the expense of women. When we turn to these critiques, we can see why Michael fails to have Vito's satisfying family life, and why his marriage fails.

But the issue is likely more complicated than Vito might appreciate. The ancient version of the public-private distinction, which Vito strives to embody, is ultimately unfulfilling to him. He cannot achieve legitimacy in the public realm as classically understood, and dies believing that his son will follow in his footsteps. In the end, neither man is satisfied with his life, and Michael's predicament in particular is driven by viewing him as caught between the past, embodied in his father, and the future, embodied in his wife.

## Vito's Ancient World

The Aristotelian version of the public-private distinction is importantly different from the liberal version in three ways. First, the public realm is constituted narrowly—it does not

include business, only government (as defined by citizen participation in debate, and holding official office). Second, Aristotle
does not see the public and private as located in specific venues
like the marketplace or the bedroom; rather, whatever is a
matter of common interest belongs to the public sphere and
whatever is a matter of private interest belongs to the private
sphere: "It is not that Aristotle never characterizes places as
private; rather in his estimation what defines a site as private
are the activities that ordinarily go on within it. If the activities promote virtue uncompromised by prevailing morality,
then the place is private" (Judith Swanson, p, 2). Third, and
most important, it sees the public and the private aspects of
our lives as interacting and mutually reinforcing much more
than the liberal view does:

> Private endeavor repays the public: families provide future citizens,
> the economy effects distribution, and the educated are able to rule
> and teach. A regime should aim to bring about such a dynamic equi-
> librium between the public and the private, for then it will be self-suf-
> ficient, "what is best." (p. 4. "What is best" is a quotation from
> Aristotle's Politics [1253a1]).

It is, strictly speaking, a misnomer to say that Aristotle sub-
scribes to a "public-private distinction," then, because the very
word "distinction" offers a modern, sharp, division between
the two spheres, which is very much an artifact of the liberal
version.

With these three features of the ancient version in mind,
we can see how Vito's leadership of the Corleone family and
the Corleone Family offered him satisfaction in the former,
and dissatisfaction in the latter. With respect to the former,
it's clear that Vito values family life as an important realm to
cultivate virtue, or moral excellence, just as Aristotle would.
This is established immediately in the wedding scene, when
he says to Johnny Fontane: "You spend time with your family?" "Sure I do." "Good. Because a man who doesn't spend
time with his family can never be a real man." Shortly before
his death, he asks Michael: "Your wife and children, are you
happy with them?" "Very happy." "That's good."

*Part II* depicts young Vito as a devoted family man throughout, even entering his life of crime because he thought that his
wife would like the rug he was offered as payment for his first
heist. He is often surrounded by large gatherings of family, and
genuinely delights in them. He seemed to know, along with
Aristotle, that

every form of private activity has . . . a telos (end or goal) of its own. Raising children, interacting with one's mate, overseeing servants, transacting business, keeping friends, and philosophizing all require virtue of some kind, and each activity can be perfected . . . For Aristotle, the raison d'être of privacy is to enable one to turn away (from the public, common wisdom) in order to achieve excellence. (pp. 2–3)

Business and friendship are both aspects of the private realm for Aristotle, which makes sense of the distinctive, and very effective, way in which Vito blends "business" and "personal" in his exchange with Bonasera, in the film's opening moments. Here, the liberal line that Hagen wants to draw between business and personal isn't merely blurred in the sense that business was transacted during an intimate, private occasion; it's that *the business itself* is presented as though it were private and intimate. This is much more intelligible according to Aristotle's framework than it is on a liberal understanding. Bonasera asks Vito to murder the men who raped and assaulted his daughter, and Vito rebukes him, not solely because of the disparity between the crime and the punishment, but because Bonasera is viewing such business in too transactional a manner. Vito says:

We've known each other many years, but this is the first time you've ever come to me for counsel, for help. I can't remember the last time that you invited me to your house for a cup of coffee. Even though my wife is godmother to your only child. But let's be frank here: you never wanted my friendship . . .

Vito goes to lengths here to insist on calling what is obviously by modern standards a transactional exchange a "friendship," even though, by his own lights, it is indeed, a transaction: "Someday and that day may never come, I may call upon you to do a service for me . . ." And we see the word "friendship" deployed again in Hagen's transaction with Woltz: "I was sent by a friend of Johnny Fontane's—his friend is my client, who'd give his undying friendship to Mr. Woltz, if Mr. Woltz would grant us a small favor." Viewed through a liberal lens, we'd be tempted to ask why Vito conducts business as if it were personal, but this is the wrong lens! For him, it is personal!

Aristotle had an idea of friendships of utility, one of his three kinds of friendship, though he considered it imperfect, because it isn't necessarily the friendship of morally virtuous people: "those who love for the sake of utility love for the sake of what is good for themselves . . . Such friendships, then are easily dissolved . . . if the one party is no longer . . . useful the other ceases to love him" (*Nicomachean Ethics*, VIII.3) Vito seems to be making good use of this sort of friendship here, and remember that both business and friendship are in the private sphere for Aristotle.

So, we see Vito excelling in the private sphere—in friendships, at least of a utilitarian sort; in family life, with what looks to be an excellent relationship with his wife, children, and grandchildren; and in business, throughout the many transactions we see in the first and second movies. But this is only one sphere, according to Aristotle's conception of the public and private, and we are only flourishing, or fulfilled, when we can exercise our virtues in both spheres. The Corleone Family is crucially not in the public sphere, in the Aristotelian sense: they are not operating in the realm of civic participation, whether that means deliberation on matters of common concern, or by holding formal political office. These activities are very important for Aristotle—"Man is by nature a political animal," he famously said (*Politics*, 1.1253a).

Since he can't operate in the public sphere, Vito instead exercises leadership in the quasi-public sphere of the five families, as evidenced in the masterful peace that he negotiates among the families after Sonny's death, and in the principled stance he takes about regulating the drug trade to keep innocent children safe. But, going by the Aristotelian conception, these leadership skills would find their highest expression in matters of true common interest, as expressed in government.

The Mafia is of course characterized in part *by the fact* that it is operating outside the law. However, the five families have interests in common that they need to negotiate, and Vito, and later Michael, prove themselves to be astute leaders here. It's noteworthy, though, that neither man finds true fulfillment in this realm, and this may be because they intuit what Aristotle felt—that the truly public, above board, common realm—what the Corleone Family calls "legitimacy"—is necessary for fulfillment. For all of their aspiration to ascend to the legitimacy of the public sphere, the Corleone Family business does not have it, and Michael's and Vito's unfulfillment arises from their dissatisfaction with this.

Shortly before his death, Vito tells Michael: "I never wanted this for you. I worked my whole life, I don't apologize, to take care of my family. And I refused to be a fool, dancing on a string held by all those big shots . . . I thought that when it was your time, that you would be the one to hold the strings: Senator

Corleone, Governor Corleone, Something." Michael affirms this: "There just wasn't enough time. We'll get there, pop. We'll get there." And indeed, the focus of *Part III* was on Michael's quest for legitimacy, in the liberal public sphere, which includes business. He attempts to divest from illegal enterprises, he seeks absolution from the Vatican, and he establishes the Vito Corleone Foundation. Both men acknowledge that a truly fulfilling life is to be found by participation in both realms, and both end up falling short—"just when I thought I was out, they pull me back in," says Michael in *Part III*, as he re-enters the quasi-public sphere of the five families.

Vito was a master of the ancient, private realm, and he strove to participate in the quasi-public, civic life of leadership in the underworld. He saw the relationship between the two as fluid and mutually reinforcing, in contrast to the liberal view that we should strictly separate the business and the personal, as Tom Hagen admonishes. And this isn't surprising—as an American lawyer who thereby has legitimacy in the public sphere, Tom embodies liberal ideals and his worldview can be expected to diverge from his boss's. Indeed, a key theme of *Part I* is to ask whether an Old World way of life can survive in the New World. What changes need to be made to do so, and can they be made while keeping one's virtue intact? It is Michael, a second-generation inhabitant of the post-war liberal moment, who is left to navigate these tricky questions. The world becomes dramatically more modern during Michael's reign, with the post-war period ushering in a renewed commitment to liberal values, and the characters have an uneasy understanding that the world is changing under their feet. This period also includes the rise of second-wave feminism, whose critique of the liberal version of the public-private distinction illuminates the unhappiness of Michael and Kay's marriage and underlies the reasons for their divorce. It also illustrates why Michael isn't afforded the consolation of Vito's satisfying private life.

## Feminist Critiques of the Liberal Public-Private Distinction

For all of the differences we've seen between the ancient and the modern senses of the public and private realms, what has remained constant is the fact that women throughout history have been relegated to the private sphere, while the public sphere is populated by men (most often, in particular, white, property-owners). This has been changing, with women in the workforce and government in steadily increasing numbers throughout the twentieth and twenty-first centuries, but it is still far from equal. Within the timeframe of the first two movies, we see substantial changes—24 percent of US women were in the workforce full-time in the 1930s, Vito's heyday, and there were about 8 women in congress. By the early 1960s, the timeframe of *Part II*, 32 percent of US women were in the workplace full-time, and 12 women were in congress—both 25 percent increases. *Parts I* and *II* were released in 1972 and 1974, respectively, the height of the second-wave feminist movement and it is crucial to remember that audiences would have been viewing Michael and Kay's marriage through the lens of the that era.

Kay is relegated to the private sphere in a way which grows increasingly anachronistic as the first two movies unfold, from 1945 to the early 1960s. We see her forgoing her progressive life as a teacher to become almost a prisoner in her own home and marriage. In *Part II*, after the assassination attempt, she asks Tom Hagen: "Am I a prisoner, is that it?" He replies: "That's not the way we look at it, Kay," but of course, she is.

Catharine MacKinnon, perhaps the most astute second-wave critic of the liberal public-private distinction, writes: "When women are segregated in private, separated from each other one at a time, a right *to* that privacy isolates women at once from each other and from public recourse. This right to privacy is a right of men "to be let alone" to oppress women one at a time" (p. 194). In other words, the "privacy" that is lauded as a hallmark of free agency by liberal accounts of the public-private distinction is revealed as a guise for the illiberal disen-francishisement and oppression that results when women are cut off from the opportunity to form solidarity with each other to resist oppression.

Further, the strict separation between the two spheres is problematized by second-wave feminists, who ask: whom does this strict separation serve? Whom does it oppress? MacKinnon answers those questions by saying: "For women the measure of the intimacy has been the measure of the oppression. This is why feminism has had to explode the private. This is why feminism has seen the personal as the political. The private is public for those for whom the personal is political" (p. 191). In other words, the liberal idea of the state being hands-off in the private sphere serves to entrench male power and allows men to operate with impunity there—a political choice is made to deem the private sphere apolitical, and second-wave feminism calls this out. Feminist critiques argue that state regulation is needed to prevent such unaccountable male behavior as domestic abuse. We see MacKinnon borne out on this point in the domestic abuse suffered both by Connie at the hands of Carlo, and by Kay, when Michael slaps her after she tells him about her abortion. Both men operate with impunity from the state here, as such violence wasn't highly regulated at the time the movies are set—the 1950s and early 1960s.

We see Kay trying to resist, though, in ways that Michael can't accommodate: each of the first two films culminates with Kay attempting to exercise feminist autonomy and agency, by breaking down the strict division of the two spheres that the liberal version of the public-private distinction imposes. At the close of the first movie, she asks Michael about his business affairs, thus attempting to break down the strict separation of public and private within liberalism, and he responds angrily. He finally acquiesces, but only to lie and tell her that he did not kill Carlo, when he did. Here, we see him struggling, not knowing which version of the public-private distinction to inhabit.

An Aristotelian model would have allowed the merging of the public and private by allowing a "private" person into the "public" world, and he wants to be true to Vito's paradigm, but he is in a different world, at a different time, as a different person; forced, however uncomfortably, to embody the liberal moment and maintain the strict separation between the spheres. Finally, he loves Kay and wants to appease her, and so he tells the lie, which serves no one. The scene illustrates how they both suffer, for related reasons: neither knows where they stand. Michael is caught between the ancient and modern styles of leadership, inhabiting neither fully, and certainly not knowing how they relate to his wife. Kay realizes that the Michael she loved—"That's my family, Kay. It's not me."—is certainly not the Michael she's now married to. She anticipates the oppression that her historical moment at the cusp of the second-wave feminist movement names—the strict separation between the liberal public-private sphere is a source of oppression and she tries to break it down.

In a thematically parallel scene, at the end of *Part II*, Kay succeeds in exercising agency and autonomy by privately getting an abortion, but is confronted with Michael's rage, culminating in domestic violence, when she confesses it. Michael had been unduly interested in the sex of the baby because he wanted an heir to the Corleone Family, and Kay had the abortion at least in part to deny him one: "I didn't want your son, Michael. I wouldn't bring another one of your sons into this world. It was an abortion, Michael. It was a son, Michael, a son and I had it killed—because this must all end." In parallel,

MacKinnon asks: "What are babies to men? On one level, men respond to women's right to abort as if confronting the possibility of their own potential nonexistence—at women's hands, no less. On another level, men's issues of potency, of continuity as a compensation for mortality, of the thrust to embody themselves or their own image in the world, underlie their relation to babies . . ." (p. 186) and this captures Michael's response quite well. Of course, this is an apt characterization of men's relation to children well before liberalism, and thus Michael views this situation through all of patriarchy, including the ancient world.

In both these scenes, then, when Kay attempts to morph the Corleone Family with the Corleone family, thus complicating the public and the private division as the feminist critiques of the liberal public-private distinction advocate, she's met with Michael's extreme discomfort and confusion as he tries to navigate the ancient, the modern, and his love for his wife, whose nascent feminism he surely cannot grasp.

## The Corleone Family and the Corleone family, Reconsidered

We see then how the second-wave feminist critique of the liberal public-private distinction drives the tensions in Michael's and Kay's marriage, and even further, shows how Michael is more thoroughly dissatisfied with his life than his father. Though both men were thwarted in their respective public spheres, Michael fails to have a satisfying private life as well, because the liberal model of the public-private distinction fails, in ways that second-wave feminism reveals, to properly value the private sphere.

In examining both the ancient and the modern versions of the public-private distinction—and how they map on to the lives of Vito and Michael, respectively—we're able to see the Corleone family's tragedy—and the Corleone Family—in a new light.

# II

---

*"I don't fear you, Michael. I dread you."*

# 7

# An Offer Michael Should Have Refused

Eddie Tafoya

Much of the beauty, richness, and poignancy of the novel and three movies that make up the *Godfather* saga grow out of the spiritual conflicts of the protagonist, Michael Corleone. A complex character who goes through a dramatic moral and spiritual evolution—or, more precisely, a de-evolution—Michael is a man of reverence, intelligence, vision, and devotion to his family while simultaneously being a cold-blooded killer and the ingenious tactician behind a crime empire.

Michael is the third of Don Vito Corleone's four children and the youngest son. When the story begins he is very much the picture of the all-American hero. He is fresh back from World War II where he was wounded while serving as a captain in the Marines, having earned both the Purple Heart and the Navy Cross. After establishing himself stateside and re-enrolling in Dartmouth College, he makes clear that he plans on staying on the straight-and-narrow and distances himself from his family, so much so that he even considers changing his name (Mario Puzo, *The Godfather*, p. 77).

After his father is wounded in an assassination attempt, however, Michael gets sucked into the Corleone organization, kills two people, and flees to Sicily to avoid retaliation and prosecution. He eventually takes control of the Corleone empire, rises to power and prominence, and over the years grows so paranoid that he orders the murder of anyone he considers an enemy, even his older brother, Fredo. Despite his genius, wealth, power, and desire to fulfill his father's dream of making the family business "completely legitimate," by the time he dies in his seventies, Michael is remorseful, guilt-ridden, haunted, and alone.

Consequently, the questions arise: What happens to Michael? Does he have a choice or does he, as his father said of other men, have "only one destiny" (p. 199)? For insight on this, we can look to Plato's "The Allegory of the Cave," which has been a centerpiece of Western philosophy for centuries. When we examine Michael's life in this light, it appears that, at least for a fleeting moment, he has a glimpse into the ideal sphere and the life he could have had if he had stayed on his original course.

## Plato's Cave

A section from *The Republic*, Plato's famous book-length collection of dialogues, "The Allegory of the Cave" involves Plato's mentor, Socrates, and Plato's older brother, Glaucon. Here, Socrates describes a cave where prisoners sit and have their heads secured in such a way that they can only look forward, at a wall on which shadows move. Above and behind the prisoners is a "raised way" where men carry objects, and behind that is a fire. Like a movie projector casting images onto a screen, the light from the fire throws shadows of these objects onto the wall. To these prisoners, the shadows are the only truth.

Socrates compares the captives to everyday people who are unable to see the ideas undergirding manifest reality. Consequently, Socrates distinguishes two realms: The World of Shadows, made up of things only perceivable through the five senses, and the World of Pure Forms, made up of elements that are only understandable through reason.

Socrates tells how the cave also has a "steep and rugged ascent" leading out of the darkness and into the World of the Sun. The philosopher's task, Socrates says, is to unchain the prisoners and show them the reality that is the three-dimensional objects on the raised way. Then, because the experience is painful and the student will not come willingly, the mentor must force the students out into the light. After their eyes adjust, these students come to understand how this metaphorical Sun is "the universal author of all things beautiful and right" and "the immediate source of reason and truth" (*Republic*, p. 475). These students, Socrates says, are best prepared to become philosopher kings, the ideal rulers.

One of the best ways to illustrate the differences between these spheres is to revisit the perennial controversy regarding the right to burn an American flag and the difference between *a flag* and *the flag*. *An* American flag is a piece of fabric with seven red stripes and six white stripes and fifty white stars on a blue field. Virtually anyone can buy one, douse it in gasoline, and hold a flame to it. To do this is to burn *a* flag, to incinerate a collection of molecules that will eventually, in one way or another, be destroyed anyway. *The* flag, however, is something very different. It is not an object we can hold in our hands but a collection of politically radical ideas that grew out of the Enlightenment and that declare how all people are created equal and have been endowed by their creator with certain unalienable rights, that among these are the rights to life, liberty, and the pursuit of happiness. It is an assemblage of philosophies concerning how people become Americans based on their allegiance to the country's founding principles rather than genetics or religious affiliation.

*The* flag cannot be destroyed any more than the fundamentals of differential calculus or Einstein's Special Theory of Relativity can be destroyed. The only way to destroy *the* flag is to wipe clean the memory banks of anybody who has been exposed to the ideas.

## The Corleones and the World of Shadows

In the *Godfather* saga we see the tension between these competing worlds, or, to put the matter in Platonic terms, the way people mistake the shadows for the pure forms. Consider, for instance, early scenes involving the reception celebrating the wedding of Carlo Rizzi and Connie Corleone, Vito's youngest child and only daughter. Here, we get a glimpse into the family's lavish lifestyle. There are hundreds of guests in attendance, including friends, relatives, politicians, gangsters, and even a pop star heartthrob.

The Italian-American Corleone family, as Vito says of another character, has "found Paradise in America." Despite appearances that they live in a sphere where, like the Biblical Eden, most of their needs and desires are met quickly, the ephemeral comforts and luxuries are the result of avarice, hubris, exploitation, and manipulation.

Add to this the way the movie immediately introduces the theme of false divinity. In the opening seconds, we see Vito, who carries the title "Godfather," an appellation with echoes of "God the Father," poised in a god-like position. While Connie's wedding reception goes on a few feet away, an undertaker, Bonasera, meets with Vito in his office requesting the Don exact revenge on two men who beat his daughter so badly they left her hospitalized and permanently disfigured. Bonasera tells how the police and justice system failed him and that the assailants not only went free immediately after their trial but also mocked him as they walked out of the courtroom.

Only after Bonasera pledges his loyalty and kisses Vito's hand does the Godfather concede to do the favor. A while later, Nazorine, the baker, visits to ask that Vito pull bureaucratic strings so that his assistant, Enzo, will not be deported to Italy. Nazorine doesn't even need to fully verbalize his request. Vito calls Nazorine "my friend" and finishes the baker's thoughts, saying, "You want Enzo to stay in this country and you want your daughter to be married" and promises to help. Bursting with joy, Nazorine grabs Vito's hand and says, "You understand everything."

The encounter with Bonasera illustrates how, like Jehovah, a deity whose main functions include righting wrongs, punishing the wicked, and rewarding the faithful, Vito can intervene and succeed where human-made institutions fail. The conversation with the baker labels Vito as omniscient and both conversations illustrate how Vito is like the Puritan god in that he demands unflinching loyalty above all else.

## Michael's Path

When we meet Michael, he makes clear that he wants little to do with his family and its crime organization. As he and his girlfriend, Kay Adams, discuss marriage, he tells her that he plans on becoming a mathematics professor (p. 78). He is, therefore, on course to climb the "steep and rugged ascent" of Plato's cave and to move toward the Good through his academic pursuit of the discipline of pure abstraction that the ancient Greeks saw as "the supreme example of true knowledge" (Lavine, *From Socrates to Sartre*, p. 44).

Michael's path changes instantly one night in late 1945, however. As he and Kay leave New York's Radio City Music Hall, Kay jokingly asks, "Would you like me better if I were a nun?" He says "no." She then asks, "Would you like me better if I were Ingrid Bergman?" He teases her, saying, "Now, that's a thought." As he speaks, they pass a newspaper kiosk and the screen goes dark for two seconds. When we see them again, Kay's expression is somber. She points out a headline announcing that Vito has been gunned down and is "feared murdered." This moment, emphasized by the seconds of darkness, throws Michael off course.

Almost instantly, he goes from being what his oldest brother, Sonny, calls "a nice college boy . . . who didn't want to get mixed up in the family business" to someone who, because of his devotion to his father, is fully committed to the Corleone organization. He crosses the street to a phone booth to call Sonny, pulling the booth door closed and shutting out Kay. This image, which will be recalled in the movie's closing seconds and again in *The Godfather Part II*, teems with meaning. It is not only his shutting out his fiancé, an all-American girl whose surname recalls the Garden of Eden and two American presidents, but also his closing the door on his plans to become a mathematics professor and continue his journey toward Plato's World of the Good.

The assassination attempt leads directly to two key moments in Michael's story, moments that virtually guarantee his being stuck in the World of Shadows. The first comes a short while later, when Michael visits his wounded father in the hospital. Michael strokes his father's head, picks up his hand, kisses it, and says, "Just lie here, Pop. I'll take care of you now. I'm with you." A tear of joy leaks out of Vito's eye. In this story that takes its title from the sponsor for a sacrament, the tear becomes the symbolic and ritualistic water of Michael's baptism into a new life in the underworld. The second moment comes when Michael "makes his bones," that is, when he proves himself a worthy gangster. This happens when, during a restaurant negotiation, Michael shoots and kills the Corleones' two rivals, Virgil "the Turk" Sollozzo and his bodyguard, the corrupt New York Police captain Mark McCluskey. After this, Michael flees to Sicily, his ancestral homeland, to avoid prosecution and retaliation.

## Michael and Apollonia

Michael's time in Sicily, the Sicilian Sequence, is different in tone and color from the rest of the movie, with the images of the Palermitan countryside taking on a fairytale-like quality. Michael's life takes another major turn there, when, after visiting Vito's hometown of Corleone, he walks through the countryside on a sunny day with his two bodyguards, Calo and Fabrizio. The three men step over a low rock wall as a group of children and women approach them. Fabrizio singles out an attractive young woman wearing a burgundy dress and a purple ribbon in her hair. He says, "Mama mia! What a beauty," and later comments that she looks "more Greek than Italian" and, in a statement foreshadowing Michael's eventual full embrace of evil, that she is so beautiful she "would tempt the devil himself."

The young woman looks over her shoulder, telling the children in Italian that they are going to "go up the mountain."

When she turns around she locks eyes with Michael. In a love-at-first-sight moment poets dream of, the two stand transfixed. Fabrizio says Michael has been struck by a "thunderbolt." Later they learn, from the woman's father, no less, that her name is Apollonia, the feminine version of "Apollo."

This sequence begins Michael's glimpse into the World of Pure Forms. For anyone familiar with Greek mythology, the connections are hard to miss: not only is Apollonia named for the god of truth and divinity who is the child of Zeus, but the ribbon in her hair is the color associated with holiness and spirituality. Her Greek features emphasize this association and Fabrizio's reference to the thunderbolt recalls Zeus's signature weapon just as her directive to go up the mountain suggests returning to Mount Olympus, home of the Greek gods. She is, mythologically speaking, the child of the father god, a status corresponding to Michael's station as the child of the Godfather. Michael has entered the divine realm and encountered his other half, his contrasexual self, his complete self, and his perfect self.

When Michael courts the angelic Apollonia, he does so with flawless decorum. He goes through great pains to show that he will remain totally respectful of her, her family, and their ways, traditions, values, and history—and therefore his family's ways, traditions, values, and history. When he visits her home, he brings gifts for Apollonia and her parents and follows strict conditions set by her father. The only other moment of their courtship captured in the film—one that borders on the comical—shows the young couple walking along a dirt road. Apollonia, in a dress and high heels, stumbles. Michael catches her. Following behind is a group of older women, presumably from Apollonia's family and village. Behind them are Fabrizio and Calo, carrying their rifles.

The placement of the Sicily section of the story asks the audience to compare Michael's life, values, and marriage in Sicily to those of his siblings in the United States. The movie quickly switches back to New York, where we see the adulterer Sonny leaving the apartment of his mistress, Lucy Mancini. The door swings open, showing her in a negligee and him with his vest unbuttoned and his tie hanging loose, the implication being that they just dressed after having had sex. Sonny then goes to his sister's house where he finds Connie with two black eyes, the result of her being beaten by Carlo.

Minutes later, we are back in Sicily where Michael and Apollonia kneel outside the church where they have just been married. The newlyweds then continue celebrating their consecrated union with a procession through the village streets and a reception that includes their first dance as a married couple.

By bookending scenes displaying the perfection of Michael's and Apollonia's storybook love with the deeply flawed relationships continued by the adulterer Sonny and the abused Connie, *The Godfather* asks the audience to note the differences between ideal love and the illusions of love. To add to this, Puzo tells us that Fredo, who has relocated to Las Vegas to learn the casino business, has become a "ladies' man," and "has knocked up" at least fifteen women, with all of the pregnancies resulting in abortions (p. 310).

By this point, however, Michael's choices have already been made, the die cast, and his fate sealed by means of the baptism at his father's hospital bedside and his killing of Sollozzo and McCluskey. Consequently, Michael's and Apollonia's relationship cannot last. One day, she climbs into their Alfa Romeo hoping to drive over to pick him up at the entryway of the estate where they live. When she turns the key in the ignition, the car explodes in a what had been an attempt to kill Michael. The storybook romance ends in a fiery blast.

The Apollonia scenes tell us that Michael's saga is a Platonic allegory, an illustration of what happens when a person is offered, but resists, the path up the Platonic "rugged ascent."

## Michael Corleone and the Final Rejection of Pure Forms

In his landmark work *Beyond Good and Evil*, nineteenth-century German philosopher Friedrich Nietzsche writes that "Christianity is Platonism for the 'people'" (*Beyond Good and Evil*, p. 6), a dynamic we see playing out neatly in *The Godfather*, especially in the way the film references Roman Catholic rituals. According to Church doctrine, the blessing of an object such as a rosary or Saint Christopher medal "is to declare it special, set apart, a vehicle of God's grace" (McFarland, p. 69) or, to put it in Platonic terms, to consecrate it into the World of Pure Forms. We also see this in the way unleavened bread is transubstantiated into the body and blood of Jesus Himself. Like the Sun in Plato's schema, the consecrated host is God Himself and therefore it is, as Socrates would say, one with "the universal cause of all that is right and beautiful" (*Republic*, p. 475).

It is only fitting, then, that the unifying motif of *The Godfather* involves Roman Catholic sacraments, those rituals that link the ordinary with the eternal. The movie begins with a celebration of matrimony and ends with a baptism. In between we see, as noted earlier, Michael's symbolic baptism at his father's hospital bedside and the blessing of Michael's and Apollonia's union in a Roman Catholic wedding. Other scenes, however, also carry subtler connotations. After visiting his father's bedside, for instance, Michael is confronted outside the hospital by Captain McCluskey, who punches him in the face, a moment recalling the ceremonial slap an archbishop gives a confirmand during Confirmation, a sacrament that often closely follows Baptism. Similarly, late in the movie and in one of its most heartfelt moments, we see Vito handing the Corleone organization's mantle over to Michael. Like a priest and a penitent, the two face each other soberly and without eye-contact. Michael asks, "What's bothering you?" much the way a confessor would ask a penitent to his confess sins. Vito, feeling his death is near, unburdens himself:

> I work my whole life . . . to take care of my family. And I refused to be a fool dancing on the string, held by all those bigshots. I don't apologize. That's my life. But I thought that when it was your time, that you would be the one to hold the strings. Senator Corleone. Governor Corleone, or something.

Ever since Michael was a child, the Don had hopes his youngest son would become a philosopher king.

Nowhere, however, is the push-and-pull between the ideal and the flawed, the evil and holy, emphasized more than in the film's climax. This begins when we see Michael and Kay carrying Connie's and Carlo's newborn child, Michael Francis, to the front of a church to be baptized. As the priest recites the baptismal prayers in a voice-over, we see members of Michael's secret army, those who have received the underworld's version of "Holy Orders," preparing to carry out a massacre. We see the Caporegime Pete Clemenza and the button men Rocco Lampone, Willie Cicci, and the former policeman Al Neri preparing to kill leaders of rival factions, among them Barzinni, Stracci, Cuneo, and the Las Vegas mobster Moe Greene.

Before they act, the assailants engage in "anointing" rituals. As he carries a shotgun concealed in a corrugated cardboard box, for instance, Clemenza stops to wipe a smudge off the quarter panel of his Cadillac Fleetwood and the scene immediately cuts back to the church and the anointing of the infant, thus connecting the two images thematically. Then we see a barber dispensing shaving cream onto his hand and rubbing it on Cicci's face. Back at the church, the priest anoints the child's forehead. The scene then switches to Neri dressed in his old police uniform and wiping his face with a handkerchief. The priest's prayers continue in the voice-over as Clemenza climbs stairs and similarly wipes his forehead with a handkerchief. We then see a Las Vegas masseuse rubbing Greene's back with oil.

The church ritual continues and the scene cuts to a hotel elevator where Clemenza waits with a sawed-off shotgun. The doors part, and out steps the Corleoe's rival Clemenza. Stracci kicks him  back into the car and fires twice, killing him. In the voice-over, the priest says "Michael Francis Rizzi, do you renounce Satan?" Michael responds, "I do renounce him" and we see an anonymous assailant swing open a glass door and shoot Greene in the eye, killing him. Back at the church, the priest asks "And all his works?" and the scene cuts to Cicci trapping Cuneo in the stall of a revolving door and pumping four bullets through the glass and into the old man's chest. Michael says "I do renounce them" and we see Lampone and another gunman kick open a hotel room door and spray bullets at Tattaglia, who is in bed with a woman. The priest asks, "and all his pomps?" and Michael responds, "I do renounce them" and we cut to the front of a courthouse, where the fake police-man Neri pulls out a pistol and shoots Barzini's chauffeur and bodyguard. As Barzini flees up the steps, Neri goes down on one knee, aims, and fires two bullets into the mob boss's back. Barzini wretches and tumbles dead down the steps. Back at the church, the priest asks, "Michael Rizzi, will you be baptized?" Michael says, "I will." As the priest concludes the Latin prayers, we see a montage of the carnage: Tattaglia and the woman bloody and riddled with bullets in the hotel bed, Cuneo dead in the revolving door stall, and the exterior of the courthouse where Barzini, his bodyguard, and his chauffeur lie murdered.

The ceremony is not only the child's baptism into the Church but Michael's complete rejection of the ideal life.

## Dancing with Perfection

Ultimately, what makes Michael's story so tragic is that, unlike the hot-tempered Sonny or obtuse Fredo who had neither the chance nor the desire to enter the world of perfection, he, at least for a moment, sees, understands, and enters the other side of Plato's cave. As a Marine captain, for instance, he risks his life for American ideals, for the truths of freedom, democracy, and the right to self-determination. Then, returning stateside, he finds those ideals undermined and greatly compromised. He sees how the family paradise he has enjoyed and that beckons him is built on the rocky foundations of greed, hubris, treachery, wrath, and other people's pain. This is under-scored when he is punched in the face by a corrupt police cap-tain who, rather than fighting to protect the ideals Michael risked his life for in the war, is a principal in a drug racketeer-ing operation and a plot to kill Michael's father.

Consequently, despite her limited screen time—which is less than seven minutes in all and with most of that in the background—Apollonia looms as the centerpiece in Michael's life, the reminder of the life he chose to reject. This is empha-sized in the closing seconds of *The Godfather Part III*, in the saga's final scene, where we see Michael, now in his seventies, sitting alone, guilt-ridden, and haunted at the estate where Apollonia was killed. Minutes before he dies, scenes from his life flash before his eyes. As Michael reflects, the movie sug-gests that he is reliving his most cherished memories: dancing with his adult daughter, Mary, and dancing with Kay, whom he has recently declared his enduring love for, even decades after their divorce.

And he recalls his moment of ideal love: he remembers his and Apollonia's wedding reception and how, for one fleeting moment, he danced with perfection itself.

# 8
# Let Them Lose Their Souls

ERIC FLEURY

E vil, in the view of many religious and philosophic traditions, is merely the absence of good. In cinema, there are few better tests of this proposition than the *Godfather* movies, a world where neither law nor religion exercise any truly meaningful influence.

The gangsters at the heart of the saga have little fear of arrest or prison, as the police and judges are also implicated in their criminal enterprises. The Catholic sacraments of marriage, baptism, and First Communion serve mainly as reaffirmations of loyalty to the Don, or as an ironic contrast with the corruption and violence that are happening at the same time. The women of *The Godfather* are seemingly innocent, but there is little opportunity for them to exhibit any virtue in the patriarchal world of the Corleones.

Most Hollywood blockbusters present clear moral distinctions, but the *Godfather* films derive their notion of right and wrong primarily from the perspective of their characters. We like the Corleones because they are entertaining figures brought to life through excellent acting, and we spend a fair amount of time with them. The movie's antagonists are not particularly villainous, at least not compared to its protagonists. Any principled differences with the other crime families vanish after Don Vito drops his opposition to the drug trade in exchange for a ceasefire with the Tattaglias and the safe return of his son Michael from exile in Sicily. In *Part II*, a young Vito objects to the cruelty of local kingpin Don Fanucci only because he inflicts it upon other Italians.

The only moral codes we can detect in *The Godfather* are the Sicilian norms of non-cooperation with authorities (*omertà*) and revenge (*vendetta*) against injuries to family and personal honor. The films give us little choice but to accept this code as our own, and so we mourn the deaths of Sonny and Luca Brasi while thrilling at Michael's annihilation of the Five Families and the traitors to his own family. Our forced identification with the Corleones is palatable because they are fiercely loyal to one another, cool-headed and courageous under severe pressure, fully aware that their life of crime is likely to end tragically, and they deal violence almost solely to those who have taken the same risks and made the same compromises as themselves. They are funny and charming, often because of and not in spite of the deadly seriousness that surrounds them.

By placing relatable characters at the center of a morally bankrupt world, *The Godfather* films illustrate that pure evil is not so much malevolent as banal. The most corrupt characters are also the least compelling, as their lack of self-awareness or inner conflict renders them static. The most significant example is Michael Corleone, who makes the most substantial transition from good to evil over the first two films. Even as we watch Michael turn from a soft-spoken college student to a cold-blooded mob boss, he is a strong protagonist so long as he is something more than the sum of his crimes. When he loses all traces of goodness, his story must come to an end or else it would be too boring and predictable to shock us or to be of much interest at all. If you don't believe me, check out *The Godfather Part III*.

## The Banality of Evil

In 1963, nine years before the release of *The Godfather,* the philosopher Hannah Arendt introduced a revolutionary new way of viewing evil with her book *Eichmann in Jerusalem: A Report on the Banality of Evil*. The book covers the war crimes trial of Adolf Eichmann, a major architect of the Holocaust who had been kidnapped by Israeli agents in Argentina and brought to Jerusalem (events depicted in the 2018 film *Operation Finale*). Arendt, a German Jew who had fled the Nazis before settling in the US, attended and reported on the trial in order to understand what kind of person could willingly serve a system that our culture still regards today as the epitome of evil.

Arendt's conclusion was that Eichmann was not a vicious anti-Semite with a psychopathic disregard for right and wrong. She instead described him as "an average, 'normal' person, neither feeble-minded nor indoctrinated nor cynical," proud that "he had done his work with a zeal far beyond the call of duty" and accordingly won the renown of "respectable society." Arendt recounts a court psychologist proclaiming Eichmann to be "normal-more normal, at any rate, than I am after having examined him." Arendt found him pathetic, sneezing in his glass cage and recounting the events of the Holocaust entirely in terms of his own rise through the bureaucratic ranks. Arendt found his most significant quality to be "inability to *think*, namely, to think from the standpoint of somebody else." He was the ultimate Company Man, constantly reiterating the self-justifying slogans of the regime and claiming to feel "free of all guilt" for the reason that none of his colleagues had any moral qualms with the machinery of mass death that they oversaw.

*The Godfather* movies parallel Arendt's account of a world in which for the individual criminal, "he and the world he lived in had once been in perfect harmony," as the greatest rewards go to the most effective criminals. Within the Nazi bureaucracy, various agencies competed for power and prestige based on their ability "to kill as many Jews as possible" and thereby win Hitler's favor. The crimes of the Five Families are much less egregious than those of Third Reich, but they are functionally similar in that their position within the social hierarchy is solely determined by their ability to provide illicit goods and services. The Corleones are nothing like other movie criminals from that time period, such as *Bonnie and Clyde* (1967) or *Butch Cassidy and the Sundance Kid* (1969). Those characters were dashing outlaws whose distinct individuality forced them into conflict with an unfeeling establishment. In *The Godfather*, the criminals *are* the establishment, accruing money and power not for their own sake but to redefine themselves as respectable, upstanding citizens.

Arendt shows us that the criminal's desire for legitimacy only magnifies the problem of evil because it inhibits an honest reckoning with the consequences of their actions. They instead suppress the recognition of their own guilt, depriving themselves of genuine self-knowledge, and settle for empty platitudes on the grim necessity of their deeds and the greater good that they will ultimately accomplish. The result is "lying self-deception combined with outrageous stupidity," as the incessant need to justify themselves becomes more important than the actual morality or effectiveness of their behavior. Like a totalitarian regime, the Corleones offer the prospect of absolute power to make things right in a world gone wrong, but nobody can pursue that kind of power without losing their capacity for introspection and empathy. The closer somebody gets to a god-like status over right and wrong, life and death, the more they reveal themselves to be an utter mediocrity.

## This Is the Business We've Chosen

One major difference between *Eichmann in Jerusalem* and *The Godfather* is the way that each handles their subject. Arendt is, as one might expect, fiercely and bitingly critical of Eichmann, regularly interlacing his words with her own ironic commentary and freely dropping insults like "everyone could see that this man was not a 'monster,' but it was difficult indeed not to suspect that he was a clown." She clearly explains the philosophical significance of the trial, and her commentary has become the primary source of reference for our knowledge of the event. Whether or not she intended it this way, a Jewish woman was able to make herself a conduit between the public and a high-profile Nazi in his effort to defend himself, so that we now remember her words much more vividly than his.

*The Godfather* movies take the opposite approach of Arendt's, centering the narrative tightly around the perspective of its characters and closing out alternative viewpoints. The films do not glorify a life of crime, but they do little to challenge the Corleones' belief that they merely act as powerful people everywhere act; everyone looks out for their own and is willing to do what's necessary to protect their interests. *Part I* opens with Don Corleone's literal point of view as Amerigo Bonasera (which translates to 'goodbye America') confesses that his faith in the American promise was misplaced. He tells the Don (and the camera) that the only justice for an immigrant like himself is the Don's system of favors owed for favors performed and retaliation for injury to family and friends.

Through Bonasera's story and profession of friendship, the audience earns entry into the Corleone sanctum, where we see very little evidence of evil in terms of malevolence or psychopathy. Even a shocking act like leaving the head of a prized racehorse in the bedroom of producer Jack Woltz (John Marley), while not exactly praiseworthy, is proportional within the terms of mob justice that Woltz clearly understands. Just as he knowingly targeted the Don's financial interests by seeking to ruin the career of singer Johnny Fontane (Al Martino), the Don targets the horse that is not merely a beloved companion, but a valued asset that he intends to retire to stud. If you're still cheering for the Corleones after that scene, as I suspect most of us are, then the movie has succeeded in getting you to accept that their code of obligation and revenge is a suitable morality for the world they inhabit.

The real problem of evil in the *Godfather* films has little to do with their bloodiest scenes, such as Michael's elimination of the Five Families or Vito's murder of Fanucci and the aged

Sicilian Don who killed his entire family when he was a child. Those spectacular moments distract us from a more ordinary kind of evil that is all the harder for viewers to detect because the characters barely acknowledge its existence. Their entire identities are formed around a set of laws they both obey and enforce, leaving precious little room for a Socratic investigation into the justice of the laws themselves and the worthiness of the kind of life that they regulate. Hyman Roth recounts that when he learned about the murder of a close friend and associate, "I let it go. And I said to myself, this is the business we've chosen. I didn't ask who gave the order, because it had nothing to do with business." But because these are complex characters and not stock movie criminals, they are not wholly indifferent to the violence that they routinely inflict and endure. Like any other "normal" person in an extreme situation, they must find ways of normalizing their surroundings. The trouble occurs when someone becomes a little too good at redefining terrible things as ordinary things, until anything is acceptable so long as they're comfortable with it.

According to Arendt, language is critical for glossing over patently evil actions with notions of necessity and even nobility, shielding the perpetrators against any irritating pangs of conscience. The architects of the Holocaust operated far from public scrutiny, and it should have been obvious to all of them that this was because they were about to perpetuate an unspeakable crime that would shock the conscience of the entire world. Their ambitions forbade such common sense, and so instead they imagined themselves as "bearers of secrets" who first engaged in humanitarian efforts to provide Jews with a "change of residence" and "resettlement" as a means of "putting firm ground under their feet." When these measures proved impracticable, they resorted to a "'permanent solution' that would 'save all European Jews from their unseemly position as a more or less undesirable guest nation in Europe." In other words, extermination. As they went about their ghoulish business, they developed a vocabulary for self-pity that magnified their own feelings so as to minimize those of their victims. Arendt summarizes this sentiment with caustic sarcasm: "What horrible things I had to witness in the pursuance of my duties, how heavily the task weighed upon my shoulders!"

To be sure, the Corleones are not committing genocide, but they similarly rely on a jargon that helps to reframe the ugliest aspects of their business into a point of shared understanding that reinforces their communal bond. As the Corleones face down the imminent prospect of war with the other families, soldier Peter Clemenza admits that it'll be "pretty goddamn bad" but then suggests that periodic warfare "helps get rid of the bad blood." He even tells Michael, who will use his status as a civilian to get close enough to two of his family's enemies to murder them and set off the war, that "you gotta stop them at the beginning. Like they should have stopped Hitler at Munich." Whether that is an appropriate comparison for a hit against a drug dealer and corrupt police captain is beside the point; Clemenza is just fishing for whatever can provide a useful rationalization at a moment of profound insecurity.

There are several moments throughout the films where the mere invocation of a phrase is sufficient to make awful things seem banal. Wandering the Sicilian town that gave him his name, Michael asks his bodyguard where all the men are, and he replies "they're all dead from vendettas" and points to a tiny sign commemorating a dead man next to a much larger poster for a local communist party. In the very next scene, they are playfully shouting "take me to America!" and names of movie stars to occupying US forces. The memorable phrase "sleeps with the fishes" reports a gruesome murder through the absurd image of a fish wrapped in a bulletproof vest. While disturbing at first, the message effectively sanitizes the deed, as no one ever mentions that or Luca Brasi ever again. If something like that happened to you, it would probably come up now and then.

The most egregious example of a *Godfather* character using particular language to whitewash a terrible evil is, fittingly enough, a nameless character making a throwaway reference to something we never see. Overall, the films offer us no insight into the details of illicit businesses or the people that they impact on a day-to-day basis, as the characters almost never discuss them. The closest we get comes during the meeting of the Five Families in *Part I*. While discussing the drug trade, one don suggests, "I don't want it near schools. I don't want it sold to children. That's *infamnia*. In my city, we would keep the traffic in the dark people-the coloreds. They're animals anyway, so let them lose their souls." Most films would make an effort to emphasize the utter wickedness of such a statement, perhaps to console their audience that they are more enlightened than the bigot on the screen. In *The Godfather*, it passes without comment or visible reaction. It only comes up again indirectly, when Don Barzini (Richard Conte) announces that "the traffic in drugs will be permitted, but controlled." This statement, entirely reasonable on its face, conceals a deliberate effort to victimize a group of people based on the sheer assertion of their inferiority. I can't think of another movie that depicts such evil in such a banal way.

## Another Pezzanovante

Michael Corleone is the definitive cinematic example of a good man becoming evil. But when exactly does he switch from one category to the other? Clearly not when he commits the double murder, as he waits to pull the trigger for the confirmation that it is necessary to protect his father against another assassination attempt. And he is already there by the time he orders the death of his brother Fredo. The climactic moment is when he receives the title of "Godfather" at his nephew's baptism, during which he also, as he tells it, "settled all family business" by wiping out his New York rivals and the obstacles to his expansion in Nevada. As he prepares to confront (and then dispatch) his brother-in-law Carlo, he enters the room with exactly half of his face in shadow, an unsubtle indication of his moral decay. That moment marks the end of Michael's antihero's journey, as his methods may have cost him a part of his soul but we're still rooting for him to succeed. Who cares about Carlo, anyway?

Apparently, his wife does. Even though Carlo is a craven and despicable abuser, his murder is tragic for Michael's sister Connie and their children regardless of whether he deserves it. After Connie's eruption, Michael's wife, Kay asks if he did the thing that he obviously did. He first screams at her for daring to ask whether he murdered a family member a few hours after standing godfather to his child. When she asks again, he takes a long pause, whispers "No," and then consoles her briefly before having his lieutenant shut the door in her face. Having gained seemingly limitless power over life and death, Michael will not discuss its moral implications with those who see its effects for what they are. He will instead surround himself with sycophants and supplicants who will help to make his power seem ordinary, and therefore immune from difficult questions.

The crux of Michael's problem at the start of the second movie is his promise to Kay that he will eventually make the Corleone family "completely legitimate." This would presumably give his children greater freedom than Michael, who could not leave the family business without deserting his father at his hour of greatest need. Yet he cannot divest from his criminal enterprises without first coercing the respect of power players like Senator Pat Geary (G.D. Spradlin) who despise his "masquerading" as a "decent American" and so will extract a heavy price for allowing Michael's entry into polite society.

Faced with this dilemma, Michael becomes what Arendt called an "inner emigrant," in reference to the countless Nazi bureaucrats who later claimed that they understood its corruption and stayed only to "mitigate" its effects from within. For many, this was no doubt a retroactive excuse for those who valued the material and social perks of office over what was sure to be a lonely stand on principle—although Arendt points out that those who did refuse to participate could usually "quit their jobs without serious consequences for themselves." Even for those who really did mean well, there was no external source of accountability, as the regime left room for only the private doubts of the mind. With only their conscience as their guide, it became incredibly easy for them to justify their own participation in the most heinous crimes on the grounds that they occasionally made exceptions to alleviate individual suffering that a "real Nazi" would never have allowed.

Michael likewise exercises a totalitarian control over his empire and his actual family, based on the premise that absolute loyalty to him is the only resolution to the contradiction of a mob boss trying to rebrand himself as a respectable CEO. The opening scenes of *Part II* in Lake Tahoe foreshadow the ultimate untenability of his dual role. Michael must resort to gangster tactics in response to Sen. Geary's attempt to "squeeze" him, and then order family capo Frank Pentangeli to stand down in his turf war with allies of Hyman Roth, whom Michael needs to secure his legitimate fortune. He ultimately resolves both problems with terrible actions which are packaged as "mitigation" compared to a worse alternative.

For Geary, Michael orders the murder of an innocent sex worker, a far crueler act than the horse head scene it echoes. When Geary wakes up in a daze next to the corpse, Michael's lawyer and adopted brother Tom Hagen comforts him that he is fortunate in that the girl had "no family" and that Tom was there to help cover the matter up. After Pentangeli believes himself betrayed and prepares to testify to the Senate against Michael, Tom again appears to offer the comparative 'mercy' of suicide to spare himself and his family the Don's wrath. In both cases, the gratitude of those receiving a favor helps to validate Michael's self-perception that his ends are just, and to ignore the victims as unavoidable collateral damage.

Just as the first *Godfather* revealed the intricate world of the underworld where Vito is the undisputed master, *Part II* shows Michael's genius in navigating the overlapping worlds of criminality, business, and politics. The journey to Cuba finds

Michael to be the very thing he dismissed in his final conversation with his father, "another *pezzanovante*" ('big shot') trading influence over human lives. We find him sitting alongside government officials and corporate heads to divide the wealth of the country among themselves. Michael makes a mockery of the Senate hearing, first with a self-serving statement and rote denials before Pentangeli's brother issues a wordless threat of *omertà*. Michael's power stops short with the two characters that he cannot join him in his efforts to blur the lines of legality because they demand treatment within the bounds of a specific human relationship rather than be picked up and discarded to suit the needs of the moment.

Fredo fails to earn the respect of either Corleone family soldiers or his own wife, but he can claim a status as Michael's older brother and the Don's eldest living son. When Michael's ties with Roth elevate profit over blood, Fredo attempts a similar betrayal to claim a piece of the pie and legitimize himself in the eyes of a brother who always viewed him as an incompetent fool. Whatever his mistakes, we recognize Fredo as the kind, gentle soul that is such a rarity in the world of organized crime. Michael's greatest crime may not be killing his brother so much as stamping out a last vestige of loving vulnerability, leaving a dreary house full of hard men whose faces are all cast in permanent shadow.

We always knew that Kay would not be satisfied with the role of a gangster's wife. We also know (mostly from Mario Puzo's novel) that Michael chose her in part as a more conventional "American" wife that would socialize well with other elites. For most of the second movie she's mostly a prop, shaking hands with Geary and his wife and then sitting silently in the Senate audience as a physical confirmation of Michael's goodness. But from the sidelines, she can see that Michael orders all of his relationships based on fear, sparing her only so long as she can produce the male heir that he imagines will grow up with no knowledge of the criminal life. She sees that Michael's attempts at legitimacy are simply covering up his latest crimes. And so she declares to him that what he regards as perfectly normal and acceptable is in fact "unholy and evil." Where his violence simply perpetuates a corrupt status quo, her abortion restores the sense of shock and outrage that Michael, and maybe the audience, had seemingly lost. In the moment, Fredo suffers the same dismal fate of so many before and after him, while Kay has the door slammed in her face once again. Yet when we last see Michael, sitting alone in a chair, he appears free to contemplate his life without the noise of familial duty and business interests forcing him into a constant mode of tactical assessment in which whatever is necessary is permissible. It's possible that he finally has the time to think about all that he has done wrong, and how he might repent.

# 9

# Does Michael's *Coda* Earn Him Forgiveness?

JOE BARTZEL

*The Godfather Part III* finds the aging Michael Corleone haunted by his brother Fredo's death, and searching desperately for redemption: In exchange for the hundred million dollar gift to the poor of Sicily that he entrusts to Archbishop Gilday, he is knighted in the Vatican's Order of St. Sebastian—a public stamp of moral approval from none other than the Pope himself. He attempts to cleanse the rest of his wealth by putting it in the Vatican Bank and going into business with the Church. Even so, when he meets with Cardinal Lamberto regarding the Immobiliare swindle, Michael remains racked with guilt. Instead of counsel regarding his business deal, though, Lamberto offers him something unexpected: forgiveness.

Lamberto quickly surmises that the stress of a bad business deal isn't all that's weighing on Michael, and he invites him to confess his sins. Michael resists at first, but it doesn't take him long to zero in on what's really on his conscience: his order to kill Fredo. Michael breaks down in tears, no longer able to avoid directly confronting that act and the guilt that has taken such a toll on his body and mind. Lamberto responds, "Your life could be redeemed, but I know that you don't believe that. You will not change." His doubt in Michael's ability to reform his life notwithstanding, Lamberto nevertheless immediately recites to Michael the traditional Roman Catholic words of forgiveness.

## Something a Little Closer

Michael doesn't remain satisfied for long with the divine forgiveness Lamberto extends to him for his life of crime. He's still broken up by the wedge his violent ways have driven between him and his family. So, when he asks Kay for her forgiveness, he says that instead of forgiveness from God, he needs "something a little closer."

There's a lot about Michael's quest for forgiveness that philosophy can shed light on, and one of the most thorough philosophical accounts of forgiveness comes in Charles Griswold's 2007 book, *Forgiveness: A Philosophical Exploration.* Griswold's discussion begins with an observation about forgiveness that might help us understand why divine forgiveness alone might not be "close" enough for Michael: forgiveness, according to Griswold, is fundamentally an interpersonal thing, something that happens between a wrongdoer and a victim. In Michael's case, he wants to heal the rift that's separated him from Kay; as such, he knows that the only forgiveness that will do him any good in this regard would have to come from Kay herself.

But when should we forgive? Not in just any circumstance, Griswold warns, for if we forgive wrongdoers when the circumstances don't warrant it, then we risk degrading forgiveness itself into some other attitude, like condoning or excusing the wrongs we've suffered. Consider, for instance, the forgiveness that Michael receives from his sister Connie. Toward the end of *The Godfather*, Michael has her husband Carlo killed for colluding with Don Barzini in Sonny's murder during the Five Families' war. *Part II* finds Connie still defiantly angry at Michael for that murder. Then, at their mother's funeral near the end of *Part II*, Connie forgives him, assuring him that she understands that, in the many violent acts he has committed, he "was just being strong for all of us, the way Papa [Vito Corleone] was." In her insistence on seeing Michael's wrongdoing as right or justified, Griswold might contend that Connie's not really forgiving Michael so much as she's just making excuses for him. And when we engage in excuse-making and rationalizing of the sort that we see from Connie in this scene, Griswold warns us that we're really just making ourselves complicit in the wrongs that we're supposedly forgiving (p. 47).

Perhaps the most striking evidence of Connie's complicity as a rationalizer of Michael's violent misdeeds follows almost immediately after his confession to Cardinal Lamberto in *Part III*: When Michael confides to Connie that he's confessed his sins to Lamberto, she reads Michael just as easily as Lamberto had read him not long before. It's not hard for her to figure out what sins Michael's talking about, and so, without any prompting from Michael, her response immediately focuses in on Fredo's death. Strikingly, she doesn't quite forgive Michael, though; instead, Connie tells him that she sometimes "still thinks of poor Fredo, drowned," even going so far as to add, "it was God's will." As we learn from a conversation between Vincent and Mary earlier in *Part III*, Michael's role in Fredo's death is still a matter of rumor and speculation, even among those very close to Michael. Does Connie really believe that Fredo's death was just "a terrible accident," or is she well aware that Michael killed him? Given how quickly she brings it up when Michael mentions confessing his sins, it's hard for me to watch the scene and not conclude that she knows what he did, and by playing along as though she still naively believes along with everyone else that Fredo's death was an accident, she's only helping Michael cover for his violent acts and evade facing up to his true, full responsibility for them.

## Seeking Forgiveness

So, if there's a moral danger in offering forgiveness when it's not warranted, then when should we forgive? For that matter, should Kay forgive Michael? Griswold lays out six things that Michael has to do in order to deserve her forgiveness: 1. acknowledge his personal responsibility for the wrong he's done, 2. disavow that he would do that wrong again, 3. express regret toward her, 4. become the sort of person who no longer inflicts injuries, 5. demonstrate understanding by listening compassionately to her account of what she's suffered, and 6. offer a narrative that explains his wrongdoing (pp. 49–51). Michael actually fares well on several of these, but he comes up short on a few as well.

In Griswold's account of forgiveness, the first two criteria (acknowledging and repudiating one's wrong actions) work in tandem with each other. We cannot rightly forgive others for things that they refuse to even admit that they did. According to Griswold, "A failure to take responsibility . . . not only adds insult to injury so far as the victim is concerned, but undermines the possibility of trusting that the offender will not turn around and repeat the injury" (p. 49). Here, too, Griswold wants to see to it that forgiveness doesn't just collapse into condoning or excusing bad behavior. Consider Connie's response to Michael after his confession to Cardinal Lamberto: By insisting that Fredo's murder was just a tragic accident, Connie is expressly inviting Michael to avoid acknowledging what he did.

But it's not enough for wrongdoers to acknowledge their wrong actions; they also have to acknowledge that those actions were in fact wrong. It's not hard to grasp, on an intuitive level, how unsatisfying a non-apology admission can be. "Yes, I injured you, but no, I wasn't wrong," isn't what most of us want to hear when we're seeking an apology from someone who's done us wrong. But Griswold thinks there's a deeper reason why forgiveness demands that a wrongdoer's admission of the deed has to be accompanied by an acknowledgment of its wrongness. When wrongdoers admit to their deeds and acknowledge that they were wrong, Griswold tells us, they're asserting a simultaneous consistency and change in their identities, relative to who they were when they committed the wrong. They're saying, in effect, "Yes, I'm undeniably the person who inflicted that injury, but I'm not that kind of person anymore, and if I had it to do over again as the person I've now become, I wouldn't do it."

Once he's gotten past his initial hesitation in his confession to Cardinal Lamberto, Michael seems to have little trouble acknowledging the wrongs he's done. In his conversation later with Kay at Don Tommasino's estate, he doesn't list all his wrongdoings, but we've seen in his confession to Lamberto that he's owning up to having done all of the horrible things he's done. And, at the reception following Michael's induction into the Order of St. Sebastian at the film's beginning, we've seen that Kay certainly knows about Fredo's death and the role Michael played in it. Thus, if we're feeling charitable, we can give Michael a passing grade on Griswold's first requirement. He also fulfills Griswold's third requirement, expressing regret toward Kay. Because forgiveness itself is an interpersonal act, Griswold tells us that if Michael wants to be forgiven, it's not enough for him just to feel regret over what he's done; he also has to express that regret to the person he's seeking forgiveness from—in this case, Kay.

Michael arguably doesn't check off Griswold's second requirement, though: disavowing or repudiating the wrongs he's committed. To better understand why, let's skip ahead to the final two things that Griswold says forgiveness demands from Michael as a wrongdoer: showing Kay that he really understands the harm he's caused her, and explaining his wrongdoing to her. According to Griswold, forgiveness requires Michael to listen to Kay's account of the harm she's suffered as a result of the wrongs he's committed. *The Godfather Part III*'s relative weakness as a film unfortunately leaves us with no satisfactory resolution to the question of whether Michael fulfills this requirement. Instead of actually talking about the many horrible things Michael has done, Kay bursts into tears and admits that she still loves him, and has loved him all along. Keep in mind, at this point, it's been clearly established that Kay knows even the very worst of what Michael has done—including

Fredo's murder. She ought to be indignant at Michael's request for forgiveness, but the movie itself fails her as a character here by instead saddling her with the melodramatic love confession. She's moved to tears, easily taken in by her Sicilian surroundings and by Michael's outward charm (the latter of which she should definitely know by now not to fall for so easily).

In any case, just as Kay might have had something to say to Michael about the effects his lifetime of immorality has had on her, they're interrupted by Michael's former bodyguard Calò who delivers news to Michael about Don Tommasino's murder. Between Kay's ill-advised diversion into melodrama and Calò's interruption, we don't really get to see whether Michael has truly, fully grasped the toll that his lifetime's worth of immorality has taken on Kay. He does seem keen to listen to what Kay has to say when he asks for her forgiveness, but the most charitable grade we might be able to give Michael on this requirement is an incomplete: it seems he might be on the way there, but he's still got a way to go.

## A Whole Different Destiny

On first glance, it seems Michael might fulfill Griswold's sixth requirement: offering a narrative that explains his wrongdoing. Not just any explanation will do here, Griswold tells us. Instead, Michael's explanation to Kay of the wrongs he's committed needs to convey three things: how Michael came to commit the wrongs he's seeking forgiveness for, why those wrongs don't capture the whole of who he is as a person, and what he's doing to better himself morally. Michael's explanation to Kay of the wrongs he's committed checks off only the first two of those three boxes. Beyond that, Griswold tells us that a wrongdoer's explanation shouldn't amount to making excuses. Griswold's intuition here is that there's a difference between a wrongdoer saying, "this is what I was thinking when I harmed you," and that same wrongdoer insisting, "and that's why what I did wasn't wrong." There can often be a fine line between explanations that just explain a wrongdoer's actions, and those that go further to try to justify those actions. Some explanations might be borderline cases which different listeners may arrive at different judgments about. And Michael's is definitely a case that leaves me uncertain about whether he really believes the heinous actions he's committed throughout the course of his life were in fact wrong.

Michael offers Kay two explanations for his wrongdoing: the first one having to do with protecting his family, and the second having to do with Sicily's long history of violence. Regarding the many murders that he carried out or ordered as he amassed and consolidated power in the Corleone family, Michael explains to Kay: "I loved my father. I swore I would never be a man like him, but I loved him. And he was in danger; what could I do? And then later, you were in danger. Our children were in danger. What could I do?" In Michael's telling, he no longer wants to be the sort of person who commits such acts; even at the time, he says now, he never wanted to commit those murders. In fact, he reminds Kay, he "had a whole different destiny planned"—a destiny in which murder and organized crime played no part. "I'm not the man that you think I am," he assures her.

Michael's comments here seem to meet the first two conditions that Griswold lays out for a forgiveness-worthy explanation. First, his explanation here does describe how he came to commit the wrongs he's done. In that regard, his explanation focuses on two points: that Michael was responsible for defending his family's safety, and when that safety was threatened, defending it with violence (and even murder) was the only viable choice he had. (Or, at the very least, he believed that at the time.) In his explanation, he also insists that those violent acts aren't all that he amounts to as a person. For one thing, he emphasizes just how ferociously he loves Kay and the rest of their family, and for another, he insists that he never wanted the life that he was thrust into to begin with.

But we, along with Kay, know by now that we shouldn't just take Michael Corleone at his word. Yes, we saw in *Part I* that Vito had different plans for Michael: to become a senator or governor, rather than be locked into the family's criminal enterprises. Michael never seemed all that interested in those plans either, as we see in his exchange with his brothers in the flashback scene at the end of *Part II*. In any case, though, let's grant that Michael's being honest about never really wanting the life of a Mafia don. Michael's murderous acts might not be all he is as a person. After all, if we agree with Griswold that no one is a true moral monster, we can understand that there's more to Michael than just his penchant for ruthless violence.

Even so, is it really true that all of the murders we've seen Michael commit were absolutely necessary to protect his family? In *Part II*, after all, Tom Hagen pushed back (unsuccessfully) against Michael's plans to kill Hyman Roth and the Rosato brothers, even after their plot against Michael had been thwarted. Michael's famous reply there was, "I don't feel I have to wipe everybody out, Tom. Just my enemies." This exchange makes clear, though, that questions have swirled around Michael for a long time, even among members of his own inner circle, about whether his use of violence is proportional. Even if we want to be charitable to Michael, and grant that at least some of his killings could be seen as defending his family's safety, we've also seen enough to know that not all of them have fit that description—least of all, Fredo's murder.

## Trapped in "This Sicilian Thing"

What about Michael's second explanation—that his violent deeds are a part of what Kay has derisively described as "this Sicilian thing"? It's no coincidence that, as he's mulling over whether to tell Connie about his confession to Cardinal Lamberto, Michael's thoughts are fixed on Sicily and its violent history. He tells Connie that the people of Sicily have "been killing each other for centuries here. For money, for pride, family. To keep from becoming the slaves of the rich *pezzonovanti*." The nearness and dearness that he feels toward Sicily come up again during his conversation with Kay at Don Tommasino's estate: When she asks him why he loves Sicily so much, he replies that "all through history, terrible things have happened to these people. Terrible injustices. But they still expect good, rather than bad, will happen to them."

Michael doesn't just admire that Sicilian resilience from afar, though; he feels a deep kinship with Sicily, its people, and its history. Even his name—Corleone—links him inextricably to this place. And the Corleone family's own history is certainly inextricably linked to Sicily's long history of violence. As *The Godfather Part II* shows, Vito's life here was indelibly marked by the murders of his own brother and mother by enforcers working for the Corleone village's local mafia chieftain, Don Ciccio. *Part II* depicts Vito's eventual vengeance against Ciccio—returning to Corleone to stab him to death at the very villa where Vito's mother was gunned down pleading for Vito's life—as solidifying his rise to power.

Michael seems to see himself as inextricably caught up in this history of violence that's shaped both Sicily and the Corleone family. This explanation conveys how he came to be the ruthless murderer he's become: His ties to family and place drew him into generational conflicts that he couldn't escape. And it shows that he doesn't think his violent acts are the full extent of who he is. He identifies some noble values in his Sicilian roots: the poor resisting the domination of the wealthy, and maintaining a resilient, optimistic perspective against all odds.

But, just as his explanation about defending his family veers perilously close to being an outright justification (in addition to just being bogus in a lot of cases), his response to Calò upon hearing of Don Tommasino's death makes it clear that he takes his entanglement in Sicily's cycle of violence to be justification for further violence. In Calò's own words, *"Sangue grida sangue"* (Blood calls for blood). Michael's actions that follow demonstrate that he wholeheartedly agrees, as he responds (in Italian) to Calò's request for revenge: "Someday, you may have to do a difficult service for me." Since Michael does still insist on justifying his violent ways, he not only fails Griswold's requirement to give an explanation that's not an excuse. He also fails Griswold's earlier requirement to repudiate his wrong-doing and admit that it was wrong.

Neither of Michael's explanations conveys the third point that Griswold says an explanation needs to include: a description of what he's doing to make himself more forgiveness-worthy. As Kay quickly and wisely figures out (making her "I still love you" melodrama from just minutes before seem all the more out of character), that's largely because Michael still hasn't done enough to morally better himself. And that brings us to the last remaining requirement for forgiveness that we haven't yet touched on: becoming the sort of person who no longer inflicts injuries. And, on that requirement, as his response to Calò's demand for vengeance demonstrates, Michael fails miserably.

## Will Michael Sin No More?

While mourning Don Tommasino's death, Michael prays aloud: "I swear on the lives of my children; give me a chance to redeem myself, and I will sin no more." He's soon interrupted by Vincent, though, who's come to inform him that he's figured out who's behind the plot against Michael and the Corleone family. Vincent asks for an order from Michael to strike back, and this is Michael's big chance to make good on his promise of repentance. Instead, though, Michael nods to Vincent, setting yet another murderous scheme into motion. And, just like that, there went the chance Michael had prayed for just minutes before. For all of his talk about not being the man that Kay thinks he is, for all his insistence that he wanted to do good instead of evil, for all his promises that his wicked and murderous ways are behind him, at the very first opportunity that arises for Michael to show that he has become a different kind of person, he makes it clear that he hasn't really changed at all.

In his quick assent to Vincent's request to move ahead with a violent attack on the Corleone family's enemies, we see what may be Michael's ultimate tragic shortcoming: In one situation after another, Michael seems to believe that he's had no choice but to meet violence with violence. And now, with Vincent requesting the go-ahead to strike back at Lucchesi and his associates, Michael's still convinced that he has no choice. Both of the explanations of his wrongdoing that he offers to Kay give us a glimpse that Michael feels trapped, with the circumstances he's encountered throughout his life demanding the violence and death that he's dealt out.

Michael's life has unquestionably been shaped by violence. He grew up the son of a Mafia don, Vito Corleone—a man whose own life was indelibly marked by the murders of his mother and brother. After returning from a world war, Michael came home to witness a gang war that nearly killed his father and did kill his eldest brother, Sonny. If it really were true that Michael never had any other choice but to continue the cycles of violence he's witnessed throughout his life, then there's nothing to be forgiven, because he never could have done anything different in the first place. And one way that we might understand the entire *Godfather* trilogy is as a demonstration of how Michael's choices do get cut off, bit by bit, until he is locked into a violent pattern that he's powerless to escape.

But we can acknowledge that Michael's options throughout his life have been shaped and limited by his circumstances, without going so far as to say that he's had no choice whatsoever in his actions. And if we think he's had genuine choices, then we have to judge his attempt at becoming the sort of person who doesn't inflict injuries to be a failure. Thus, Cardinal Lamberto's assessment of Michael proves correct: He doesn't change. It's not that he can't; opportunities to show that he's changed do come Michael's way, culminating with Vincent's request for the green light on Lucchesi and his co-conspirators.

So, if Michael hasn't really changed in the end, what should we make of Lamberto's offer of forgiveness to him? Does that turn out to be the most scandalous act in the entire movie? It may turn out that God forgives for God's own reasons, and there's something powerful happening in that interaction that goes beyond human reason. But, on the question of whether Kay owes Michael the forgiveness he seeks from her, Griswold's answer at least is clear: Michael continues to find justifications for his evil ways, and he hasn't really changed those ways at all.

In the end, the possibility of Kay's forgiveness is permanently foreclosed by Mary's death by a bullet that her killer, the

assassin Mosca of Montelepre, had meant for her father. Even
before that horrific act, though, Michael had made it clear that
he hasn't earned Kay's forgiveness. Our final look at Michael
Corleone, then, comes years later, with Michael all alone at Don
Tommasino's estate. Mary's dead, and rather than forgiving
Michael, Kay and Anthony have presumably written him off for
good. At least as far as they're concerned, Lamberto's initial
response to Michael's confession gets the last word: "Your sins
are terrible, and it is just that you suffer."

# 10
# The Self and This Sicilian Thing

ALEXANDRA ROMANYSHYN

"A man who doesn't spend time with his family can never be a real man." For Vito Corleone, family, and by extension, kinship, is the linchpin that holds everything together. After all, his purported reason for getting into the criminal world in the first place was to protect his family and other Italians from mobsters who pick on their own.

This commendable dedication to family seems to be a common thread among a number of others in the Mafia; even Clemenza, after knocking off Paulie, remembers his promise to pick up dessert for his wife: "Leave the gun, take the cannoli." But what happens when the family business gets in the way of, well, your family? The unfolding stories of Michael and Vito over the course of *The Godfather Part I* and *II* show disparate ways of handling conflict within the self that arises—for instance—when you have all your enemies wacked while simultaneously vowing to renounce Satan and all his works.

Though Vito's identity as the magnanimous, noble family head seems to remain relatively intact, we see a profound transformation in Michael from the sweet hero Christmas shopping with Kay to the ruthless mobster who sends Fredo fishing.

## The Mobster and the True Self

The concept of the "true self" is one that fascinates academic philosophers and folk psychologists alike. Broadly speaking, this term refers to the set of features that distinguish an individual from others or that make them unique. Many of us have an intuitive grasp on what it is—enough to know that Michael Corleone, the once starry-eyed war hero, has lost his true self by the end of *The Godfather*. One common view (Strohminger,

**91**

Knobe, and Newman) is that the true self is also the more moral self, and so Michael has lost his because he's become an immoral person. At the same time, if someone has been a criminal their whole life, it might seem odd to say that their *true* self is so completely different from anything they have ever been. That would be like saying Luca Brasi's *true* self is nonviolent; never mind all the assassinations. The intuition here is that the true self shouldn't be completely divorced from how the person actually lives.

Philosopher Harry Frankfurt identifies the true self with the integration of the will. According to this picture, we're characterized by the things we desire and care about. Our will is integrated when we're able to resolve conflicting desires and make choices wholeheartedly. Moreover, it is *good* for us to be integrated around what we want, in the sense that we will have a happier life if that is the case. Think of it this way: let's say you are deciding whether to have a cannoli or not. The catch is that you're lactose intolerant, and so you have to decide between your desire for the cannoli, and your desire not to be sick. On Frankfurt's picture, the part of you that wants a cannoli is metaphorically pitted against the part of you that wants not to be sick. Whatever you decide, one part of you doesn't get to have its way. If you cave in and have a cannoli, at least part of you will suffer as a consequence. Having integrated desires one way or the other benefits you, then, because you get what *all* of you wants.

You can have integrated desires for pretty much anything—cannoli, or the demise of all the heads of the competing families. Simply put, as long as you don't have conflicting desires, you get to be integrated. But there are some problems with this picture. One thing, pointed out by Brad Hooker, is that getting what you want may not always be good for you; someone who wanted to do nothing but count blades of grass his whole life would not be well-off, even if they got to do exactly what they wanted. At the end of *The Godfather Part II,* Michael in many ways gets what he wants: he wipes out all his enemies, a desire that he was highly integrated around. Yet he is more miserable than ever. Integration of the will isn't doing him much good.

## The Integrated Don

Some scholars think that it's good for us to be integrated, but that integration of the self has nothing to do with consistent desires. Instead, you are integrated when you have little compartmentalization within the psyche. Sometimes we feel the need to compartmentalize different identities that make up who we are in order to avoid some negative outcome, and the more we do so, the less happy we tend to be, and the less integrated we are. While we all likely have some degree of compartmentalization (I tell fewer corny puns around co-workers than I do around my husband, for instance), extreme compartmentalization that is motivated by negative emotions, like fear, is a problem. For example, suppose a ruthless mobster who is also a loving husband and father feels the need to compartmentalize these two identities: in their business environment, they might wish to hide the gentler, more loving aspect of themselves, for fear that it would damage their intimidating persona. In the more loving, family arena, they might feel the need to conceal their identity as a ruthless mobster for fear of horrifying their family. Michael has this sort of compartmentalization because he wishes to perpetuate a narrative that "that's my family, Kay— that's not me." Because Michael is so committed to hiding his business dealings from Kay, he has to hide a significant part of his identity from her. This concealment, though, is part of what destroys their marriage. We see the epitome of a compartmentalized self at the end of *The Godfather:* Connie hints to Kay that her husband is in fact behind all the assassinations of the other New York dons, prompting Kay to ask Michael,

"Is it true?"

"Don't ask me about my business, Kay," he tells her, repeatedly. Finally, he assents: "This one time—this one time I'll let you ask me about my affairs."

"Is it true?"

"No."

This scene demonstrates just how much Michael needs to keep business and family compartmentalized. He won't even let Kay *ask* him about his affairs. In the moment when you think maybe—just maybe—he'll let her into his world, the compartmentalization is preserved with a lie.

Michael shuts Kay out—literally—as Clemenza hails him "Don Corleone" and Al Neri closes the door on her. Michael's need to severely compartmentalize business and family, and by extension don and husband, materializes in this act of shutting her out. But does a mobster necessarily have to have that sort of compartmentalization? And if not, why does Michael feel such a strong need to keep Kay completely in the dark?

To answer this question, we should rewind to our first glimpse of Vito Corleone. In the first scene of *The Godfather,* we see a psyche so integrated around being Don Corleone that the thought of accepting money for a hitjob is repugnant to him: "Bonasera, Bonasera. What have I ever done to make you treat me so disrespectfully? If you had come to me in friendship, then the scum that ruined your daughter would be suffering this very day." Accepting a hitjob is decidedly *not* just business, for Vito. There he sits, casually playing with a grey cat on his daughter's wedding day; in that moment, Bonasera's request is about relationships, friendship, and most importantly of all, family. The Godfather observes, sadly, "I can't remember the last time that you invited me to your house for a cup of coffee, even though my wife is godmother to your only child." Vito is not two-sided; the self he shows to Bonasera is the same self he shows his family.

Though he does have worries and regrets, they are not for himself and the way he has lived his own life: they are for Michael and who he eventually becomes. "I never wanted this for you," Vito tells him. "I worked my whole life—I won't apologize—to take care of my family. And I refused to be a fool dancing on the string held by all those bigshots. I don't apologize, that's my lot. But I thought that when it was your time, that you'd be the one to hold the strings. Senator Corleone, Governor Corleone." He sighs, "Just wasn't enough time, Michael. Wasn't enough time."

Vito accepted his lot; he accepted that he had to step into the role of Don Corleone to care for his family. The family business, for him, was integrally bound up with—well, the family! But for Michael, the story was—and is—rather different. Michael was not raised to be a criminal. This is the insight into Michael's compartmentalized self: he was not meant to succeed his father, and his attempt to reconcile the disparity between what he was intended for and what he is ("We'll get there, Pop") results in this narrative where just one more murder, just one more crime, will make the family safe enough that he can leave all this behind. Except he can't.

Compartmentalization within the self happens for two reasons: one, to deceive others, and two, to deceive yourself. It happens when we are in a position where acknowledging one of our identities will yield negative outcomes, so rather than deal with these outcomes, we try to conceal part of who we are. In Michael's case, the more Kay knows what he has become, the more he loses her, and the more he has to acknowledge that he isn't actually making the family business a clean, legitimate enterprise. The walls stay up.

## La Famiglia and the Self

As we have seen, many accounts of the self focus on what's going on within the individual: compartmentalization of identities, or integration of the will. Some philosophers, though, have observed that the self is not just an individualistic entity, because it is dependent upon others. To use the language of Hilde Lindemann, our friends and family "hold" us in certain identities. The stories they tell about us, as well as the way they treat us, mold and reinforce our sense of who we are. For example, part of the reason Don Vito has the identity of a magnanimous family man is that his wife and children all treat him like a magnanimous family man. Identities that other people do not corroborate are harder to maintain. Notice how unstable Fredo's identity is, for instance. He insists that he's smart, despite the way his family treats him, but he's far from confident in that assertion. He isn't even certain of his identity as a Corleone. In *The Godfather Part II,* he recalls that his mother used to say he was dropped off by gypsies, and sometimes he thinks she was right. In this brief comment, we see the power others possess in establishing our identities and determining how we think about ourselves. This relational component of the self fits well with Sicilian culture; if we were to rephrase Vito's quote about family, we'd say: "A man who doesn't spend time with his family can never be a real *self.*"

Part of why Michael loses his self, but Vito doesn't, is because Michael loses his family. In *The Godfather Part II* Michael comments that he can trust his people because he's essentially bought their loyalty. But once Fredo breaks his heart, he begins to realize that he can *only* trust those people. His own family could betray him, yet he can rely on Al Neri to be loyal. In the end, the only people holding Michael in any kind of identity are the ones hailing him "Don Corleone." All the other facets of his self die with the relationships that sustained them.

## Transformative Experience in Louis Restaurant

Whichever picture of the self we adopt—integrated, true, compartmentalized, relational, or some combination of all—one thing is clear: Michael undergoes a radical transformation of the self in *The Godfather Part I* and *II.* A question emerges: what causes such radical transformations of the self? It is nothing unusual for people to change throughout their lives, though most changes (hopefully) aren't quite as drastic as Michael's. In Michael's case, the transformation is so severe that we might simply say he's become a completely different person. This is because he's undergone what Laurie Paul calls a "personally transformative experience."

A personally transformative experience has two distin-guishing features: you don't know what it's like until you've had it, and once you've had it, it radically alters your percep-tion of the world around you and of yourself. There are lots of things that have the first distinguishing feature, but not the second. For example, if I have never tasted the Italian delicacy *trippa alla romana,* no amount of description from people who have tasted it will give me an accurate idea of what it's like or whether I'll enjoy it. Someone might tell me that it's disgust-ing, but that doesn't mean I will experience it as disgusting, and since the flavor is so unique, I probably won't be able to imagine it accurately. The only way for me to know what it's like to eat tripe is to, well, eat tripe. But it isn't clear what rea-son there is to try this entirely novel thing, since I can't know in advance whether I'll like it.

Personally transformative experiences have an added com-ponent: not only is it impossible for you to know what they'll be like in advance, but also they change you as a person. For many people, becoming a parent might be such an experience, since it significantly alters your values, goals, and even your sense of who you are. While there may not be much at stake for me in ordering the tripe versus pasta fagioli, our very identity is at stake in the case of a personally transformative experience. In the case of Michael, we can chalk up the radical shift in his self to one specific transformative experience in Louis Restaurant.

When Sollozzo and Tataglia (or really, Barzini—since "Tataglia's a pimp") make an attempt on Vito's life, Michael's world shifts away from Kay, towards helping his family. This is understandable for anyone, but especially for Michael, who has such a profound bond with his father; almost the only times we see Vito smile are with his son, and Michael, who dons an eter-nally serious face, smiles broadly while talking to Vito about his son reading the funny papers. When Michael arrives at the hos-pital and finds his father alone and without protection, he leaps into action. With the help of Enzo, the baker, Michael creates a bluff to scare away the hitmen who are coming to take his father's life. While Enzo is left shaken, unable to light a cigarette, Michael is visibly struck by the steadiness of his own hands as he holds out a lighter. Though he has seen war, this is arguably when he realizes that maybe he has the stomach for Mafia life, too. From this point on, Michael is in the process of transformation, from the "civilian" of the family to its eventual don.

When Michael learns from Sonny and Tom that Sollozzo and McCluskey, the corrupt cop who abetted Vito's attempted assassination, wish to meet with him, his burgeoning transformation becomes even more clear: with callous, business-like determination, he proposes killing them both. Clemenza, then Sonny, find this laughable, but Michael is unwavering. He needs a "guarantee" that no more attempts will be made on his father. Sonny accuses him of taking things too personally, to which Michael responds, "It's not personal, Sonny. It's strictly business." Even here, the need to compartmentalize has begun: doing what he feels he must to protect his father isn't acknowledged as a personal matter, for Michael. His nonchalant, businesslike demeanor continues while Clemenza coaches him on the details of the assassination, asking him if he knows what to do after the shooting. Michael replies, "Sit down and finish my dinner." When the time comes to shoot both men, Michael does experience turmoil, indicating just how momentous this experience is for him; the rattle of nearby subway cars overwhelms viewers as Michael finally pulls the trigger and runs out of Louis Restaurant.

This act of killing Sollozzo and McCluskey is a transformative experience for two reasons. It is evident that no amount of preparation could tell him what it would *actually* feel like to pull the trigger. Just like I cannot know what tripe will taste like until I've actually tried it, Michael cannot know what shooting someone at point-blank range is like until it's done. As Sonny tries to warn him, this isn't war: "Whadya think this is, the army where you shoot 'em a mile away? You gotta get up close like this and bada-BING you blow their brains all over your nice Ivy League suit." Michael is clearly distraught after the shooting, tossing away his gun and sprinting out of the restaurant, ignoring Clemenza's advice: "Just let your hand drop to your side, now let the gun slip out. Everyone will still think you've got it. They're gonna be staring at your face, Mike. So walk out of the place real fast, but you don't run." Once this scene is completed, there is no going back to the "civilian" he used to be; Michael is now, forever, a part of the family business. It is in this sequence that we see the death of Michael the good college boy, and the birth of Don Corleone.

Transformative experiences change you, unpredictably and irreversibly. Some people may regret having them, but there is no undoing them. Just as new parents can't go back to their former, less encumbered lives, Michael cannot go back to his former self. But the difference is, no one wanted Michael to undergo this transformation. The tragedy and finality of it is evident in Vito Corleone's face, when he is finally informed that it was Michael who killed Sollozzo and McCluskey—he turns away, teary-eyed. He knows, in that moment, that Michael can never go back. Whether Michael knows this is yet to be determined.

## Alienation and Elimination of the Self

When there is tension and fragmentation within the self, there are a couple ways to handle it. Some people learn to live with the tension. Vito Corleone preserves his magnanimous, family-oriented persona, and is seemingly unperturbed by the questionable strategies that preserve his family's safety and status. When the Hollywood producer, Jack Woltz, awakes to a severed horse head in his bed, the Godfather's response is a mere raise of the eyebrows, as if he has just been informed of an interesting—albeit unusual—business strategy on Tom's part. As we saw earlier, he's accepted his lot. Vito reconciles these two disparate identities.

Michael, on the other hand, feels the tension between his family, and the family business. In a poignant scene with his mother in *Part II*, Michael asks her about his father: "What did Papa think, deep in his heart? He was being strong . . . strong for his family. But by being strong for his family, could he . . . lose it?" When his mother reassures him that you can never lose your family, he simply replies, "Times are changing." Michael shows himself to be prescient, here, as he does end up losing most of his family by the end of the film.

Kay has an abortion because *"This* must all end!" and Michael ostracizes her from the family; Fredo is shot by Al Neri as punishment for betraying Michael; everyone else, with the exception of Connie and Tom, is dead. Michael's self-alienation alienates Kay, and he's been shutting her out for so long that it comes as no surprise when he coldly closes the kitchen door in her face after he catches her visiting their children. Even Tom, who remains, is alienated from Michael. He gets cut out in *The Godfather*, and in *Part II*, when Tom tries to argue that it's not worth killing Roth, Michael coldly asks, "Are you gonna come along with me in these things I have to do or what? Because if not you can take your wife, your family, and your mistress and move them all to Las Vegas." Tom's reply, "Why do you hurt me, Michael? I've always been loyal to you," suggests that he feels the insult of perpetually being left out, not just in this one moment, but ever since Michael demoted him from consiglieri.

In Michael's compartmentalized psyche, business ultimately wins. He cannot be both a cutthroat mobster and a loving husband, and the lie he perpetuates even moments before kicking Kay out ("I'll change. I've learned that I have the strength to change.") isn't fooling anyone. You can't undo a transformative experience; you can't change back. At the end of the day, Michael may have some integration, but it isn't with respect to his family: if anything, his will is integrated around wiping out his enemies, even if that means estranging his wife and having his brother wacked.

We can regret the loss of our former self. People who have undergone life-shattering hardships often miss the more care-free, content self they used to be.[1] Michael clearly regrets his loss. *Part II* ends with Michael sitting, alone, remembering his father's birthday. Surrounded by his two brothers, Tessio, and Carlo, all of whom are now dead (and mostly by Michael's own doing), he tells them that he has enlisted in the army. He's gone explicitly against his father's wishes, but he's done so to forge his own path in life, to live out his own vision for his future. In forging his own path, he ultimately estranges all the people who made him who he was.

---

[1] See, for example, Susan Brison, "Aftermath: Violence and the Remaking of a Self," (Princeton: Princeton University Press: 2002).

# III

---

*"Finance is a gun; politics is knowing when to pull the trigger."*

# 11
# Machiavelli Corleone

WALTER BARTA AND ARLENE BHUIYAN KHAN

In the *Godfather* trilogy, Michael Corleone is a Machiavellian leader. Whether keeping his family safe or expanding his business empire, Michael's rise to power is largely due to his adroit scheming, unabashed use of violence and political maneuvering, which are skills of deliberately honed Machiavellianism.

But who was Machiavelli? The Renaissance political philosopher, Niccolò Machiavelli is best known for his political treatise, *The Prince,* a handbook for those, like Michael Corleone, seeking power and success within the power structure. Like the Corleone family, Machiavelli was Italian; he was born and lived most of his life in Florence during the fifteenth and sixteenth centuries. He rose to prominence when appointed Second Chancellor, a position similar to the "consigliere" of a crime family, of the Republic of Florence and for the next fourteen years he travelled all through Europe on various diplomatic missions, witnessing the rise and fall of myriads of rulers. At this time the Italian peninsula was a collection of city-states ruled by noble families feuding for territory, not unlike families of the mafia. After one such regime change Machiavelli was imprisoned, tortured, and banished from the city of Florence.

During this time of disfavor, he retiring to a rural estate— somewhat like Michael Corleone while in hiding after his own run-in with law—Machiavelli turned to writing the lessons learned from his career: what became *The Prince.* Dedicated to the ruler of Florence, perhaps to regain favor, Machiavelli's writing offers insight into how to obtain and maintain power, based on his observations of the successes and failures of past rulers. Contrary to the prevailing thought of his time, Machiavelli advised practical political realism in contrast to well-intentioned political idealism.

To Machiavelli, and Michael would surely agree, being a good and honest person may be precisely what makes for being a weak ruler because strong leadership sometimes requires acts that may not always be considered conventionally moral. Misunderstood and demonized, the name "Machiavelli" became synonymous with power-hungry self-glorification. However, far from advocating immorality, Machiavelli suggested his advice could lead to the security of the state, resulting in better lives for its citizens.

According to Machiavelli's philosophy, the state would best flourish under a strong ruler, thwarting threats from outside, unencumbered by unrealistic expectations and foolhardy ideals. Far from being limited to feudal princedoms, Machiavelli's methods have since been adopted by modern politicians, entrepreneurs, and mobsters alike—anyone, like the Corleones, seeking political success in the face of difficult realities.

Machiavelli described a great ruler, or his ideal "Prince," as one having "virtù," the mastery of how to possess and apply power, not to be confused with "virtue," the qualities of moral character, which are possessed by a good person. A ruler with virtù is astute, cunning, and adaptable. According to Machiavelli, a Prince would have an "ends justify the means" philosophy, willing to compromise morals and commit necessary evils to obtain and maintain power.

A Prince would respond boldly to fortune, be loved and feared, apply appropriate force, and use and detect deception, all the while appearing to be good. As can be shown, through his actions and attitudes throughout *The Godfather* trilogy, Michael Corleone is an excellent example of a Machiavellian leader, embodying the qualities of virtù, willing to do whatever it takes to achieve his goals.

## Take Accidents as A Personal Insult

For Machiavelli, a Prince must be opportunistic and master their fortune. According to Machiavelli, "Fortune is the arbiter of one-half of our actions"—or more (*The Prince*, XXV). Normally thought of as a force randomly affecting human affairs, Machiavelli thought of fortune as the goddess Fortuna, who like a torrential river destroys everything in its path, against which a Prince should prepare during calmer times or quickly change course to avoid destruction.

Since fortune is usually bad and always out of their control, a Prince must respond proactively and adaptably in the face of changing circumstances, even if it means undermining former plans and principles. A poor ruler ignores fortune or is taken by it in contrast with a great ruler who is a master of fortune, rather than a victim of it, and exploits it to advantage. For example, in an instance of pure chance, when in hiding in Sicily, Michael survives a car bomb intended to kill him when his first wife Apollonia accidentally triggers it instead, upending his life and ending hers. This event demonstrates how even powerful families like the Corleones are not immune to the whimsies of fate. As a boss might say, "If anything in this life is certain, . . . it's that you can kill anyone." In other words, no matter how protected you are, fortune can still wipe you out.

Thus, not having a mastery of fortune leads to weakness. For instance, the decline of Michael's father, Vito Corleone, is largely attributable to his inability to adapt to the times. When Virgil "The Turk" Sollozzo offers him a part in the up-and-coming narcotics business, Vito not only turns down the opportunity, but gives the impression that he is stuck in the olden times, making himself a hindrance to the business, unwilling to embrace fortune.

Machiavelli further noted that a Prince can obtain power either by "hereditary" titles or by "arms and ability," though both involve good fortune (II, VI). The former is easily gotten but is a matter of the luck of good birth; the latter is more difficult and depends on one's ability and adaptability; but of course, neither guarantees long term power. All this can be seen in the difference in deference shown to Vito's children: Sonny, Fredo, Tom, Connie, and Michael.

When Vito is hospitalized, Sonny is initially thrust into leadership as he is the first-born son, but he loses it due to his rash decision-making and the inability to control his emotions. Tom Hagen rises high in the family due to ability and even becomes consigliere; but Tom's unfortunate birth, as an orphan with Irish heritage, never allows him to rise to the position of Don himself. Fredo, the second son, is a playboy in Las Vegas and is therefore not seen as serious, strong, or able enough to become Don. Connie, as the Don's daughter, does not share the same privileges as his sons; nor does her husband, Carlo Rizzi, as a mere son-in-law. Michael on the other hand, although but a third son, earns his title both by inheritance and by accomplishment, insuring his place as Don.

Michael shows great flexibility and opportunism from the very beginning. Introduced as a character who doesn't fit into the violent mobster underworld, Michael changes his behavior to preserve his family and business. Early on he avenges his father's attack by shedding his non-violent principles and adapting to the needs of the moment. Walking into the hospital late in the evening just as his father is about to be murdered, Michael assesses and reacts to the situation quickly. He calls for back-up, asks the nurse for help to move his father, and enlists Enzo, the baker's son, who happens to be passing by. Much later, after securing himself the title of Don and defeating the Five Families in New York, Michael seizes as many opportunities as he can; he expands the family business by tapping into the gambling industry, leaving olive oil behind. He is willing to change with the times and adapt to the opportunities at hand, unlike his father. Machiavelli would approve of Michael's ability to master his fortune. Michael is patient and punctual, he waits for the opportunity and reacts quickly when it presents itself. He also considers other possible outcomes, which gives him an upper hand over others when situations unfold unpredictably.

## Keep Your Friends Close and Your Enemies Closer

Another important rule for Machiavelli is that a Prince must inspire the respect of subjects. Regarding whether it is better to be respected by being feared or loved, Machiavelli said that "one should wish to be both, but . . ., it is much safer to be feared than loved" (XVII). Furthermore, the Prince should "avoid those things which will make him hated" (XIX). Love and fear encourage loyalty, but hate and contempt encourage revolt. Thus, both mercy and revenge may sometimes be errors if they weaken the state. Also, a Prince should only employ loyal soldiers since "mercenaries and auxiliaries are useless and dangerous" as they can turn at a moment's notice (XII). For example, when Sonny hires men to guard his father at the hospital, they are unreliable; in contrast, when Michael enlists Enzo, a mere baker's assistant, for the same task, Enzo stays because he is a loyal friend to the Corleones.

Vito is a Don that is loved and feared, lording over the family with a generous but dangerous presence. Vito initially gains respect by murdering Don Fanucci, a much-hated local mafia boss. Afterward, instead of asking for Fanucci's dues for himself, Vito further solidifies his reputation by doling out favors with the understanding that favors may be asked in return. His demeanor is always warm and calm and he is known to be able to reason with unreasonable people. His relationships are based on love, but with an undercurrent of fear: he treats his friends kindly, but his enemies brutally, which inspires fear in friend and enemy alike. For example, Vito demonstrates a merciful and loving character when he helps Amerigo Bonasera get revenge, even though Bonasera had not shown him respect. However, Vito's words are intimidating and cold, instilling fear in Bonasera and ensuring loyalty.

Vito similarly handles the mistakes of his family members in a merciful manner. He doesn't always retaliate using force, even for grave injuries, like the death of his first-born son, Sonny. As his son Michael says of the matter, "Never hate your enemies. It affects your judgment." Sparing lives and forgiving are the calculated means by which Vito garners love and avoids hate. As a result of this trait, Vito maintains loyalty from politicians and Dons to a degree that Michael and Sonny do not. However, due to Vito's sometimes merciful character, his enemies grow to fear him less and he is gunned down as a result.

Worse still, some of his allies—Paulie Gatto and Salvatore Tessio—betray Vito for personal advancement, in spite of their love for him. Machiavelli would have predicted this, for as he says, "men more quickly forget the death of their father than the loss of their patrimony" (XVII).

Michael attempts to invoke love and fear through many of his actions, but as Michael becomes more powerful and more vicious, he is loved less and feared more. Michael initially gains the admiration of his own mafia family by killing Sollozzo and then massacring the heads of other families in New York. After this, his loyal capos come to pay their respects by kissing his ring and calling him "Don Corleone." However, Michael's demeanor is not as warm as Vito's and the fear he instills in his followers eventually becomes hate. Hyman Roth, a business partner and fellow mobster, hates Michael and attempts to assassinate him in retaliation for the murder of Moe Greene, a rival casino owner. Even Michael's own family avoids and alienates him. His sister Connie resents him and his own wife Kay divorces him and has an abortion out of spite.

Machiavelli would approve of both Vito's and Michael's general approach to their followers. However, Machiavelli would point to the weaknesses of their extremes: Vito is too soft and Michael is too hard. Ultimately, the strengths and weaknesses of both lead to their rise and decline in power.

## I Don't Like Violence; Blood Is a Big Expense

Furthermore, according to Machiavelli, a Prince must use violence as an instrument to seize control and maintain power. He advises the use of adequate force to annihilate the enemy quickly and permanently, so they can never retaliate, instead of a drawn-out process of small injuries over time. He warns, however, against the over-use of violence as it can lead to hatred, distrust, and revolt. In his words, "men ought either to be well treated or crushed, because they can avenge themselves of lighter injuries, of more serious ones they cannot" (III). Machiavelli further advises to be both man and beast. The beast, he described, would be a lion or a fox as circumstances dictated, the former because it is strong and scares wolves and the latter because it can detect and avoid traps.

Vito and Sonny both use force but in different and opposite ways. While Vito uses force carefully, rarely and for only specific occasions, Sonny is more trigger happy and unhinged. Vito prefers to use intimidation, instrumentally but indirectly. For example, rather than hurting him outright, Vito threatens a movie producer by decapitating his prized horse and leaving the head in his bed. Furthermore, Vito covers his tracks. Rather than confronting him directly, Vito trails the mob boss Fanucci until there are no witnesses, surprises him with a quick and deadly gunshot, and discretely disposes of the weapon. Vito also sometimes rejects calls to extreme violence. For example, when Bonasera requests help in avenging the cruelty shown to his daughter, Vito refuses to commit murder, instead settling for assault. However, Vito sometimes underestimates the need for protection. He is shot on more than one occasion due to inadequate bodyguards. Vito pays for his underuse of force.

Sonny, on the other hand, is violent and hot headed, having gained his ruthless reputation during a turf war with the Irish mob. In the aftermath of his father's assassination attempt, Sonny goes into a fit of rage and orders many people killed, including Don Tattaglia's son, guaranteeing hatred and revenge from the other families, as predicted by Machiavelli. Conversely, when the enemy is not attacked with adequate force, they are more apt to regroup and come back stronger. This is exactly what leads to the demise of Sonny. Later, when Sonny's brother-in-law Carlo assaults his sister Connie, Sonny beats him to a pulp in retaliation, but does not kill him. This gives an opening to the Tattaglias, who convince Carlo to work with them to take Sonny out, leading to Sonny's violent death in a rain of machinegun fire. Sonny pays for his overuse and underuse of force

In contrast, Michael's use of force is precise and sufficient to thwart retaliation, as recommended by Machiavelli. When his father is almost killed, Michael kills Sollozzo quickly and cleanly, with minimal necessary use of force. The best Machiavellian example, however, is when Michael orchestrates the assassination of all the other heads of families in New York and their co-conspirators. The strike is as quick as it is comprehensive: the killings all occur at the same time, catching everyone by surprise, leaving no one powerful left to seek revenge. As Michael says of the matter, "I don't feel like I have to wipe everybody out. Just my enemies" (*The Godfather Part II*). Machiavelli himself tells a similar story as an example, that of Agathocles the Sicilian, who rose to power through a similar massacre. One morning, Agathocles called all senators and rich men of Sicily to an assembly. They were meant to discuss a political matter, but instead he signaled the military to kill everyone present. Having eliminated everyone powerful, he declared himself king.

However, Machiavelli also warns against savage, cruel, inhumane, and excessive force, even if it gives one power like Agathocles, because it doesn't give glory. In other words, one remains inferior to other excellent rulers that are able to acquire the same success by more measured means. As Michael gets entrenched in the family business, his use of force gets demonstrably excessive. He goes after Hyman Roth and the Rosato brothers even as Tom Hagen assures the security of his family position and suggests against pursuing personal vendettas. Michael also orders the assassination of his brother-in-law Carlo and his brother Fredo, actions which haunt him for the rest of his life.

Throughout the *Godfather* saga, Michael, Vito, and Sonny use force to establish power, regain security, and avenge personal vendettas. When applying force as suggested by Machiavelli, just enough to annihilate the enemy, they are all successful; however, when force is over- or underused it leads to grave mistakes that ultimately lead to their downfall.

## Never Let Anyone Know What You're Thinking

Finally, and perhaps most controversially, Machiavelli says that a Prince should be skilled in the art of deception: to be able to discern when to keep their word, perform good acts, and when not to. As Machiavelli puts it, "it is unnecessary for a prince to have all the good qualities . . . , but it is very necessary to appear to have them" (XVIII). Though refraining from casting moral judgements about the behaviors of rulers, Machiavelli does consider a ruler justified for deceiving subjects, as they themselves are likely equally wicked. He highly encourages rulers to be good when they can but to be bad when they must and to always appear good either way.

This includes the keeping up of religious appearances. Rulers should only speak in terms of peace and faith, attend religious services, and take part in religious ceremonies, because subjects judge superficially and will assume a ruler is inherently good if they look the part. These deceptions are not only allowed, they are imperative, being the only way to ensure the loyalty of subjects and stability of the state.

Failure to use such deception or discretion can have bad results. For example, Sonny inadvertently reveals to Sollozzo that he favors the narcotics trade, unlike his father Vito. Sonny thus shows his hand to his enemy. This knowledge directly leads Sollozzo to plot to murder Vito so that the family can be taken over by Sonny. If Sonny had played his cards closer to his chest, had he kept his emotions and thoughts under control, Sollozzo's assassination attempt on Vito may never have happened.

In contrast, Michael excels in the art of deception. Early on he creates the illusion that his father is well-protected even though in reality he was abandoned. Michael deduces that Sollozzo is working with corrupt police led by Captain McCluskey. He then deceives both into thinking he is just a "civilian," uninterested and uninvolved in the mafia. Later, pretending he is unarmed, Michael is able to grab a secretly planted gun from the bathroom stall, effectively without risk of capture. Sollozzo himself attempts to deceive Michael too when he claims that he is "not that clever," feigning ignorance; but Sollozzo inadvertently proves himself right when he lets his guard down so much that Michael is able to kill him single handedly.

As Michael becomes more involved in the family business his need to deceive even those most close to him grows. Michael uses deception to lay traps for Carlo, even lying to his face. Michael also becomes better at detecting deception from others, keenly deducing that Fredo had been lying to him all along. As recommended by Machiavelli, Michael also maintains an appearance of goodness. He tells everyone that he will make his family's business legitimate, though he never quite does. He also passes as a good Catholic and even accepts the role of Godfather for his nephew. In perhaps his most Machiavellian moment, Michael attends his nephew's baptism at a crowded church at the exact moment that his henchmen murder all his enemies; thus, he keeps up the appearance of goodness and ensures himself an alibi, even as he performs one of the greatest massacres in his family's history. Afterward, when his wife

Kay asks about his involvement in the crimes, he lies and closes the door on her, ensuring that she can never betray his schemes. Just as Machiavelli would advise, a successful leader like Michael is able to do what needs to be done, at worst deceptively and at best discretely, and always under the guise of goodness.

## The Ends Justify the Means?

Throughout *The Godfather* trilogy, Michael Corleone follows Machiavelli's doctrine of leadership, although he never says it (but true Machiavellians would never admit that they are Machiavellians, after all). Michael advances "virtù" rather than "virtue": political expediency rather than moral beneficence. Specifically, his means to power include opportunism, love, fear, force, and deception.

In the end, as one might expect, Michael's scheming leads to precisely the results that Machiavelli predicts: power, wealth, and influence. However, we also see the pitfalls of such a strategy, as Michael achieves a Pyrrhic victory, alienating himself from his family in the process of protecting it. Being Machiavellian has its benefits, but these may come at the expense of other important moral values and virtues: family, legitimacy, and conscience.

Either way, Machiavelli has achieved his own lasting influence: his philosophy of political realism continues to affect real-world politics to this day.

# 12

# The Government Is My Family

JENNIFER KLING

During much of the first two *Godfather* movies, Don Vito rules New York. Sure, there are the police and there are off-screen political officials like judges and the mayor, but Vito is the man in charge. He's the one pulling the strings to make things happen and ensure justice is done. (Well, his notion of justice, anyway. But isn't that true of all political authorities? They all do what *they* think is just.) As Michael tells Kay, "My father is no different than any other powerful man . . . any man who's responsible for other people, like a senator or a president."

Kay disagrees with Michael's point of view, so much so that she refuses to give birth to their third child and instead chooses to have an abortion in *The Godfather Part II*. But Michael's point tracks—Vito, and later Michael Corleone himself, function basically as heads of state. The Corleone Dons, as well as the Dons of the other Five Families, provide protection to those under their jurisdiction, grant aid to those who ask and are deemed worthy, maintain levels of organization and bureaucracy that ensure that life is more-or-less predictable for those who follow their rules, and publicly act as moral exemplars within their communities. They also back their claims to authoritative rule with the threat of overwhelming force and violence. As Michael could've said in response to Kay's disagreement, if it looks like a cannoli and tastes like a cannoli . . .

But, we should be careful in our judgment here. Are Vito, Michael, and the other Dons really the true rulers of New York? They do run the city; there is no question about that. But do they have the right, or, we might say, the standing, to do so? Or, are they simply political pretenders, barking orders backed by force and nothing more? At the end of the day, what is the difference between the heads of the Five Families and the heads of the government?

## Elections, Duh

Dons are not elected; this much we know. No one voted Vito or Michael into office. There was no possibility of a referendum on the question of whether the Five Families should move into the drug trade, and no way to appeal Michael's decision to move the family to Nevada. By contrast, presidents, senators, mayors, and the like are all selected by the people, at least in theory. Political legitimacy, or the right and standing to rule, is conferred by the process of being freely and fairly elected. The rallying cry of American democracy is that ultimate political power resides in the people—we choose who leads us, not the other way around, and we'll go to the mattresses against anyone who tries to take over without our consent. It's not personal; it's just business: the business of freedom.

But for there to really be a democratic political system, everyone needs to have roughly equal political power at the outset. Part of being free is being able, by right, to exercise the same measures of political control as everyone else. You don't have to exercise your political power, of course—you're free *not* to vote, or protest, or participate in referendums, or appeal to the courts. You simply have to have the ability to do so without penalty. In the United States, though, it is not, and never has been, true that all ordinary citizens have this freedom. Some people have, and always have had, more power and ability to impact collective political decision-making than others.

The theory is one person, one vote; but that's just a story we tell ourselves. In reality, we don't all have equal political power. Take blue-collar workers, for example (who are disproportionately Americans of color). Their hourly positions mean that they often can't get time off to go vote, or to go to city council meetings, or to visit a lawyer to file an injunction. (Who's got the time? Or the money?) Technically, they can do these things, of course—but not without serious penalty. In the United States at least, losing your job, having your pay docked, or spending all your savings and time to sue those damn boys who beat up your daughter, puts you perilously close to turning to a life of petty theft to get by. And, if there's no real possibility of exercising your supposed democratic rights without penalty, it's hard to say you have those rights at all.

We think that whoever is officially voted into office has the will of the people on their side: they are legitimately in charge because we the people put them there. But as of 2020, according to The Sentencing Project (sentencingproject.org), over 6.2 percent of Black Americans cannot vote, permanently, because they have been convicted of a felony. Compare this to the 1.7 percent of non-Black Americans who are disenfranchised. And, what makes these stats even more troubling is that a felony can be anything from murder, to stealing $500 worth of stuff (in Kentucky), to illegally camping on state property (in Tennessee), to cheating at the lottery to win $1500 (in Nebraska). The list goes on. The point is that Black Americans are disproportionately convicted of felonies, and so disproportionately lose their right to vote. It is not clear whether these laws are still intentionally targeted at imprisoning and disenfranchising Black Americans, as they were in the past, or whether current Black disenfranchisement is an unintended, deeply harmful result of the structure of the American criminal justice system. Regardless, in both Florida and Alabama, over 15 percent of the Black population is disenfranchised—so can we really say that Florida and Alabama politicians legitimately speak for them? I believe in America, but I don't think so.

These profound disparities in political power—which are just a few of a much larger set also including corporate money in politics, gerrymandering, the Electoral College, etc.—mean that our presidents, senators, mayors and the like have *never* really been freely and fairly elected by the people over which they have jurisdiction. They don't rule because (or with all) of our consent. Just like Michael, they rule because they are simply the heirs who took up the mantle when it was their time. (Or, like Vito, they took power from the old guard with a powerful, if not deadly, blow.) Just like the Dons, government officials rule because they've got power, and wealth, and have select people willing to support their rule with money and violence. With apologies for quoting *Godfather III*, "Politics and crime. They're the same thing."

## Who's Being Naive?

Unlike senators and presidents, Kay tries to tell Michael, men like Michael's father have men killed. Politicians just make grumpy speeches attacking mafiosi, or flowery speeches praising Italian Americans on the House floor. *That's* the key difference between the two, you might argue. The *Godfather* movies are full of violence; although "women are more dangerous than shotguns," the guns (and knives and fists) do a lot of damage, and solve a lot of problems for the Dons. In the background of their business is always the threat of deadly force. Don't do what we want, or don't do it our way? We'll make you an offer you can't refuse, and by that we mean we'll put a horse head in your bed to scare you into complying. Either your brains or your signature will be on that contract.

Of course, this doesn't sound entirely dissimilar to American domestic and foreign policy. During the Portland Black Lives Matter protests of 2020, federal officers dressed in plainclothes and tactical gear pulled peaceful protesters into unmarked vans and held them, sometimes for hours, before arresting them or letting them go. Arrests in these cases, according to *NPR*, were based on whether the protestors resisted being pulled into the vans. (For the record, if someone who looks like Luca Brasi pulls me into a van, you bet I'm resisting! I've seen *The Godfather*, I know how these things sometimes end.)

After calls to regulate and defund the police gained traction in 2020, NYPD Police Union Chief Patrick Lynch responded by urging police officers to follow every regulation that guides their conduct and behavior to the letter. According to *The New Yorker*, Lynch argued that if liberal protestors wanted regulation, then police would show them regulation. While some regulation is good—we don't want a bunch of Captain McCluskeys running the police—Lynch's response is, and clearly was meant to be, a hell of a threat. Comply, or we'll find ways to make your life hell until you comply. Continue to refuse to dance on the strings held by the government? We'll make it clear that we can make you disappear.

These are contemporary examples, but historical cases of the government controlling its population through the threat and use of violence aren't difficult to find. March for civil rights? The police will set the dogs on you and burn crosses on your lawn. Try to carry a gun while Black? An officer will shoot you. Unionize? Federal agents will throw rocks and try to blackmail you into committing suicide. To be fair, professional police forces and domestic federal enforcement agencies in the United States were originally formed to protect nineteenth-century businessmen, politicians, and their interests. Perhaps it's not surprising they act like mafia enforcers. The point here is not to assign blame for how this came to be; it is simply that the American government cannot claim innocence in regard to using (sometimes deadly) force in order to enforce its will on its own people in a way that is analogous to the tactics of the most ruthless mafia Dons.

Something very similar can be said in regard to American foreign policy. As US President Teddy Roosevelt described it in

1901, the United States should "speak softly, and carry a big stick" in the international community. While it's not so elegant as a shiv or garrot, the point is the same. Attempt to reason first—you want to talk business? Let's talk business—and if that doesn't work, turn to violence to achieve your goals of protecting and empowering your family, err, your country. At the extreme, execute coordinated killings, or wars, to get rid of the Moe Greenes Hyman Roths of the world who are standing in the way of the United States. Of course, sometimes these killings don't succeed—like Pentangeli, Fidel Castro survived numerous CIA assassination attempts—and that causes all sorts of complications. But in general, we might think that this kind of violence on the international stage is acceptable, because after all, it's in the interests of the country. Like Michael, the United States simply does what it thinks is necessary to protect its interests, regardless of what anyone else in the family, or citizenry, has to say about it.

Using violence to solve problems, though, is not how legitimate countries are supposed to act. They are supposed to be better, or at least different, than crime bosses in that they are supposed to use diplomacy and law rather than violence and deadly force. If we accept that "anything goes" in the realm of American foreign policy, so long as it is in the country's best interests (as decided by those in charge), then there is no practical difference between the mafia and the American government. Save perhaps that the Dons and their families are more efficient and effective in their work. Similarly, when we recognize that American domestic political authority is backed ultimately by the threat of violence and deadly force, rather than by the consent of the people, it becomes clear that there is no relevant difference between the heads of the Five Families and the heads of state. The American government is a poorly managed mafia family.

## *Realpolitik* and the Rule of Law

At this point, we might conclude that the Dons have an even greater right, or standing, to rule than our presidents, senators, mayors, and the like. If all we have are options between tyrants, there are pragmatic reasons to go for the more transparent, efficient, and effective ones. The Dons are more realistic about what role they *really* play, and they get the job done with the minimum of necessary fuss, because blood is a big expense. They're realists; they're not holding themselves to any independent moral or ethical standards. They are careful though to do whatever maintains and grows their and their families' power to operate with impunity in their communities. This kind of freedom inevitably requires violence, but it's not personal; again, it's strictly business.

This is the realpolitik attitude made famous by the "Iron Chancellor," Otto von Bismarck, who helmed the unification of Germany in 1871. He employed ruthless diplomacy and charm, as well as violence and military force, to maintain both domestic control and the German Empire's powerful position in Europe for his almost thirty-year tenure. Bismarck would fit right in—just like Tom Hagen—with the Sicilians depicted by Coppola and Puzo. Bismarck, or Vito or Michael Corleone for that matter, would've stopped Hitler at Munich. Forget rights and legitimacy and justice; perhaps it's better to have those who are openly realists in charge, who are willing to do what stops the war before it gets out of hand.

The downside of the realpolitik approach is that it requires an endless cycle of violence. There are business killings, revenge killings, counter-killings for the revenge and business killings, beatdowns, rough-ups . . . the list goes on. Realists are willing to do whatever it takes to win; in their world, violence is inevitable because it will often appear to be the most expedient response and there are no external standards impeding its use. The realpolitik style can, and sometimes does, create stability and order. Before Michael instigated the war among the Five Families, things in New York were fairly calm—everyone in their communities just followed the Dons' orders, because everyone knew what would happen to them if they didn't. This is order, yes, but it's at the expense of true justice and peace.

True justice and peace require something more than order. Justice requires rule of law, not of people. Peace requires the presence of social support systems that serve the whole population, not merely those subsets of the population that happen to be in the good graces of the rulers. Vito Corleone is nicer than Don Fanucci; the people love him in part because of that. But Vito—like all the Dons—still deals in favors. To get what you need, whether it's start-up money, or to prevent your immigrant apprentice from being deported, or to have your daughter's assailants beaten up, you must be his friend (read: be willing to do what the Don wants, should he call on you). And even still, the Don can refuse, as Vito does in negotiations with Sollozzo. The Dons have complete discretion in how they respond to requests, based on their own preferences. When the undertaker goes to Don Corleone, he's not really getting justice.

He's simply getting what Vito is willing to give, on this, the day of his daughter's wedding.

Although it would go against Sicilian tradition, Vito could have refused the undertaker, and there would be nothing the undertaker could do. This is the rule of men, not laws (emphasis on *men* as in the patriarchal world of the *Godfather,* only men rule. There are no Lady Dons. But, I digress sans apology). Were the Dons bound by rule of law, there would be some things they must do, and other things they could not do. The law would have ascendancy; it would constrain and control the Dons, not the other way around. Where there is rule of law, there is public agreement about what the law is—no rulers making decisions purely based on their preferences or their own personal views of justice!—and agreement that everyone is subject to the same set of laws, even when they disagree with it or it conflicts with their interests. Also, under rule of law, everyone has access to the law. They can use it to settle disputes, uphold their rights, and protect themselves and others against abuses of power, regardless of whether they can bake a cake for the judge or provide fresh oranges for the lawyers.

## Big Plans and High Hopes

We don't live in a world that has full rule of law. But, we could. The American government has the potential to be more than a poorly managed mafia family. It was originally conceived of as a country based on the rule of law, where the consent of the people, not the threat of violence and deadly force, would provide the authorities with the right and standing to rule. Now, those who came before us had their own plans for the future, and so our country has never lived up to these founding ideals.

The story of the *Godfather* films is the story of America. We have tried so hard to be legitimate, but every time we think we're out, they pull us back in. We end slavery—and then get Jim Crow. We end Jim Crow—and then get mass incarceration. We ensure that women and non-landowners can vote—and then refuse to make Election Day a holiday. We provide public education for all—and then refuse to fund it adequately. We call for avoiding foreign entanglements—and then endlessly interfere in Central and South American countries. We depose a dictator in Iraq—and then install a puppet government that falls as soon as we leave. Our track record is not great.

But our history does not determine our future. We could redeem ourselves by working to create a government that upholds the rule of law. We could put social support systems in place that help everyone (everyone! Even the Fredos of the world), and we could refuse to let the powerful create exceptions for themselves and their friends. Sure, nothing is ever perfect in the real world—there will always be exceptions and people who slip through the cracks—but we could work to overcome the corruption, the cycles of violence and favors, by aiming to bring about the rule of law in our country. If we did this, then there would be a difference between the heads of the Five Families and the heads of the government.

The rule of law isn't personal, and it's more than strictly business: it's the key to true justice and peace.

# 13

# Plato's Philosopher King and Coppola's Godfather

Bruno Ćurko and Antonio Kovačević

Let's be honest, who wouldn't want to be ruled by a perfect person? Someone wise, someone just, someone, perhaps, with a face and posture like that of Marlon Brando? Indeed, if you wish to live in a perfect state, it's kind of logical that its ruler must be a perfect human.

Today, we can see flaws in this. There's no perfection. We can only hope that every four years or so, as a consolation prize, we manage to pick the best temporary ruler. A ruler who will be as wise as possible and who will be just. Or, at least, just-*ish*. Looking like Marlon Brando is usually neglected as a prerequisite for ruling nowadays.

However, some 2,500 years ago, ancient Greeks were still full of optimism. Having enough time on their hands, while the concept of democracy was still young, and while the city-states were small enough that almost everyone could say something and be heard, their philosophers went to work, imagining what an ideal state would look like. Rarely anyone took them quite seriously, and why would they?

Here's what some of those weirdos did: Socrates walked barefoot everywhere and was sentenced to death because he "corrupted the youth," Diogenes slept in a barrel on the streets and shouted at kings, and Demonax . . . well, he was pretty chill. So chill, in fact, that he stopped eating and starved himself to death. Some of them, still, were highly regarded in society. Pythagoras, for instance, had his own cult and, to return the favor, gave us math. Aristotle had his own school, and was the teacher of Alexander the Great—he gave us a huge scientific basis on which later brainiacs like Nicolaus Copernicus and René Descartes developed their work. And Aristotle's teacher, Plato, also gave us a lot of stuff to think about; so much stuff, in fact, that we can't stop thinking about it, even as we're watching *The Godfather*. He also gave us an occasional migraine.

## Plato's Quick Guide to Becoming a Philosopher King

Plato thought and wrote about an ideal state, and with it, the notion of *justice*. In his capital work *The Republic* (around 375 B.C.E.), Plato imagines an alternative system of power with an ideal head of state—the philosopher king. In this idealistic alternative to the realistic situation, he outlines the qualities which this ideal ruler must possess: truthfulness, temperance, justice, and a good memory—all obtained through political skill and philosophical study. It's safe to say that no one was surprised when Plato, as a philosopher, suggested that philosophers would be the best rulers, isn't it? But let's rewind the historical tape a bit.

Since humans began organizing themselves in communities, and since civilizations began to emerge, there has always been either a ruler, or a group of people who ruled, at the head of these communities. From the earliest human settlements through, let's say, the unification of the Upper and Lower Egypt kingdoms around 3100 B.C.E., to today's democratic governments; from the first known Egyptian ruler, the pharaoh Narmer, to the (currently) last known US President Joe Biden.

During these five thousand years, there were different approaches to the idea of ruling, but most of them had something in common—most of them claimed to rule justly. And while different kings, emperors, chieftains, and despots tried to impose their idea of justice on their subordinates, philosophers sat in the corner, scratching their heads. What the heck *is* justice? Philosophers started to ask this question some 2600 years ago, starting with the pre-Socratic schools, and haven't stopped asking it to this day. Plato was quite interested in this question as well, offering his answer in *The Republic*.

According to Plato, justice and governance were strongly intertwined—justice is ensured through righteous rule providing the maximum possible happiness for all citizens. But what would justice look like in practice, who would be at the steering wheel of a just system? Would Plato approve of the way that, let's say, the USA elects its presidents, or would he be more inclined to the idea of the Godfather? It has to be a trick question, right? I mean, Plato, a super smart and progressive ancient Greek raised in Athens, cradle of democracy, would surely choose Dwight D. Eisenhower over Don Vito Corleone?

Surprisingly—no! Plato wasn't a big fan of democracy, and the rule of the people by the people didn't sit well with him. In his metaphor "The Ship of State" he tries to explain that democracy is the rule of incompetence:

> The sailors are quarrelling with one another about the steering—everyone is of the opinion that he has a right to steer, though he has never learned the art of navigation . . . the true pilot must pay attention to the year and seasons and sky and stars and winds, and whatever else belongs to his art, if he intends to be really qualified for the command of a ship, and that he must and will be the steerer . . . (Plato, The Republic, Book VI)

To be able to rule well and to rule justly, a leader has to be competent, he has to be educated for the throne. Similarly, as an ordinary sailor shouldn't have an opinion about steering the ship, why should an ordinary citizen have a word in ruling? Harsh as it may be, Plato argued that the only people fit to be "captains of the ship" are philosopher kings, in his words, benevolent men with absolute power. It's easy to draw this parallel with the Godfather, at least the part about the absolute power. Benevolence, well, can wait for now.

## Justice for All, or Just for a Philosopher King

So far, we could see that the ideal rule and justice are connected. The reason why Plato insisted on introducing philosopher kings as ideal statesmen lies in this connection. He saw justice as the answer to the problem of human behavior, and only those who possessed this virtue were eligible for ruling. He goes on to say:

> Until philosophers are kings, or the kings and princes of this world have the spirit and power of philosophy . . . cities will never have rest from their evils—no, nor the human race, as I believe—and then only will this our State have a possibility of life and behold the light of day. (Plato, The Republic, Book V)

Why was he so insistent on pushing philosophers as kings, and why should they be, of all people, the best choice for rulers? And what has this got to do with *The Godfather*? For Plato, to be a perfect ruler, a person must possess a set of main virtues, which are: wisdom, prudence, prowess, and justice. Wisdom, being the crown of all virtues, is essential in developing all the others. As only philosophers, through their training and love for wisdom ('philosophy' literally means 'love of wisdom') have the knowledge of the absolute truth, they are the only ones qualified to rule—they are able to apply their wisdom and knowledge for the common good of the state. Can we consider that Don Vito Corleone has all of the characteristics of Plato's philosopher king: wisdom, prudence, prowess, and justice? Surely he's a man with absolute power at the helm of his ship, and surely, his rule has more similarities with the rule of kings than it has to the rule of contemporary democratically elected presidents.

## For Justice, We Must go to Corleone

In search of the Godfather's virtues, we can start right at the beginning of the first movie, as Sicilian immigrant Amerigo Bonasera enters the "palace," seeking audience. A simple undertaker has come to ask a favor from the "king."

"I believe in America," he starts. America made him his fortune, and he raised his daughter in the American fashion, giving her freedom, but still teaching her never to dishonor her family. His daughter had found a non-Italian boyfriend, who's taking her to the movies and making her stay late, which Bonasera didn't protest at the time. Some two months before the audience with the Godfather, Bonasera's daughter was taken for a drive by her boyfriend and his friend. They got her drunk and tried to rape her. When she resisted, they beat her badly. "She will never be beautiful again," Bonasera weeps in front of the Godfather, continuing: "I, I went to the police, like a good American."

He believed that the State would punish the boys who defiled his daughter, but the court made a fool out of him—the boys walked away free the same day. Bonasera felt betrayed. And in that moment, he said to his wife: "For justice, we must go to Don Corleone."

Although he went to the police first, placing his faith in the State, the official government, he perceives, failed him. His daughter was brutally beaten and mutilated by two young men who weren't properly punished for the crime they committed. And now, when he feels that Uncle Sam let him down, Bonasera seeks retribution from the other system of power—he comes to the Godfather.

As many others before him, he pleads with Don Vito Corleone for justice; as many others before him, when the official structure abandoned him, he turned to the alternative one—one that can be observed as an opposition to the official

State, arising from the perceived incompetence of the latter. Similarly, as Plato outlines the rule of philosopher kings as an ideal alternative to the Athenian democracy, Coppola here placed the Godfather as a realistic born-out-of-necessity alternative to the US democracy.

Bonasera's words reveal the psychology of abandonment. Someone believed that the State would protect him, someone believed that the System is powerful and righteous enough to, at least, right the wrongs. This faith has been betrayed. Now what? Should the individual resign and accept his destiny? Or should he seek justice?

If you know that there's another system, close to you, a system which allows pleading your case directly to the source of the Power, shouldn't you do everything possible to get justice? This is where the Godfather's true might resides. It resides in ordinary citizens, who perceive that the US has failed them, and who decide that they will submit themselves to the other power. In a sense, the Godfather is, indeed, elected. He's elected every time someone comes to ask him for a favor, progressively affirming his authority, one favor at a time.

## Vote for the Godfather!

The connection between the authority of the President and the Godfather is even underscored by Michael Corleone, when in conversation with his wife Kay he concludes: "My father's no different than any other powerful man . . . Any man who's responsible for other people. Like a senator or a president." When Kay remarks that senators and presidents don't have men killed, Michael almost smirks: "Oh, who's being naive, Kay?" Michael is well aware of the structures of power, as well as the differences between them. He knows the distinction between the President and the Godfather. But, what is more important, he understands their similarities as well. They are both responsible for other people. They both have loyal subjects, vassals or citizens under them, people who are trusting in their protection. And Michael knows how easily this loyalty can be lost if justice is not satisfied.

In his own way, we see, the Godfather is just. His system is not as developed or sophisticated as other, formal ones. He has no judicial hierarchy, he has no laws that guide his rule. His notion of justice stems from a very simple, if not primitive, ethical system which can be dated all the way back to ancient Babylon and the rule of Hammurabi (around 1800 B.C.E.)—an eye for an eye. Someone broke your hand? We'll break his.

Someone stole from you? We'll steal from him.

No, Corleone said to Bonasera, when he begged him to kill the boys that mutilated his daughter—your daughter is still alive. Punishment must be proportionate to the crime—they will be punished, and they will be beaten badly. An eye for an eye. The first condition of being a philosopher king is satisfied. The Godfather might be seen as just. Undoubtedly, he can also be seen as wise, adapting and problem-solving throughout the movie left and right. But, can we consider that Corleone is a prudent man? After Barzini's men kill his oldest son Sonny, rather than seek revenge for his killing, Don Corleone meets with the heads of the Five Families to negotiate a cease-fire:

> How did things ever get so far? I don't know. It was so unfortunate . . . so unnecessary. Tattaglia lost a son and I lost a son. We're quits. And if Tattaglia agrees, then I'm willing to let things go on the way they were before . . .

The whole scene is Corleone's display of prudence, overcoming extremely strong emotions in order to find the peace between Mafia families at that moment. This is also intertwined with the virtue of prowess—he's sitting at the table with the people that tried to kill him and who killed his first-born, coming to a cold headed agreement, but also setting up boundaries, with his old-school, tit-for-tat, almost Old Testament definition of justice, saying:

> I forgo the vengeance of my son. But I have selfish reasons. My youngest son was forced to leave this country . . . and I have to make arrangements to bring him back here safely—cleared of all these false charges. But I'm a superstitious man and if some unlucky accident should befall him . . . if he should get shot in the head by a police officer or if he should hang himself in his jail cell or if he's struck by a bolt of lightning then I'm going to blame some of the people in this room. And that, I do not forgive.

It seems, at least at first, that Don Corleone could pass Plato's requirements for being a philosopher king. He is wise, prudent, has prowess, and is, in his own way, righteous and just. To be perfectly clear, once again, most of the courts, lawmakers, various priests, holy men, and philosophers, wouldn't accept the notion that the Godfather is just, because, in the end, he runs a criminal enterprise.

He is, in the eyes of the official state—a criminal. But this word means nothing to the Godfather. He has his own state to govern and his laws which he abides. The laws that the Godfather follows were not set by him—the Mafia code of conduct was set up sometime during Prohibition, with solidified division and structure of "families," as well as procedures for resolving disputes. Their set of rules imported from Sicily was strict and hierarchical, demanding an oath of silence (*omertà*), forbidding any cooperation with authorities or government, and punishing oath breakers swiftly and mercilessly. Here's that Old Testament approach that the Godfather sometimes uses.

So, again, if Plato gave the Godfather a checklist of the necessary virtues that he has to have in order to apply for the role of a philosopher king, undoubtedly Vito Corleone would check out on all four. But surely, there would come a moment, maybe during the second round of in-depth face-to-face interviews, where Plato would drop Corleone out of the audition for the philosopher king? There would come a moment when Plato just couldn't keep turning a blind eye, where he would stand up, shake Vito's hand and send him home. He could maybe have accepted the fact that Don Vito Corleone wasn't a philosopher, because the latter compensated for this with a natural gift of wisdom, Plato may have even tried to overlook the fact that the Godfather's and his ideas of justice are going in different directions, but possibly the biggest differentiation between Plato's ideal state and Godfather's approach to government is family.

## (Un)importance of the Family

The core of everything the Godfather does is family, it's the basis of his values, the motivation behind his actions, and one of the pillars on which he builds his ethical system: "because a man who doesn't spend time with his family can never be a real man." Plato, well, had a radically different approach. In his ideal state, philosopher kings live together, as a separate class, which Plato called the "Guardians." They would live as soldiers in camps, simply and communally, and the ruling men and women should mate on the city's orders. Imagine telling that to the Don.

Qualified women, philosopher queens, and, qualified men, philosopher kings, in Plato's ideal scenario reproduce for the benefit of their state. Children being born out of these actions would be raised communally, and all Guardians would be considered to be their parents. The core of the Godfather's strength, his family, in this scenario, would be nullified. In Plato's vision of a perfect state, children mustn't be attached to a private family household—they should be raised by a class of philosopher kings and queens, educated, trained, and tested, and only the most virtuous ones, wisest, most prudent and just, will become rulers.

Closing a complete class of people like this in a micro-society, and raising them in a camp where everyone is your parent raises a few eyebrows in modern discussions. Today, we consider family to be the foundation of society, but this usual contemporary understanding of the concept of family in the Ancient Greece was barely recognizable. It seems that the Greeks had two complementary institutions co-existing at the same time: *family*, which took care of all the "material" things, including reproduction and continuation of the blood line, and *pederasty*, which took care of the "affective," and to a degree the "intellectual," side of a man's intimate life.

Family was certainly no center of the upper-class Greek's emotional life, and Plato's writings only highlighted this notion even more. His philosopher kings and queens organized as a ruling class can have neither private property nor their own family, and strictness and obedience are ensured by eugenics and euthanasia. Plato argued that if rulers began to want to own land, houses, and money, and to set up domestic treasuries and private love-nests, they would begin to fail as guardians of the people, and the city will start to degenerate. Well, decent argument as that may be, there is little doubt that Vito Corleone would answer to this with "a man who doesn't spend time with his family can never be a real man."

The institution of family seems not only important to the Godfather individually, but to the whole society built around the Mafia, which can be proven, again, with the beginning of the movie by asking a simple question: why did Don Barzini, Corleone's rival, attend Connie's and Carlo's wedding? Because it would be in bad taste not to invite him! And, even more, it would be in very bad taste if Don Barzini attempted to do anything sketchy during that day of celebration. We can see the backbone of the Italian-American community here, as the only issue, and only altercation which happened was the fact that the FBI and the Press were outside the premises. Inside, the community held together, celebrating the expansion of one family. No plots that day, and no killing and fighting between Italians, no, thank you.

In the Godfather's version of justice, a real mafioso, a real man needs to handle his responsibilities as a husband, father, brother, and son. He needs to take care of his family, and all the family members should be obedient and loyal to the "head of the family." This is almost a mantra of the Godfather, and as

Marcia J. Citron wrote: "The Corleones may be a criminal family, but their ties to relatives are strong, and Coppola's style plays up the closeness of the family unit." Family in the *Godfather* story is not only about blood relations, but, more importantly, crime and trust relations—that's why Tom Hagen is the consigliere of the whole family, and Fredo is sent to Las Vegas.

Reliability and trustworthiness brought a lot of family members closer to the family, although they are not necessarily blood related. Further, bringing back that Old Testament eye-for-an-eye approach, betraying your family is the worst thing a man can do. This is a major difference between Plato's idealistic aspirations and the Godfather's criminal kingdom—Plato identified having too strong familial ties as bad for the community, and attempted to cut them completely, dispersing the notion of family as an institution.

In *The Godfather*, the family is the basis upon which the whole system functions properly. To conclude and to encapsulate the relationship between justice and family, and the notion of the other power opposing the real state, a quote from the Godfather seems to fit perfectly at the end:

> I work my whole life, I don't apologize, to take care of my family. And I refused to be a fool dancing on the string, held by all those bigshots. I don't apologize that's my life but I thought that . . . that when it was your time . . . that you [Michael] would be the one to hold the strings. Senator Corleone. Governor Corleone, or something . . .

# 14
# More Dangerous than Shotguns

SAMANTHA SEYBOLD

Michael Corleone is having a rough go of it. Admittedly, this is the running theme in all three *Godfather* films, but this is his first serious foray into the family business. He's just killed a crooked police captain and is laying low in Sicily, away from his family, his girlfriend Kay, and everything he's ever known. It will be more than a year until he can safely return. So, when a mysteriously beautiful—and mysteriously silent—young Italian woman crosses his path, he's understandably smitten.

One of his bodyguards notices and, after gawking awhile himself, instructs Michael: "In Sicily, women are more dangerous than shotguns." Dangerous, indeed. This woman, Apollonia Vitelli, captivates Michael and soon becomes his wife. However, a bomb intended for Michael cuts her life tragically short.

Apollonia's story is shocking but not unusual when it comes to the *Godfather*'s female characters. For the typical woman in Coppola's world, day to day existence seems to amount to little more than being a sex object or homemaker. Her life is dominated, directed, and driven by men. This arrangement frequently has devastatingly tragic, even deadly, consequences for her. Yet she stays with the murderous boyfriend, the abusive husband, and the conniving brother, even as we audience members plead with her to get out while she can, *if* she still can.

Being a woman in the *Godfather* movies is a major liability. Yet, these women also do remarkably daring things in an effort to assert their autonomy: to seize control over their own lives and challenge men's efforts to control them. They're not always successful as there are plenty of formidable obstacles standing in their way: obstinate men, sexist power plays, extensive corruption, and threats of physical violence abound. But, if we write the women of *The Godfather* off as mere victims, we risk overlooking the power that their choices hold. Every time she chooses for herself, she threatens the patriarchal social order on which the Mafia is founded.

## An Offer She Can't Refuse?

The brutalization and victimization of women is pervasive in the *Godfather* movies. Senseless violence against daughters bookends the trilogy, which opens with the famous scene where undertaker Bonasera pleads with the Godfather to avenge his daughter's beating, and closes with Mary Corleone's hapless death during a botched attempt on Michael's life. We watch as Tom has a nameless prostitute brutally murdered in order to gain leverage over Senator Geary, and Don Fanucci holds "Senza Mama" actress Carla at knifepoint to extort her father. We quickly learn that the world of *The Godfather* is a world of violence, coercion, and brute force. Women are particularly vulnerable. They are kept in the dark about the "family business," but readily exploited and abused by it nonetheless.

Do the female characters in *The Godfather* have *agency*? In its broadest sense, *agency* refers to intentional action, the capacity that defines what it means to be an agent. The agent is one who is able to freely set an intention or goal, and then freely act on it. Agency is particularly important when it comes to questions about moral responsibility. We typically think that an agent can be held responsible for what they do because they have freely and intentionally chosen to do it. For instance, we hold Michael responsible for Fredo's death because he set an intention (to murder Fredo for betraying him to Hyman Roth) and acted in line with that intention (ordering Al Neri to off Fredo on an innocent fishing trip).

The thinking here is that Michael, as an agent, is accountable for what he did because what he did was entirely up to him. There are some problems with this account, however. Feminist philosophers have pointed out that this notion of agency overlooks the *relational* nature of agency. Agency is relational in the sense that our capacity to set goals and act on them depends on the actions of others. Kay may have decided to break things off with Michael after he disappeared to Sicily, but her love for him—along with his smooth talking and promises of eventual legitimacy—leads her to change her mind and agree to marry him. Vito Corleone had grand plans for Michael to stay out of the family business and be a senator one day, but a fruit stand hit and a corrupt police department left a power vacuum that Michael had to fill to protect his hospitalized father (*Godfather I*).

In his quest to turn the family business legitimate, Michael famously laments how there is no escape from the Mafia underworld: "Just when I thought I was out, they pull me back in!" Examples like these support the feminist critique that philosophy's traditional notion of agency doesn't reflect the real life circumstances of decision making. Things are too messy. Another person can respect and enable your choice to leave, *or* they might do everything in their power to drag you back in.

Feminist philosophers propose replacing talk of *agency* with talk about *relational autonomy* to acknowledge the others-dependent nature of intentional action. At its core, relational autonomy refers to self-direction, where the self is understood not as purely self-sufficient but as an individual who is "socially and historically embedded" (Natalie Stoljar) and thus shaped by her position in society. According to feminist philosophers, thinking about choice in these terms allows us to pay attention to how social factors influence what individuals want and do. We inevitably bump up against the expectations of other people and social structures. For the women of *The Godfather*, sexism represents the most severe limitation to their autonomy.

## I'll Use Everything in My Power to Keep You from Leaving

From the first scene in *The Godfather*, Coppola swiftly plunges us into an intensely patriarchal world. We watch as two men—Vito Corleone, a deeply revered and very powerful man, and Bonasera, who gushes deference and fear in order to get his help—discuss how to handle the brutal beating of Bonasera's daughter. Little is known about this nameless girl: when she refused her boyfriend's advances, he and a friend viciously assaulted her, and Bonasera laments that "she will never be beautiful again." Bonasera trusted the US legal system to bring justice to his daughter but watched in horror as her attackers walked free. Now, despite his reservations about dealing with the Mafia, he is desperate for Corleone's help. Anything to make them pay for what they did to his daughter. In particular, he wants them dead.

This scene brilliantly captures the stiff hierarchy that governs the mafia world. The terms of any dealings with the Godfather are clear: deference, respect, and a blank check to pay him back at any point in the future. Don Corleone is the alpha male, with a cadre of tough guys in dark suits ready to carry out his orders. In exchange for that protection, he demands unquestioning loyalty. Otherwise, all bets are off.

Lucky for Bonasera, the day he approaches the Don is a special one. On the day he's marrying off his daughter Connie, Corleone has a special obligation to grant whatever requests he receives.

This opening exchange establishes the world of the Mafia as a world of patriarchy. In a patriarchal social arrangement, women are deemed inferior to men by virtue of their gender. This cleaves society into two separate and definitively *unequal* classes, like what we see in the *Godfather* films. Male control and decision-making are the order of the day, and one's gender dictates one's role in the Mafia family. Men run the family business and answer to one male family head or Don. They work in a world governed by overtly masculine values like physical violence, honor, aggression, and competition. Women are excluded from the family business and kept fully in the dark about its proceedings. Instead, we typically see them relegated to the kitchen or the bedroom—often only a door away from a dark office of men in suits plotting the next deal. They prepare food, carry and raise children, and generally don't ask questions.

Except, sometimes they do. When Connie discovers that her husband Carlo is dead, she bursts into Michael's office and lets him have it. "You lousy bastard!" she screams, "You never gave a thought about me!" In shock, Kay tries to convince Connie otherwise. Surely Michael didn't kill family, not after he just became the godfather to Connie and Carlo's child. But the realization dawns on her. She turns to Michael, steeling herself for the question: "Is it true?" "Don't ask me about my business, Kay," Michael replies curtly. Kay presses him further until he seems to give in. "This one time, I'll let you ask me about my affairs," he says, then flatly denies his involvement in Carlo's death. As Kay leaves the office, she turns to look back at her husband. Several hit men surround the newly-minted Don Corleone. One of them notices her looking in, walks to the door, and closes it. Michael has full control. She is shut out and alone.

Scenes like this capture the fragile nature of patriarchy—it isn't something that just happens, but must be continuously, systematically enforced. According to philosopher Kate Manne, *misogyny* is the means by which this is accomplished. Typically, "misogyny" signals a fringe attitude held by a few bizarre individuals who hate women. But Manne argues that repurposing the term allows us to better convey the coercive nature of gender inequality. She redefines misogyny as "the system that operates within a patriarchal social order to police and enforce women's subordination and uphold male dominance" (*Down Girl*. p. 33). This system manifests differently in different social contexts, but the end goal is always the same: to keep women in their place (p. 77).

As the Luca Brasi of sexist ideology, misogyny enlists two main strategies for enforcing gender inequality. The first is punishing deviance. This makes going against the gender hierarchy costly to some degree, ranging from social snubbing to physical violence. Signora Andolini's death is a tragic example of misogynistic punishment in action. When Don Ciccio refuses to spare her son Vito, she holds the despicable Mafia lord at knife point so that Vito can escape. Ciccio meets her bold resistance with blunt force and executes her immediately. His action encapsulates the simple purpose of misogynistic punishment: *to put her in her place again* (p. 77).

The second strategy of misogyny is rewarding compliance. Ideally, women fulfill sexist expectations in a manner that is "as natural and freely chosen as possible" (p. 47). Rewards ensure that when women "play along" and do what they're told—preferably without even being told—things are easier and more pleasant for *everyone*. This is a powerful but easily overlooked reason for why women in *The Godfather* stay in the Mafia. An Italian-American woman in the mid-1900s was regarded as a second-class citizen both inside and outside of the Mafia. Yet she had a lot to gain by staying in the Mafia and submitting to its demanding gender roles because, unlike mainstream US society, it offered her a place of value and safety. The *Godfather* movies highlight this give-and-take of Mafia life well. To be the wife, daughter, or love interest of a gangster supplies financial security, material comfort, protection, and status that would be difficult or even impossible to have otherwise. Granted, this puts her in the unpredictable crossfires of male violence, jealousy, and greed. But she has much to gain by staying in the mafia, and much more to lose if she leaves.

Both of these strategies reveal the inherently *coercive* nature of misogyny (p. 47). The mechanisms of misogyny do not necessarily force women to submit. Rather, they make her refusal to do so particularly costly. Misogyny thus erodes her autonomy rather than canceling it outright. It constitutes the patriarchal version of an offer she can't refuse. Yet there are moments when we get to witness her courageous refusal firsthand.

## Watch Yourself

Sonny is two-timing Sandra and she knows it. She refuses to look away when he openly flirts with one of Connie's bridesmaids, Lucy Mancini. Her look challenges his status as the unquestioned head of the household. When Sonny realizes the scrutiny of her gaze, he barks a command that reminds her of her place: "Watch the kids." Sandra tersely responds with a warning of her own: "Watch yourself."

If Manne is right about the pervasive nature of misogyny, then moments like these—though they occur on the fringes of the films' "real" action—are deeply significant. Sandra faces a lot of pressure to keep her head down. She may live her life at the mercy of the burgeoning egos and wallets of the Mafia, but the cost of defying this role is higher still. Sonny is her provider, the father of her children, and has an infamously short fuse. This all makes it easier for Sandra to let his infidelity slide. But in this moment, she reminds him that she has power, too. In doing so, Sandra asserts her autonomy: her life is her own, not Sonny's. She does this in spite of the intense pressure to comply, which makes her act all the more captivating.

Sadly, in Sandra's case her reminder falls short of pulling Sonny back from his lurid affair with Lucy. Yet it pushes us to ask: what space remains for the *Godfather* woman to seize some control by challenging the terms of the role she's been relegated to, *in spite of* the mechanisms in place that are intended to ensure her compliance? Her self-assertion may be undermined or overruled faster than Altobello scarfs down cannoli in *Part III*. But these discouraging odds make her resistance all the more significant.

Take Connie, whose mettle is downright inspiring. Unlike other Mafia women, she refuses to turn a blind eye to her male family members' dealings. She tries time and again to control her hotheaded brothers' outbursts. She fights back against her abusive husband, even pulling a knife on him as he chases her while pregnant around their home. She gains Michael's trust, becoming his confidante and consigliere by *Part III*—an unprecedented level of involvement in the family business for a woman. She personally orchestrates a cannoli-themed hit against her malicious godfather Altobello and gives the final approval to kill Joey Zasa when Michael is hospitalized (much to his dismay). Compared to the naive bride decked out in frothy white at the beginning of the movie trilogy, the Connie of *Part III* has made a place for herself, in spite of constant pressure for her to defer to the men in her life.

One of the most compelling (and perhaps overlooked) displays of Connie's autonomy occurs in the aftermath of Kay's split from Michael. Connie is living with Michael and caring for his children, Mary and Anthony. Against Michael's wishes, she helps sneak Kay into the house so that Kay can see her own children. Unfortunately, Michael comes home early and is enraged to discover his ex-wife in his home. Stonily silent, he shuts Kay out of the house without a word despite her pleading. In this moment, we see what Connie was willing to give up on Kay's behalf. She risks being discovered and facing Michael's ire at her blatant disregard of his wishes. Yet Connie does it anyway. She acts on her own desires rather than out of fear of what Michael will do.

Like Connie, Kay's persistent rejection of the Mafia's gender roles is a constant through the films. But unlike Connie, Kay is better positioned to do so since she is a white woman from mainstream US society. It's clear from the beginning that she is an outsider—with her fair hair and skin and warm, bright clothes, she visually stands out from the dark, somber world of the Mafia. Similarly, the Mafia's stark gender roles are foreign to Kay. This generates friction between her and Michael throughout their marriage. From the moment we meet Kay at Connie's wedding, she is not content with accepting Michael's vague answers about the family business and expects him to make good on his promise to make the Corleone family legitimate.

This friction climaxes in the aftermath of Hyman Roth's terrifying hit on her home. Michael floods the family compound with guards and jets off solo to the Caribbean, leaving Kay and the children locked down at the house. After a particularly unnerving close call at the RICO hearings, Kay tells Michael that she is leaving with the children. Michael is incredulous, then irate. He insists that she isn't listening to him and that "things between men and women will never change." He cuts her off when she tries to explain herself and outright orders her to stay. Kay says that she no longer loves Michael; all she feels toward him is dread. "In time, you'll feel differently," he says. Then Kay reveals that her miscarriage was an abortion. She couldn't bear to subject another child to the Corleone family dysfunction. As Michael's anger grows, she says she did it because she knew he would never forgive her for killing their son "because of this Sicilian thing that's been going on for two thousand years." Michael strikes her: "You won't take my children." Kay does leave, but is forced to leave her children behind. She gives up her marriage, the Corleone family's wealth and influence, and her children because she refuses to live trapped in this world of Michael's making.

Kay's decisions set her on a very different trajectory than her Italian American counterparts. As a white, educated, Anglo-Saxon woman, Kay has privilege and opportunity that women like Connie do not. Kay had a life outside the Mafia and can freely return to it when things get bad. As a result, she takes red flags like Michael's lies and controlling behavior for what they are: indicators that she needs to leave. She can do this because for her, leaving is far less costly: as a white woman, she is not as vulnerable to abuse and exploitation in mainstream US society, and thus not as willing to tolerate the abuse and exploitation that accompanies her life with Michael. These social dynamics consequently impact Kay's capacity for autonomy. Her social position is far less precarious than Connie's or Sandra's, which gives her more freedom. Even though her self-assertion is still costly, she risks less when she stands up to Michael.

## Women Can't Be Careless, Either

As he prepares to hand off the title of Don to Michael, Vito offers an iconic piece of advice: "Women and children can be careless, but men can't." But Vito's words of wisdom miss the mark somewhat—women may be kept in the dark about the family business, but they cannot afford to be careless, either. Life in the Mafia is a dangerous place where a woman can lose everything, even her own life, at a moment's notice. She faces incredible pressures to submit to male authority without question. Despite the often terror-filled nature of life in the Mafia, most women stay because they have something to gain by staying—and much, much more to lose if they leave.

In spite of this, we see these women take steps to seize control of their own lives and assert their autonomy. Many of the *Godfather*'s women are brutalized, victimized, and silenced, seeming to have little control over their lives. Yet the films let us glimpse some of these women courageously fighting back. Connie and Kay represent the most visible, and perhaps most successful, instances of rebellion against the Mafia's stark gender roles. But even when a female character's efforts to direct her own life are thwarted, she was courageous enough and self-assured enough to try. Remember Bonasera's daughter? Her refusal to submit to her boyfriend's advances cost her dearly. The assault that her boyfriend and his accomplice subjected her to is a classic example of misogyny at work: these young men used violence to put the woman who refused to cooperate back in her place. Yet we cannot overlook the fact that she *still* refused to give in. She refused to let their cruelty override the choice she had made to turn down her boyfriend's advances.

Like Bonasera's daughter, the women of *The Godfather* all experience victimization to some degree as they live out their lives in the Mafia. But they are not all *merely* victims. We also see them assert their autonomy in the face of immense, even life-threatening pressures to give up and give in. They know as well as we do that rejecting the Mafia order is costly. This makes their defiance—whether successful or not—even more threatening to the patriarchy. Such women are indeed dangerous.

# IV

"... for old times' sake."

# 15
# Frank Pentangeli's Stoic Suicide

JOSHUA HETER

A mid to high-ranking member of an immeasurably powerful organization is caught up in a plot to bring down its leader. After the conspiracy—involving everyone from senators to military officials—is revealed and suppressed, the alleged conspirator takes his own life at the behest of his (still very much in power) figurehead by "opening up his veins" in a warm bath allowing the life to drain from his body.

For fans of the *Godfather* franchise, this story will sound particularly familiar as it is at least in part that of Frankie "Five Angels" Pentangeli, the New York City capo of the Corleone crime family. Sometime after the Corleones' move to Nevada, Frankie took over the New York operation from Peter Clemenza who died, either from a heart attack or from something meant to resemble one. Eventually, Frankie comes to Michael, head of the family, to ask his permission to take out the Rosato Brothers, Frankie's primary rivals in the city. However, Michael—hoping to avoid an open conflict with his business partner, Hyman Roth—refuses as the Rosatos are backed by Roth.

When the Rosato Brothers then make an attempt on *his* life while adding "Michael Corleone says hello!", Frankie turns state's evidence and testifies against Michael to the authorities. It's only when Michael ominously arrives at a Senate hearing (at which Frankie is to publicly identify Michael as the head of the Corleone crime family) with Frankie's brother in tow that he reverses course and rebuts his own sworn testimony, ostensibly clearing Michael of any wrongdoing.

Soon after, Tom Hagen, Michael's *consigliere* visits Frankie, still in federal protective custody, where the two casually reflect on lessons from history, both recent as well as ancient.

> **Tom:** Frankie, when a plot against the Roman emperor failed, the plotters were always given a chance to let their families keep their fortunes. Right?
>
> **Frankie:** Yeah, but only the rich guys, Tom. The little guys, they got knocked off, and all their estates went to the emperors. Unless they went home and killed themselves, then nothing happened. And their families; their families were taken care of, Tom.
>
> **Tom:** That was a good break, a nice deal.
>
> **Frankie:** Yeah, they went home and sat in a hot bath, opened up their veins, and bled to death. And, sometimes they had a little party before they did it!
>
> **Tom:** Don't worry about anything, Frankie Five Angels.
>
> **Frankie:** Thanks, Tom. Thanks.

With this conversation firmly in mind, in what seems to be an outcome orchestrated by Tom via Michael himself, Frankie takes this same course of action; he acquiesces, slits his wrists, and dies in a hot bath.

Of course, as Tom and Frankie both acknowledge, this is far from the only time the plot against a powerful man has ended with a failed conspirator being offered the opportunity to end his own life in a somewhat strange act of grace, giving him the chance to leave this world with at least some modicum of honor and self-determination. With this in mind, this broad story is not only that of Frankie Five Angels. It's also the story of Lucius Annaeus Seneca or "Seneca the Younger," the first-century Roman statesman, playwright, and (perhaps most importantly for the purposes of this book) Stoic philosopher. In fact, as we'll see, it may be at least in part Seneca's story to which Tom and Frankie are alluding in their conversation about the fate of unsuccessful plotters during the time of the Roman Empire.

## Seneca the Younger

Seneca the Younger was (perhaps unsurprisingly) the son of Seneca the Elder. Born in Hispania (what is modern day Spain) in 4 B.C., he was taken to Rome by his aunt as a young boy where he would study rhetoric and philosophy. Eventually, as well as writing a great deal of philosophy and a number of tragedies, Seneca would spend time serving as a magistrate, as a praetor (a type of judicial officer), and for a time as the tutor of Nero. This final position is especially significant as it almost certainly led to Seneca becoming one of Nero's closest advisors when Nero became Emperor of Rome.

Initially, Nero's administration and Seneca's role in it were generally successful. However, for a variety of reasons, Nero's behavior eventually became increasingly erratic and morally questionable (to put it nicely) which led to instability. Upon the death of Sextus Afranius Burrus—another advisor to Nero and a staunch supporter of Seneca—sometime after A.D. 62, Seneca left Nero's court and retired to the countryside. Unfortunately for Seneca however, this was not the end of his story.

In A.D. 65 Roman statesman Gaius Calpurnius Piso led what would become known as the Pisonian Conspiracy. The conspiracy—which included senators and members of the military—was a plot to assassinate Nero. It's unclear what role (if any) Seneca played in it, but when the plot was revealed, he was one of forty-one named conspirators. Having been ordered to take his own life by Nero as punishment, Seneca went home, severed a number of his veins, took poison (to cover all of his bases, I suppose), eventually immersed himself in a warm bath to lessen the pain and hasten the blood draining from his body, and died. However, this was not before Seneca hosted one final dinner party for his friends with his wife, Paulina ("Seneca and His World").

As we can see, Seneca's ultimate fate has a number of parallels with that of Frankie Five Angels. Both men—once wealthy and at least somewhat influential, embedded within the power structures of massively influential organizations—took their own life by bleeding to death in a hot bath at the behest of their leader after being caught up in an attempt to bring down that leader. However, Seneca's story also comes with an added twisted irony in that throughout his life, he was particularly interested in suicide. Indeed, Seneca had a great deal to say about death in general and suicide in particular. Some have even gone so far as to say that Seneca had an obsession with the topic and that he is the preeminent philosopher on self-killing. With this in mind, it's worth asking, what would Seneca have to say about Frankie's suicide? Would he approve of Frankie taking his own life? Would he see it as a cowardly act? Or, would he see it as the rational conclusion of a life arrived at through thoughtful deliberation (as he almost certainly viewed his own death)?

## Stoic Living and Dying

To understand Seneca's view of suicide and how he may have viewed the suicide of Frankie Five Angels, we must first have at least a basic understanding of Stoic ethics—Stoicism being the school of thought to which Seneca subscribed. Stoicism emerged in the Hellenistic period around 300 B.C. and was most prominent in ancient Greece and Rome. One of the most important ideas in Stoic thought is that a good life is one that is lived in accordance or in harmony with nature. And it is living in harmony with nature that will allow us to achieve true happiness.

In *Letters from a Stoic*, Seneca himself writes "Let us keep to the way which Nature has mapped out for us, and let us not swerve therefrom. If we combat Nature, our life differs not a whit from that of men who row against the current" (*Letters* 122.19). Thus, for the Stoics, what is morally good and bad is nothing more than vice and virtue. Virtues—for example: wisdom, justice, courage, and moderation—are those things which necessarily contribute to living in harmony with nature. Vices—for example: foolishness, injustice, cowardice, and intemperance—are those things which are necessarily opposed to living in harmony with nature. All else, according to the Stoics, can be labeled as "indifferents."

An indifferent is any aspect of life which does not *inherently* contribute to or impede living in harmony with nature. However, according to the Stoics, we can divide indifferents into preferred and dispreferred indifferents. Preferred indifferents—for example: health, pleasure, beauty, wealth, strength, and noble birth—are those things which only *typically* (though not universally) aid in having a good life (living in harmony with nature). Things like wealth and strength might *often* be good and desirable, but even these are merely indifferents because there are at least some instances in which they are neither good nor desirable. If the wealth and strength that comes from being the Corleone brothers end up ruining the family and tearing it apart, it may have been better to not have had them.

Similarly, dispreferred indifferents—for example: disease, pain, ugliness, weakness, poverty, and ignoble birth—are those things which only *typically* (though not universally) impede having a good life. Things like poverty and ignoble birth might *often* be bad or undesirable, but even these are merely indifferents because there are at least some instances in which they are neither bad nor undesirable. If poverty and an ignoble birth can (at least in part) play a role in leading a young Sicilian boy to flee to America where he will start his family and build his fortune, it may have been better to have had them. The crucial point is that indifferents have no value in themselves. Whether preferred or dispreferred, they only have value when they are attached to virtue.

It is this distinction between preferred and dispreferred indifferents which can help us understand a great deal about Stoic ethics. For the Stoics, activities that are directed toward living in harmony with nature (which often enough includes securing preferred indifferents) are our proper functions, duties, or *kathêkonta*. They are actions which are befitting of our natures. Of the *kathêkonta*, there are those that are appropriate regardless of the circumstances and those which may only be appropriate in rare or unusual circumstances. For the Stoics as well as Seneca in particular, suicide (or acts of physical self-harm generally) fall into this latter category. That is, there are at least some circumstances—infrequent as they may be—in which taking one's own life is the rational and proper course of action.

These are most frequently instances in which a person experiences an imbalance of indifferents great enough that it makes it impossible for him to live in harmony with nature and achieve happiness. That is, when one experiences an imbalance of indifferents such that the dispreferred grossly outweigh the preferred, self-killing may be the rational or proper course of action, so say the Stoics. As Cicero (influenced by the Stoics) puts it: "When a man has a preponderance of the things in accordance with nature, it is his proper function to remain alive; when he has or foresees a preponderance of their opposites, it is his proper function to depart from life" (*De Finibus* 3.60).

## Seneca on Frankie's Suicide

Seneca, in line with the Stoic thought which preceded him, held that there are a number of types of (perhaps infrequent) circumstances in which suicide was the proper course of action. Put differently, according to Seneca, there are a number of ways in which there may be an imbalance of indifferents such that self-killing is the rational thing to do. He argues that self-killing may be justified when one faces the effects of chronic disease, pain, the ravages of old age, and other maladies which may make virtuous living impossible (*Letters* 61, 58.32–37). However, to understand how Seneca may have viewed the suicide of Frankie "Five Angels" Pentangeli in particular which mirrors his own suicide so closely, we need only take a closer look at two such sets of circumstances.

First, according to Seneca, suicide can be the rational and proper course of action when taking your own life can preserve your *dignitas* (or dignity). In *Letter* 77.14, Seneca recounts the story of a young Spartan boy who is captured and made a slave.

When the boy is asked to perform a demeaning, degrading task (fetching a chamber pot), he shouts "I will not be a slave!" and runs his head into a wall, which kills him. Seneca describes the boy's actions as brave and generally praises those who would choose this fate as opposed to "weakly yielding" and living without freedom.

Elsewhere, Seneca praises a murder-suicide in which a slave kills his master and then himself as well as the suicide of a gladiator-in-training who kills himself by shoving a stick down his throat and choking to death. Of this latter case, Seneca writes:

> It was not a very elegant or becoming way to die; but what is more foolish than to be over-nice about dying? What a brave fellow! He surely deserved to be allowed to choose his fate! How bravely he would have wielded a sword! With what courage he would have hurled himself into the depths of the sea, or down a precipice! Cut off from resources on every hand, he yet found a way to furnish himself with death, and with a weapon for death. Hence you can understand that nothing but the will need postpone death. Let each man judge the deed of this most zealous fellow as he likes, provided we agree on this point,—that the foulest death is preferable to the fairest slavery. (*Letters* 70.21)

What is perhaps most striking about this passage is the enthusiasm with which Seneca discusses suicide. And, while the Stoics had a reputation for taking pleasure in defending that which was broadly seen as macabre, if living as a slave (or under slave-like conditions) is a genuine and insurmountable impediment to living in harmony with nature, it's not difficult to see how Seneca might think that such enthusiasm is called for.

Nevertheless, to be sure, at the end of *The Godfather Part II*, Frankie is not living as a slave, but he is living in a state in which he has surrendered (perhaps out of necessity) a great deal of his freedom. After nearly testifying against Michael to the Senate, he is living under federal protective custody in a heavily guarded army barracks. It is unclear how long this specific arrangement will last, but what is clear is that—under threat from the Corleones—Frankie's life (and importantly his freedom) moving forward will not resemble anything to which he has become accustom as a capo of the family.

Whether he continues living in the barracks indefinitely under almost prison-like conditions or he lives out his days in hiding elsewhere, it is not a stretch to think that his life into the future, were he not to commit suicide, would come with a great deal of indignity. What makes his situation even more perilous is that his recanted testimony against Michael might lead him to have to live not under prison-*like* conditions but in a literal prison. And, should that be his fate, and should Frankie be able to survive in prison at all, the prison life of a rat will almost certainly be especially punishing for him. With this loss of freedom, with this indignity, Frankie's act may be just the sort of thing Seneca would praise him for, for freeing himself through his act of self-killing.

Second, according to Seneca, suicide can be the rational and proper course of action when taking one's own life is an act of self-sacrifice for his country or friends. Seneca calls true friendship the type of friendship "in which and for the sake of which men meet death." (*Letters* 6.2) And, he praises those who are willing to die for their country and fellow citizens (*Letters* 76.27). This is consistent with the stoic line of thought—often attributed to the stoic thinker, Chrysippus—which compares life to a party. There are only a finite number of ways in which one can reasonably depart (or remove oneself) from a party, one of which is when a partygoer must do so in order to fulfill his obligations to his friends. So too (as the analogy goes), there are only a finite number of ways in which one can reasonably remove oneself from this life through suicide, one of which is when doing so is required to fulfill the obligations one has to others.

When Tom visits Frankie at the army barracks where he is under protective custody, the reason for Tom's visit is thinly veiled. He is there under instruction from Michael to let Frankie know (in not so many words) that were he to remove himself from his current circumstances—presumably, by taking his own life—his family back in New York would be able to keep the wealth he accumulated through his work with the Corleones. Again, this is not unlike the "good break" and "nice deal" the plotters against Roman emperors were given to which both Tom and Frankie allude.

A man like Frankie has significant responsibilities to a number of people, not only to those members of the Corleone crime family who have served under him but more importantly to his literal, blood relatives. It is these responsibilities to which Frankie refers when he confronts Michael about not being allowed to take out the Rosato brothers because of their association with Hyman Roth: "My family doesn't eat here [in Lake Tahoe], doesn't eat in Las Vegas, and doesn't eat in Miami with Hyman Roth!"

Frankie's family "eats" in New York because of the work he's done for the Corleones; should Frankie's work be disrupted by the Rosatos, he argues, his family may suffer. After he has betrayed Michael, it is made clear that Frankie's family will be allowed to keep their fortune, should Frankie take his own life. Should he not do so, his family may very well become destitute. It also seems likely that, should Frankie commit suicide, as Michael via Tom implies he should, Michael won't pursue any further revenge against Frankie's family in addition to allowing them to keep their wealth.

So, Frankie's unique set of circumstances includes two important features which Seneca takes to be relevant to the question of the propriety of suicide. Should Frankie not take his own life, he may be forced to continue on in a state of indignity. And, committing suicide may be the only way in which Frankie can fulfill his responsibilities to his family. With these considerations in mind, it isn't difficult to imagine how Seneca might judge Frankie's final act.

The philosophical issues surrounding suicide cannot be fully cataloged (much less addressed) in a chapter on the suicide of Frankie "Five Angels" Pentangeli. Even if we are only considering the morality of self-killing, there are a number of perspectives to take into consideration on the topic beyond those of a small albeit influential school of philosophy from the Hellenistic world.

Nevertheless, there is a strong case to be made that Seneca would judge Frankie's suicide as the rational or proper course of action, given Frankie's unique set of circumstances. It is not just that Frankie's suicide resembles Seneca's so closely, it is that Frankie's circumstances won't allow him to live a virtuous life or in harmony with nature. Taking his own life may very well be a reasonable act, or at least so Seneca would argue.

# 16
# The Three Parts of Michael's Soul

CHRISTOPHER JANAWAY

What would Plato think of Michael Corleone? This is an odd question. It's possible to imagine that Michael may have heard of the great Greek philosopher in school, but there's no chance the other way around, and not just because Michael's a fictional character.

From a distance of two and a half thousand years, Plato is at some disadvantage when it comes to knowing about organized crime in the 1940s and 1950s. But part of what makes Plato great, and why so many people still read him, is that his ideas often possess a kind of universal wisdom. They stretch out over times and places and can help us think through things today. One of his most important questions is: what is the best kind of life to lead, the best kind of human being to be? His answer is: someone who is governed by reason, not appetite or emotion.

Michael Corleone, as portrayed by Al Pacino in *The Godfather I* and *II*, might seem to fit this profile. In stark contrast with his brothers Sonny and Fredo, he is able to conduct himself with supreme, self-controlled rationality. But we shall see how he is in fact quite the opposite of what Plato recommends.

## Michael's Tragedy

Michael's arc through *The Godfather I* and *II* is tragic. At the end, he's alone in the boathouse, having ordered his brother's death, alienated his wife, and lost the unborn son she has aborted. He has destroyed everything that he had been fighting to build and keep. "You can never lose your family," his mother tells him right near the end: a biting irony because it's abundantly clear that he knows this is precisely what has happened. But, is Michael a tragic hero?

Plato's pupil, the equally great Greek philosopher Aristotle, who wrote a famous treatise on tragedy called *Poetics*, might well think that he is. Of all the art forms the ancient Greeks invented, the tragic plays they wrote for performance in their amphitheaters were perhaps the greatest. Aristotle analyzed what makes tragedy an important art form and what makes a tragic story work. In short, he said, it's a kind of story in which someone who has power, success, and a lot to lose, loses it all through his or her own deliberate but mistaken actions. It works when we see how those actions have consequences, and how the consequences have further consequences, until the tragic protagonist's life is ruined. As the story unfolds step by step, we feel fear, and by the end we feel pity for the protagonist. By grasping how the events unfold and feeling how they lead to painful ruin, we learn something profound about life, and find the experience satisfying.

Aristotle is very strict about what kind of story will work. It can't be that a totally virtuous person gets their life ruined. That's just distressing. It can't be that a total villain faces adversity but gets away with everything in the end. That's repulsive. But equally it isn't a *tragic* story, says Aristotle, if an out-and-out evil person ends up in disaster, because then we just think "Good, he deserved that" and don't feel any pity. I think we can feel pity for Michael. Maybe not everyone does, but if you do, that means you can't be thinking of him just as an out-and-out evil villain.

Michael performs evil actions, and ultimately becomes a monster. He deserves to be caught and punished by the justice system. But the *Godfather* movies brilliantly keep us identified enough with Michael that part of us can sympathize with the inner pain he has caused himself. And as a person, he has some seemingly admirable qualities. He brought tragedy on himself not because he was weak, cowardly, disorganized, or dissolute, but because he was rational, restrained, decisive and loyal. Others around him floundered and philandered, but he took responsibility and pursued his life logically. Plato, in his great book *The Republic*, praises the person who is governed by reason as the one who has the best life. So, is that applicable to Michael Corleone? To see why it's not, we shall have to find out what "governed by reason" means.

## Parts of the Soul

In *The Republic*, Plato argues that the human soul (or psyche, his word) consist of three parts that can either be in conflict or harmony with one another. They are the reasoning part, the part that has appetites, and the spirited or emotional part "with which we get angry." It's best to think of the soul as a person's mind or character, not anything supernatural. Plato argues that we should think of this soul as having different parts because we experience internal conflicts. We often loosely talk this way in ordinary life: "part of me wishes I hadn't given up playing the piano" (but part of me thinks "Why bother? I'd never have been any good"); "part of me thinks I'm overpaid for the job I'm doing" (but most of me is quite happy with the money). Earlier on there was another example when I casually said that part of us sympathizes with Michael.

Plato thinks that some of this talk about parts of ourselves must be literally true, and that there are three specific parts to each of us. He asks, "Do we learn with one part, get angry with another, and with some third part desire the pleasures of food, drink, sex, and the others that are closely akin to them?" After some interesting reasoning he answers that yes, there must be just these three distinct parts of the psyche in each of us: a rational, thinking part, an emotional part that looks after our honor and esteem, and a part that has raw appetites for things such as food, drink, and sex.

Why must these three parts be distinct from one another? Because they can fight against one another—which, Plato argues, could not happen if the psyche was just one unitary, simple thing. So, for example, sometimes we might want to eat or drink something, while at the very same time we might think it would be unwise to do so. Imagine an enticing cool beer in front of you. You want it. But say you've already had a few drinks, then part of you maybe thinks, "I'm driving home, and I can't be drunk." So, in a way you want the drink and at the same time you don't want it. If the psyche were one single thing, says Plato, it would be impossible for it to be pro and con toward the very same thing at the same time. So, there must be an appetitive part of you (a part with appetites) and another, distinct rational part of you that thinks about what it is best to do.

Plato makes a subtle point here. When your appetitive part wants a drink, it doesn't want it because it's *good*. It just wants it. Whether the action of satisfying your appetite is good or not is left to your reasoning part to think through. The same would apply to lust. Sometimes people just want sexual gratification without any thought about whether it would be a good thing to go for. Fortunately, it's also possible for most people to entertain the question whether it would be the best thing to do at this particular time with this particular person, and so on. So the rational part can fight with the appetitive part.

Also, the emotional or "spirited" part, the part of us "with which we get angry" can fight against appetite. Suppose your appetite comes out stronger and you drink that enticing beer regardless. Then you might get angry that you've done it. You might feel angry that you'd let yourself down or embarrassed yourself in front of others, or just because you've messed up and have to get an expensive taxi home. You're angry about what your appetite made you do. Your emotional part would then be fighting against your appetitive part, and so again Plato's reasoning is that the two cannot be the same thing, but must be separate parts of us.

Finally, the angry part can be at odds with the rational part. Plato refers to a story from the ancient epic poem, the *Odyssey*. Odysseus has been away at the war and taken many years to return home. He arrives, in disguise, to find rival noblemen living it up in his palace and trying to get his wife to marry them. He is enraged at his honor being insulted so grossly, and feels like rushing in to attack them all. But, says the poet, he refrained: "He struck his chest and spoke to his heart: 'Endure, my heart, you have suffered more shameful things than this'." This is his rational part speaking to his angry part, calculating that the better course of action is to bide his time, get allies, get a plan in place, and strike his enemies effectively at the right time. So reason fights with appetite, anger fights with appetite, and in this last case reason fights with anger. Hence, by Plato's reasoning, there are these three distinct parts to the soul.

There are many questions we could ask about the soundness of the reasoning here, and, for that matter, what it really means for something like a "soul" to have "parts" anyway. But what seems important in the examples is that there are different kinds of desire, which can be in conflict with one another. We desire things out of sheer appetite, we desire things because of our emotional reactions, and we desire things because we work out that they represent the best course of action. Each kind of desire can win out over the others, and if one kind habitually wins out, that defines your motivations in life. It defines what kind of person you are.

Are you governed by appetite? Do you just go after whatever the sensual desire of the moment draws you to? Are you governed by anger? Are you constantly moved to action by feeling your honor and esteem threatened? Or are you governed by reason? Do you desire to do whatever your reason tells you is best in the circumstances, overriding conflicting desires that your appetites or anger might throw up? Plato is absolutely clear that this last kind of person is the best. Reason is the noblest part of the soul, and its defining role is to govern. Appetites and emotions will be there in all of us, but reason should preside over them in kingly fashion. That brings harmony to the whole soul. By contrast, if appetite or anger takes control, the soul becomes unbalanced, unhealthy, and unhappy. The best and most healthy soul is the one that is governed by its reasoning part.

## Michael and His Brothers

If you've just come from reading these ideas in Plato, the *Godfather* movies seem to offer some perfect test cases. With uncanny precision, the films mark out Sonny, Fredo, and Michael as governed respectively by anger, appetite, and reason. Sonny is presented as sexually promiscuous at the beginning, but in the ensuing scenes the key to his character is his susceptibility to anger, a ruling trait so blatant that it leads directly to his death. He is so easy to trap because he functions the opposite way from Odysseus: his anger at Connie's treatment by Carlo springs him into instant action with no thought at all about the wisdom of what he's doing. His enemies can manipulate him because he is so obviously governed by his angry part.

The movie goes out of its way to point up the contrast between Sonny and Michael. On the way to the fateful restaurant meeting that will be Michael's big turning-point, Sollozzo says to Michael, "I hope you're not a hothead like your brother." Sollozzo should have hoped that Michael *was* a hothead, because then he would have been a weaker adversary. From this point on we see Michael again and again succeed in his aims through steely self-control and calculation. Anger is there in Michael, and also intense fear as he approaches the shooting of Sollozzo and McCluskey, but he is not governed by the emotions of the moment, and is always working towards a rational plan which allows him, unlike Sonny, to outwit those who would manipulate him.

Fredo is a different character again. The first time we see him at the wedding, he's already drunk, while Michael is absolutely in control. Fredo is then disgraced by his wife's drunken behavior on the dance floor, but he cannot even act out of anger to save his honor: someone else has to deal with the situation for him. When he's angry, as in one of the most poignant scenes towards the end of the second movie, it is with the impotent, resentful anger of a helpless victim ("I'm smart, and I want respect!"). Unlike Sonny, his anger can't motivate him into action. Instead, Fredo is a person governed by his appetites, always hankering for a banana daiquiri or some "real drink," or, in Moe Greene's memorable words, "banging cocktail waitresses two at a time." He is the guy who's good at showing visitors a good time, but satisfying his and others' appetites is all he seems to understand. He so misjudges Michael that he lays on a reception for him in Las Vegas complete with girls, booze, and an accordion band. Again, the scene graphically displays the contrast between the brothers. Michael barely gives all this paraphernalia a glance: it is a ridiculous distraction from the business at hand. No emotion, no gratification can stand in the way of his relentless, logical course of action.

## Governed by Reason

So now, the odd question with which we started: what would Plato think? He says that to be the best kind of person, you must be governed by the reasoning part of yourself, not by either of the other two parts. But what does that really mean? There are at least two different senses we could give to "governed by reason." One would be describing someone's *modus operandi*—how do they go about getting what it is they are pursuing? In this sense, using reasoning and calculation is often *instrumentally* good. In other words, it's a good *means* to an end. But it doesn't really matter what your end, your overall goal, is. If your end is to save many lives, it's best to work out a plan that gives you the best way of achieving that. If your end is to rob a bank, likewise. In very many situations in life, using reason tends to be instrumentally good. But Plato actually has something quite different in mind, another sense of being governed by reason. He thinks the reasoning part of the soul should set your *values*, the things that are your most important governing goals in life, or the things that you most profoundly love. It's noblest to value learning, rational inquiry, a life of taking thought for what is true and what is the best course of action.

When he comes to the question of which kind of person is happiest, Plato again uses a threefold division, with a slight modification. He assumes that if your supreme value in life is satisfying your various appetites, you will set great store by material acquisition, and so you will be a money-loving person. The other two types fall into place naturally in light of the earlier discussion:

> It seems to me that there are three pleasures corresponding to the three parts of the soul, one peculiar to each part, and similarly with desires and kinds of rule. . . . The first, we say, is the part with which a person learns, and the second the part with which he gets angry. As for the third, we had no one special name for it, since it's multiform, so we named it after the biggest and strongest thing in it. Hence we called it the appetitive part, because of the intensity of its appetites for food, drink, sex, and all the things associated with them, but we also called it the money-loving part, because such appetites are most easily satisfied by means of money. . . . What about the spirited part? Don't we say that it is wholly dedicated to the pursuit of control, victory, and high repute? Then wouldn't it be appropriate for us to call it victory-loving and honor-loving? . . . Now, it is clear to everyone that the part with which we learn is always wholly straining to know where the truth lies and that, of the three parts, it cares least for money and reputation. . . . Then wouldn't it be appropriate for us to call it learning-loving and philosophical? . . . And doesn't this part rule in some people's souls, while one of the other parts—whichever it happens to be—rules in other people's? (*Plato: Complete Works*)

Learning is learning the truth, and in particular learning the truth about how best to life your life. If that is your *love*, your *value*, then you will be a philosopher, and that (perhaps not surprisingly) is the best and happiest kind of person to be in Plato's eyes. You care more for truth and what is truly good than you do for satisfying your appetites or aggressively guarding your honor. The rational part of you is "wholly straining to know where the truth lies," and it rules by subordinating all other parts of you to this most valued goal.

By contrast, if your highest value is gratification of your appetites, or concern for your reputation, then the parts of your soul other than reason are ruling over the whole of you, setting the ends that you value. But notice something important: an appetite-loving person, someone whose highest value is some kind of sensual gratification, can probably get it more effectively by behaving rationally—*in the instrumental sense*. Instead of sitting around hoping for food, drink, or sex to come to you at random, have a rational plan, calculate how much money you'll need, work hard to get it, and then you can have banana daiquiris and the rest whenever you want. In other words, this person's dominant goal of satisfying appetites can be better achieved by using reason as an instrument.

But now we should be able to see clearly how unlike Plato's ideal this kind of rational appetite-lover would be. This person's actions follow a rational plan, but their most valued end has nothing to do with reason, learning, or truth. The person is using reason instrumentally in order to "strain after" something else.

## Michael's Values

Michael Corleone is a clever, self-controlled reasoner, but he is no philosopher. He succeeds, to begin with, through suppressing emotions and appetites, and pursuing his course with cool rationality. It begins in the scene where he defends his father in hospital, moves through the shooting of Sollozzo and McCluskey, and culminates in his utterly assured establishment of himself as the new Godfather. In Pacino's performance, especially in *The Godfather II*, the cool rationality gradually transmutes into a forbidding, ice-cold tenacity of purpose. Reason, calculation, self-control, helps him to succeed.

But why is he doing all this, ultimately? What is it that Michael most highly *values*? The obvious word that comes to mind is *family*. Michael's most fundamental drive initially seems to be that of protecting and enhancing the lives of his close blood-relatives: he saves his father's life and later reveres his memory, he loves his siblings, he nurtures his children. Are these not truly among the goods of life? On the other hand, "family" is an ambiguous term throughout the narrative. The Corleone family, like all the five families, is a ruthless crime organization. To prosper, the organization must compete aggressively against its rival families, and against governments and law-enforcers that stand in its way. Michael's mantra is "It's business, not personal." But in truth he is unable to divorce the two. Michael is so identified with the organization that the struggle for his own honor and recognition eventually becomes his innermost personal value.

Beneath all Michael's self-control there is seething anger, which eventually comes to the surface after bullets fly into his bedroom. Driven on by his rage at the disrespect this shows to himself, Michael emerges as a paradigm of Plato's type who is "wholly dedicated to the pursuit of control, victory, and high repute." His keen rational abilities are used as means towards the control and revenge that his angry part is "straining after." He strikes Kay out of pure rage. He kills Fredo via a well thought out set of instructions, not in a wild passionate frenzy. But he kills him out of anger all the same. Had he been ruled by reason in Plato's sense, Michael would have wanted, more than anything, to know what was truly the right way to live, the right thing to do. But there is no room in his soul to ask that question, let alone to regulate his behavior in line with any answer he might discover.

Michael leads an unhappy life because, under the guise of an impersonal "business," the whole of him succumbs to the rule of a rampant angry part that values only recognition, victory, and control. And the consequences for his family and for himself are all the more unhappy precisely because he pursues these values with such perfect instrumental rationality.

# 17

# The Godfather, the Son, and World Spirit

LANDON FRIM

> Your father, his thinking is old-fashioned. You must understand why I had to do that. Now let's work through where we go from here.
>
> —VIRGIL SOLLOZZO on the attempted assassination of Vito Corleone, *The Godfather Part I*

Part of what makes *The Godfather* such a great American drama is that it takes change so seriously. The story slogs a bloody path through the vendettas of Old-World Sicily, to the petty rackets of 1900s Hell's Kitchen, to the million dollar deals of mid-century Las Vegas, Havana, and beyond. Its characters aren't static pieces of furniture on a stage, but are compelling precisely because they evolve along with their shifting environments. Throughout the series, one singular truth asserts itself: *change is coming*.

In this way, *The Godfather* movies are profoundly 'dialectical'. They recognize that nothing stands still. And even the most powerfully drawn characters can't freely dictate events by decree. Instead, history moves by way of negation—the contradictions of one epoch are what gives birth to the next. And within this process, new characters and personalities are called into existence.

The Mafia of the Old World couldn't last forever. Its ethos of blood feuds and honor killings, of "never going against the family," and paying tribute to the local chieftain, fell apart. This system crumbled under the weight of its own contradictions. No matter how feared or respected the local Mafia don may have been, they ultimately couldn't keep pace with modern industry and trade. Personal ties of respect and reciprocity, of honor, loyalty, and protection, just aren't compatible with a maximum return on investment.

But the Mafia didn't disappear; It merely evolved. Outmoded, quasi-feudal traditions were finally displaced by a New World focus on profits and the bottom line. Here, the mantra is always, "It's not personal . . . It's strictly business." And so the warm, personable rule of the *original* godfather, Don Vito Corleone, passes to the cool, more bureaucratic management of his son, Michael.

We see in *The Godfather Part II,* a Mafia which mimics the patterns of American big business. The Corleone's pivot from direct extortion and local racketeering to global investment, especially in the capitalist playground of pre-revolutionary Cuba. Alongside representatives of mining, fruit, and telephone firms, the Corleones plot to carve up the wealth of the tropical island nation. All the while, they are aided in their plunder by the corrupt and vicious regime of Fulgencio Batista. In the words of Corleone associate Hyman Roth, "what . . . we have now is what we have always needed, real partnership with the government."

But New World capitalism is shot through with contradictions of its own. Left out of this cozy relationship, between big business and corrupt government, is the mass of exploited working people. In a movie series which focuses on back-room deals, pinstripe suits, and high-stakes intrigue, 'the people' are rarely represented as a distinct force of their own. This abruptly changes in the most intense scenes of *Part II* when revolutionary crowds storm Havana. Businessmen, visiting US senators, and assorted mafiosi are forced to rapidly abandon the country along with much of their wealth. Here, dialectics— the constant march of "world spirit"—takes another decisive step forward, this time toward socialist revolution.

Why does it come to this? What is the motor of world history which transforms old, feudal-style relations into modern capitalism, and then brings market capitalism to the point of crisis and collapse? Consciously or not, *The Godfather* trilogy unpacks these transitions in unflinching, often brutal detail. But to truly understand this evolution of values, politics, and economy, we have to start at the beginning.

## The Old World

Before Michael and Vito, was Don Francesco "Ciccio", a quintessential Old-World Mafia boss. The films introduce Ciccio in 1901, flanked by armed guards in his villa compound. He rules over the small Sicilian town of Corleone in the manner of a medieval lord. Ciccio demands that the villagers pay him personal fealty as well as financial tribute for "protection." But one man, Antonio Andolini, refuses to pay. In response, the don has Andolini killed, prompting a spiral of violence that would lead to the deaths of Andolini's wife and eldest son. Only his youngest son, Vito, manages to escape this vicious cycle of vendetta by boarding a ship to the New World. At Ellis Island, immigration officials incorrectly transcribe the boy's name as Vito *Corleone*, after his hometown. Thus, the eponymous "godfather" character is born.

But Ciccio, himself, is an interesting case. It would be easy to write off his actions as the result of a spiteful and malicious nature. Alternatively, one might be tempted to exoticize the concept of 'vendetta' as a peculiarly Sicilian practice. Such readings would be a mistake. For they ignore the deep, structural reasons behind Ciccio's decisions.

Don Ciccio's status is only held in place by violence and the implicit threat of violence. He is a parasite, producing nothing for the village of Corleone, but only skimming wealth from the labor of others. In this way, Ciccio really is in the mold of a feudal lord; they too were social parasites. The medieval aristocrat planted no crops and baked no bread, neither did they weave or forge, or build. What the old nobility did, in the name of the king or queen, was to offer "protection'" in exchange for tribute. And it didn't matter if there was an actual threat which required this service of protection. What these social relations really amount to is direct and ruthless extortion. Those with the hired thugs (whether they carry swords and pikes, or modern rifles) have the ability to extract payment from everyone else.

Constant acts of violence are highly disruptive and generally bad for business. So the *clever* lord (or don) will rely more on 'soft power' to bolster their position. Ostentatious shows of magnanimity or *noblesse-oblige* (such as charity and public festivals) are to be met with declarations of loyalty from the common folk. That's how you know everyone's on the same page. In this premodern arrangement, where there is no modern state, no uniform laws, and no independent courts or contracts, reputation is everything. This holds true even in turn-of-the-century Sicily, where modern capitalism and the unified Italian state hadn't yet come into their own. In the words of the Italian Marxist Antonio Gramsci, "The South of Italy can be defined as a great social disintegration" (p. 178). Informal displays of respect are what hold everything together.

Likewise, signs of *disrespect* have to be swiftly put down. For these can be deadly. Once people stop praising the ruler's name, the ruler's utterly useless and parasitic nature is laid bare. And once the emperor (or lord, or don) is seen to 'have no clothes', it won't be long until they have no head either! That's why Don Ciccio had to make an example of Antonio Andolini when he proudly refused to pay tribute. One small crack in the veneer of the don's legitimacy could lead to a flood of non-payment and popular rebellion. No matter how many armed thugs are at the boss's disposal, they can't take on the whole population at once.

In this context, the notion of 'vendetta', or blood feud, makes perfect sense. Absent a functional, modern state with uniform laws, reputation is critical. 'Respect' is the real currency backing up everything else. So, a serious insult has to be avenged at the risk of losing face before the community. And it doesn't take long for one act of vengeance to elicit another in response, sometimes lasting for generations. Consequently, blood feuds, far from being a Sicilian peculiarity, were commonplace throughout pre-modern civilization. This was especially true among the nobility—from the 'robber barons' of the Holy Roman Empire to the Samurai class of feudal Japan. In turn-of-the-century Sicily, where capitalism and the modern, unified state were still weak, the local mafia boss occupied a similar role.

*The Godfather* movies show how these pre-modern relations are imported to the New World. When the young Vito Corleone lands in America, he takes up residence in the working class, immigrant neighborhood of Hell's Kitchen. There, he encounters yet another Old World–style mafioso, one Don Fanucci (*The Godfather Part II*). When Karl Marx insisted that history repeats itself, "first as tragedy . . . second as farce," he may as well have been referring to Fanucci. This don has all the markers of Old-World feudalism, only in exaggerated, ridiculous form. He struts around the neighborhood like a true aristocrat, sporting an ostentatious white hat, suit, and long coat. Fanucci sponsors the 'festa' honoring Saint Rocco, and waves on cheers and praise from the assembled crowd, accepting tributes of food and jewelry as he goes by. Finally, he makes a grand display of pinning money on the statue of Saint Rocco to yet more popular adulation.

All the while, it's clear that Fanucci's power is outmoded and brittle. He extorts the residents of Hell's Kitchen, but doesn't have the muscle to back up all his threats. When trying to take his cut from the young Vito Corleone, Fanucci threatens to get the police involved if Vito and his crew don't pay up. This move would be unthinkable for an authentic Old World don. And later it's discovered that two bookies from the neighborhood refused to pay Fanucci altogether. Exposed for the jumped-up thug that he is, Vito arrives at the obvious question: "He's got guns. We've got guns. Why should we give him the money we sweated for?" Soon thereafter, Vito assassinates Fanucci, ultimately taking his place as the local don.

The upstart boss is certainly better at playing the role. Vito tries to be useful in mediating neighborhood conflicts and handing out charity to those less fortunate (at one point saving a widow from eviction by paying a portion of her rent). And he extends his "protection" for general declarations of loyalty, and the promise to repay these favors should the time ever come. This is an improvement over Don Fanucci's obnoxious, heavy-handed shakedowns of street vendors, store clerks, and theater owners.

But a beloved, neighborhood parasite is a parasite none-theless. The operative question is this: how does the young Vito Corleone make his money? How does he finance his lifestyle and his ability to dole out charity to the poor denizens of Hell's Kitchen? The answer is undeniable. Vito's money is siphoned from the pockets of his neighbors. Only, this brute, economic fact is obscured by Old-World displays of personal reciprocity, 'friendship', and honor.

This veil of honor is crucial for maintaining the system. It is why a mature, well-established Vito refuses to take cash payment from Amerigo Bonasera when he seeks revenge on those who brutalized his daughter. Like a true aristocrat, Vito doesn't want one-time customers, but lifelong, indentured sup-plicants. Hence his famous response to a reluctant Bonasera: "Some day, and that day may never come, I'll call upon you to do a service for me."

Still, this Old World manner of doing business—based on direct, personal relationships—isn't sustainable in the long-term. It can't keep pace with modern mass industry and economies of scale. And behind this ideology of friendship, honor, and respect, is the constant need for violence to back it all up. Vito Corleone's income is the result of 'extra-economic' coercion. In other words, it's not a return on investment *within* a business; Rather, it's a physical demand for payment *outside* of commercial activity. Put simply, it's a shakedown.

So anyone (any future Bonaseras) who can escape this kind of direct, personal extortion will surely do so. They will find other ways to satisfy their needs for justice and security. And "escape" is far easier in America, as compared to Old-World Sicily. Here, developed markets and the rule of law increasingly

spell the end for the old way of doing things. The Mafia will
have to evolve or die.

## The New World

Vito, himself, can see the writing on the wall. He laments to his
youngest son, Michael: "I never wanted this for you . . . I
thought that . . . when it was your time, that *you* would be the
one to hold the strings . . . Senator Corleone, Governor
Corleone." Vito knows that the future is in legitimate business
and political control, not blood feuds and dodging police.

And this shift in thinking is particularly evident in the
character of Tom Hagen, a non-Sicilian of German-Irish
extraction whom Vito adopted as a small boy. As an adult, Tom
earns a law degree and was elevated to the position of
*consigliere* (advisor) to the Corleone family. It is this character,
hand-picked by Vito, who is the constant voice of cool,
deliberate reason—a foil to Michael's hotheaded, older brother,
Sonny.

But old beliefs die hard. In the closing scene of *Part II*, set
in 1941, a young Michael announces his plans to join the
marines following the Japanese attack on Pearl Harbor. Sonny
(a living relic of "Old-World" values) is incensed at the prospect.
He has nothing but contempt for those enlisting:

**Sonny:** They're saps because they risk their lives for strangers.

**Michael:** They risk their lives for their country.

**Sonny:** Your country ain't your blood. You remember that.

But Michael will do things his own way, signaling a shift to the
New-World values of profits and patriotism over blood and
clan. He fights in the war, returns a hero, and ultimately marries his long-time girlfriend, Kay Adams (a conspicuously *non-
Sicilian* outsider). The constant theme of their conversations is
his promise to make the family business fully "legitimate within five years."

Yet even before this conscious shift, the "family business"
has been gradually transforming. Instead of avoiding the
official state, New World mafiosi co-opt, bribe, and corrupt the
state by paying off cops, journalists, judges, and politicians
(Captain McCluskey and Senator Geary being the prime
examples of this). Vito Corleone is said to carry politicians in
his pocket, "like so many nickels and dimes." And instead of
just ripping off businesses, the Corleones open up legitimate

firms, like the Genco Olive Oil Company, as fronts for their illegal ventures. Even murder is spoken about in capitalist, cost-benefit terms, like when the villainous Sollozzo calmly asserts, "I'm a businessman; blood is a big expense."

Eventually, legitimate businesses are no longer mere 'fronts', but instead become the main sources of revenue. The whole model gets inverted: Crime becomes a mere adjunct to legitimate trade. This is especially true in the move out to Nevada, where the Corleones invest in Las Vegas hotels and casinos. Yes, there's still killing, blackmail, and extortion. But these acts are in the service of legal businesses and contracts—not the other way around. So, casino magnate Moe Green is shot through the eye in a Vegas massage parlor. But why? It's so the Corleones can take control of his legal casino outfit.

The most dramatic example of this shift toward capitalist legitimacy comes during the communion party for Michael's son in *Part II*, held at his sprawling Lake Tahoe estate. One of the guests, Frank Pentangeli, makes a drunken scene. He is a high-ranking *caporegime*, left in charge of the family's affairs back in New York, ever since Michael and the major players moved out West. But now, the illegal rackets of the old neighborhood are an increasingly small (and embarrassing) revenue stream compared to their main interests in gaming and hospitality.

Pentangeli, who staggers around the fashionable party and drinks from a garden hose, can't even get an audience with Michael. He loudly complains, "What do I gotta do? Do I have to get a letter of introduction to get a sit-down? . . . *He's got me waiting in the lobby!*" This dynamic, of the Old-World being displaced (and disrespected) by the New, is punctuated by Pentangeli's attempt to get the party band to play some traditional *tarantella* music; Instead, they mock him with an upbeat version of "Pop Goes the Weasel." This also foreshadows Frank's betrayal of Michael before Senate hearings on organized crime, that is, his becoming a "weasel."

Finally, in *Part III*, a now elderly Michael completes the transition entirely. He pours money into Immobiliare, a European real-estate firm. To get a controlling stake, Michael plans to buy out the Vatican's interest (worth $600 million). But to make this deal, he has to convince Vatican officials that he is no longer invested in the gambling business. "We've sold the casinos, all businesses having to do with gambling. We have no interests or investment in anything illegitimate." Now, even being *adjacent* to criminal activity is unacceptable.

If the Mafia don was once in the mold of a petty, feudal lord, he is now a calculating CEO. As Michael categorically puts it in the same Vatican conversation, *"Friendship and money; Oil and water."* In other words, the two don't mix. What matters is a return on investment, not pledges of loyalty, friendship, and honor. Michael perfectly embodies this modern, bourgeois ideal. In the words of the Communist Manifesto:

> The bourgeoisie, wherever it has got the upper hand, has put an end to all feudal, patriarchal, idyllic relations. It has pitilessly torn asunder the motley feudal ties that bound man to his "natural superiors," and has left remaining no other nexus between man and man than naked self-interest, than callous "cash payment." (*The Communist Manifesto*, p. 20)

The days of long coats, hats, and strutting through the public *festa* are over, now replaced with nondescript black suits and boardroom deals. Here, the movement is a characteristically dialectical one: Michael becomes so good—so efficient—at being "Godfather" that he transforms into something else entirely.

This change in values and style only mirrors the new economic realities: In the New World, capitalist way of doing things, money isn't taken by brute force, as an "extra-economic" shakedown. Instead, profits are taken *during the normal course of doing business*, the result of investments in land, materials, and most especially, *labor*.

Some things, to be sure, remain the same. Just like in the old neighborhood rackets, the boss makes his living by extracting wealth from the only people who actually create it—the workers. Only now, there's no need for intimidation or breaking thumbs. Workers voluntarily agree to receive back in wages less value than they produce. That's where profits come from, after all. But the coercion here is entirely above-board, all recorded in freely signed contracts, and backed up by impartial laws, courts, and police. Workers willingly sign up to do jobs where the capitalist's cut is taken out in advance—not because anyone is threatening them with direct, physical violence, but because otherwise they'll starve. The worker can flee this or that boss, but they can't escape the capitalist class as a whole. As Tom Hagen would put it, "It's not personal . . . It's strictly business."

## The World to Come

The contradictions of New World capitalism are clear: Eschewing direct, brute force, the capitalist remains a parasite all the same. They extract billions of dollars of value without producing anything themselves. At the same time, they leverage their considerable wealth to shape laws and policies for their own benefit. There's no need to pay off individual cops, journalists, or judges; the whole character of the modern state is dictated by the needs of business.

This dynamic takes on cartoonish dimensions in the capitalist paradise of pre-revolutionary Cuba. Vividly depicted in *Part II*, we see representatives of various Mafia families assemble at the birthday party of Hyman Roth, a longtime associate of the Corleones and major player in the Cuban hotel and casino industry. In a moment of obvious symbolism, a cake with a picture of Cuba is literally carved up and divided amongst the guests.

It's at this event that Roth speaks of "real partnership with the Cuban government." But his prosaic speech is indistinguishable from that of any CEO or corporate lobbyist: "This kind of government knows how to help business, to encourage it . . . and has relaxed restrictions on imports." And Roth's ambitions don't end in Cuba. As he gleefully boasts to Michael, their syndicate is powerful enough to capture the heights of political power in Washington as well. "Just one small step; Looking for a man that wants to be president of the United States and having the cash to make it possible. Michael, we're bigger than US Steel."

This gathering of mafiosi is then mirrored by an official summit of "legitimate" businessmen, hosted by Cuban dictator Fulgencio Batista. Representatives of the General Fruit Company, United Telephone and Telegraph, The Pan-American Mining Corporation, and South American Sugar sit around a large wooden table in a lavish hall. Michael and Hyman Roth are, of course, in attendance as well, representing "tourism and leisure activities."

Conspicuously left out of the meetings are the laborers who sustain those very businesses. There are no fruit pickers or miners, no telephone exchange operators or hotel staff present. The great mass of working-poor have no voice here at all, and are essentially invisible. At most, news of approaching Communist rebels casts a subliminal anxiety over the proceedings. And herein lies the dialectical brilliance of *The Godfather Part II*. It shows the irresistible force of historical change, precisely when it's operating behind people's backs.

But the working class isn't invisible for long. On New Year's Eve 1958, Communist rebels flood into Havana, propelled by an explosive cocktail of hope and rage. Similarly *The Godfather Part I* originally included a scene depicting Italian

Communists marching at Portella della Ginestra, in Sicily. Cut from the final version, this scene foreshadows the events in Havana in *Part II*. This was  response to the infamous 1947 massacre of peasants, socialists, and Communists by right-wing forces—likely supported by large landowners, fascists, Christian Democrats, and members of the Sicilian Mafia itself (Coppola, *The Godfather*, Deleted Scene). The scenes depict a militant working class who will no longer pit up with exploitation and victimhood.

In some sense, these events in Cuba were predictable, even inevitable. They merely resolve the contradictions of New-World capitalism, where political power is monopolized by a tiny elite who, themselves, produce nothing for society. Still, the revolution comes as a violent, surprising shock to many. And *Part II* artfully showcases this stark divide between the objective unfolding of history and the subjective expectations of individuals on the ground.

Inside a lavish New Year's Eve gala, hosted by Batista himself, guests in formal attire saunter around the hall aimlessly. There's no energy left in the room. Batista's New Year's Eve address is received with yawns, and his toast of "Salud, Salud, Salud!" is met with an indifferent, stony silence. Outside, Rebels engage in exuberant cheers of "Freedom, Freedom, Freedom!" Sensing something is amiss, guests start to trickle out of the hall. Panicked senators and businessmen seek sanctuary in the American embassy. The party, in every sense of the word, is over. World Spirit is on the march, dashing the carefully-arranged plans of Roth, big business, and their government allies.

Michael, perhaps because of his dispassionate nature, can see before everyone else the way that history would unfold. He is the first one to leave the gala, while Batista is still in the middle of his speech. And even earlier, at Hyman Roth's birthday party, Michael has a moment of uncommon prescience: There's a *reason* why the Communists will succeed in Cuba. They're fighting for more than money.

> **Michael:** It occurred to me: The soldiers are paid to fight; the rebels aren't.
>
> **Roth:** What does that tell you?
>
> **Michael:** *They can win.*

We see in all this a characteristically *dialectical* movement of world history. First, local, communal ties of blood and family are broken up—*negated*—by the irresistible logic of the New World. Global capitalism reduces everything to a question of investment, profits, and cash payment. But when the contradictions of the New World reach a boiling point, when the global market leaves millions destitute and without political voice, this triggers a renewed focus on direct human needs and welfare. After all, who cares about the stock exchange when you can't even afford to eat? *The negation is, itself, negated.*

Only, this is not a simple retreat to a parochial past. There is no going back. The world is too connected, and the productive capacities of industry are just too great. Giant factories, air travel, and mass communications are starkly incompatible with a humanity divided up on rural estates and small villages. Instead, human needs can only be met through direct, workers' control of the existing means of production. The values of Old World, communal life don't disappear, but are transformed into the modern specter of World Communism.

# 18
# The Twelve Mobsters

MICHEL LE GALL AND CHARLES TALIAFERRO

From the earliest times, philosophers—from Socrates in ancient Greece and Musonius in ancient Rome onward—have warned us about the damage charismatic individuals can inflict in their pursuit of wealth and power.

In ancient Rome, there were some outstanding cases of noble and disinterested conduct. Cincinnatus (sixth century B.C.E.) left his farm to become a supreme commander of Roman forces and, after a victorious military campaign, resigned and returned to his farm (Cincinnati, Ohio, is named after him).

Despite such inspiring examples, and with the rise of the Empire, the world of the Caesars (including Julius, Augustus, Caligula, and Nero) became not unlike that of the Corleone family and its rival five crime families. Imperial Rome was crowded with individuals seeking power by means of calculated violence, including murder and intimidation, using family allegiance, marriage, and religion to solidify alliances, prizing loyalty to themselves and their and families, while punishing those they suspected of betrayal. We know a lot about this from the second-century work, *De vita Caesarum*, popularly known as *The Twelve Caesars*, by Suetonius.

The parallels between ancient Romans and Sicilian Americans are illuminating, and in *Godfather II*, Tom Hagen and Pentangeli discuss the fate of failed conspirators against the Roman emperor. These parallels should incline us to take seriously the critique of violent power politics advanced in the name of philosophy, by Socrates and Musonius. Perhaps influenced by the example of Cincinnatus, Musonius praised peaceful farming as opposed to urban striving for domination.

We can look at the *Godfather* movies the way Suetonius looks at the Caesars, simply laying out the acts with minimum commentary so that you can infer any lessons for yourselves. Let's observe the most conspicuous parallels between Godfathers and Caesars:

1. **Ceremony, homage, and loyalty**
2. **Prudence**
3. **Family**
4. **Exile and execution**
5. **Religion**
6. **Demeanor, lust, and madness.**

While in the last category, *The Godfather* movies do not plumb the depths of sexual depravity as found in Suetonius, the movies do (as the public intellectual Gore Vidal said of Suetonius) hold up a mirror to ourselves: "Most of the world today is governed by Caesars . . . Suetonius, in holding up a mirror to those Caesars of diverting legends, reflects not only them but ourselves, half-tempted creatures, whose great moral task it is to hold in balance the angel and the monster within—for we are both, and to ignore this duality is to court disaster."

## Ceremony, Homage, and Loyalty

The first *Godfather* movie is bookended by a marriage and a funeral; the second by a funeral and the ritual execution of Fredo; the third by a reception in honor of Michael and the shoot out on the Opera House steps, a scene reminiscent of the Odessa steps sequence in Eisenstein's "Battleship Potemkin." Central to these six scenes is the notion of ceremony as a vehicle for manifesting power and authority, and confirming homage and obedience. Or depending on the protagonist's course of action, suffering the consequences of betrayal.

*The Godfather* begins with an Italian immigrant professing his love for the United States of America. He has found prosperity and enjoys his children, until his daughter is brutally attacked, and the courts provide no justice. Don Corleone rejects Bonasera's request for a revenge killing of his daughter's assailants yet finally takes pity on Bonasera. But only after Bonasera surrenders, kisses the Don's hand, and calls him "Godfather."

The setting for this scene is the celebration of the marriage of Connie, the Don's daughter. As the celebration proceeds, in his darkened office, Don Corleone receives the homage of two others who, unlike Bonasera, fully appreciate the ritual of homage. The first is Johnny Fontane, a popular crooner. Heralded as an idol by the young women outside, inside another reality emerges: Johnny as supplicant. On the verge of tears because he's been rejected for a movie role, Don Corleone brings him back to reality with a reprimand "Act like a man!" and an admonition against Johnny's becoming a "Hollywood finocchio"—Hollywood "fennel," Italian for the slang, "pansy." Johnny's loyalty pays off and he secures the role. The other retainer, Luca Brasi, wins the Don's heart since he is loyal, no questions asked.

As Suetonius demonstrates, emperors tended to elicit loyalty, especially among the populace, through triumphs or bread and circuses. Julius Caesar (XXXVII), was without peer in capitalizing on the pageantry and power of ceremony—particularly the triumphs. His five separate triumphs, "all differed from each other in their varied pomp and pageantry."

But that was not enough. Loyalty of the army and praetorian guard had to be purchased. Julius Caesar (XXXVI) "doubled the pay of the legions in perpetuity . . . and sometimes distributed to every soldier in his army a slave, and a portion of land" For his part, Mark Antony (LXXXIV) played up the theme of loyalty at his funeral. A herald "proclaimed to the people the decree of the senate . . . with the oath by which they had engaged themselves for the defense of his person." Antony's post-mortem solicitation of loyalty provides a counterpoint to Luca Brasi. In politics as in crime, characters with Luca's resolute loyalty are few. Only money and access to power assure loyalty. And when future prospects dim, all bets are off.

## Prudence

We typically associate prudence with Victorian virtues. Prudence is inherently prim and proper. It's very sound announces restraint, caution, and self-discipline. But in the *Godfather* movies, as in Suetonius, prudence (Latin *prudentia*) suggests something different. It means "knowledge" or "skill." Derived from "*providens*" it can also mean "one who foresees."

In *The Godfather*, prudence is the ability to foretell the consequences of actions, particularly violence. Both Sonny and Fredo lack prudence; they think short-term. Sonny plots revenge against Sollozzo and co. after the failed attempt on

Don Corleone's life ("The Tattaglia family's going to eat dirt. I don't care if we all go down together.") and later Fredo falls in with Hyman Roth to get his fair share. Both these protagonists are the authors of their own demise. They fall victim to emotion, anger, or in Fredo's case self-doubt and pity. But let's not assume prudence equates to restraint in the use of violence.

Michael is far from restrained in his use of violence. Rather, he wields it judiciously. When he volunteers to murder Sollozzo and Captain McCluskey at Louis's restaurant, he has already mapped out his play. He will escape to Italy, Corleone-backed newspapers will discredit McCluskey and justify the murders. And when calm returns, Michael will return. Similarly, in the final scenes of *The Godfather*, Michael's henchmen terminate his rivals. These are strategic killings. Michael has bet that by going all in—or "going to the mattresses"—his authority will emerge uncontested. Prudence always fully sees the path forward.

Suetonius provides many examples of prudence. The most famous case of the balance between action and prudence is Julius Caesar's crossing of the Rubicon (XXXII). That event is now an expression describing an irreversible decision. Yet in Suetonius, Caesar is not perturbed by the irreversibility of a decision. Instead, he concentrates on the consequences of his action. Simply put, Caesar weighs events not strictly in terms of outcomes, because he betrays little self-doubt, but rather their implications and repercussions. Here's how Caesar framed it: "We can retreat now, but once we cross that little bridge, then the whole matter becomes one of the sword (Latin: *omnia armis agenda erunt.*)" The future agenda is all about force; negotiation has no role. Caesar never overtly expresses doubt.

Prudence manifests itself in the *Godfather* movies in other ways—from choosing a wife to picking an enforcer. For example, Don Corleone entrusts Clemenza ("I want reliable people. People who aren't going to be carried away.") with roughing up the men who assaulted Bonasera's daughter. Invariably, prudence and domination are inextricably intertwined. But foresight is the singular skill that enables political and criminal actors to succeed. Yet, when they let their guard down, or compromise prudence by believing their flatterers, their demise is sealed.

## Family

Let's begin by clearing up another misconception. While loyalty to the family is atop the list of obligations, there are definite limits. Dedication to the family is more than sustaining the strength of the family at all costs. For the ambitious, it's also a vehicle for advancing one's own interests. And when the family fails you, you seek recourse elsewhere.

Whether in *The Godfather* or Suetonius, families are invariably extended families. Blood ties run deep, yet they don't determine the limits of family. Tom Hagen is a telling example. An orphan, he was raised alongside Michael and Sonny. When Sonny challenges Tom by saying, "That's easy to say; it's not your father," Tom responds, "I was as good a son to him as you or Mike." Similarly, politics define family for Suetonius, just as much as blood. We learn that for political reasons Augustus Caesar (XVII) spared the offspring of Antony and Cleopatra and "reared them . . . as if they were his own kin."

How do we capture the power and purpose of family? In all three *Godfather* movies, family is literally an image—a photographic image, whether it's a wedding, a first communion, or the family photo at Michael's party. Photographs are important because they cement a formal ideal of family, one that everyday life frequently belies.

In the most obvious sense, for the Corleones and their criminal counterparts, family represents a community of financial and corporate interests—shares in illegal enterprises. So being part of a family requires loyalty and delivering the goods to the Don himself, or a capo, in return for protection.

For their part, women have a special function in the family. Women embody the mandate of upholding honor. So, whether it's Sonny defending his sister Connie from an abusive husband or Connie's wayward behavior, women need protection. When Connie confronts Michael and challenges his authority by suggesting she may run off with Merle Johnson (the real-life name of the closeted actor, Troy Donohue, who plays Merle), Michael's resolve, as well as Connie's concern for Fredo, ultimately force her to repent and seek forgiveness.

In a pivotal scene, Connie performs an act of homage, renouncing her ill-begotten ways ("I want to stay close to home now, is that alright? . . . I hated you for so long, Michael, for so many years. I think I did things to myself, to hurt myself, so that you would know—and you would be hurt too . . . You were being strong for all of us, like Papa was."). In the end, for Connie, family provides for her as a widow and for her children.

Contrast that with Kay's unyielding confrontation with Michael: she breaks her ties with him as husband and head of "the family" only later to reconcile. But first, Kay aims a figurative shotgun at Michael—the news of an aborted male child.

The complexities of Roman political families far exceed anything the Corleone family can muster. Since primogeniture was not accepted political practice, emperors constantly guarded against family plots, pretenders, and astute wives or mothers. We know Augustus Caesar (LXV) "bore the death of his kin with far more resignation than their misconduct." But family was precarious: "At the height of his happiness and confidence in his family . . . fortune proved fickle . . . his daughter and granddaughter were guilty of every kind of vice, so he banished them." Family ties bore, for the Romans and the Corleone family, an inherent contradiction. By blood, they were strong, but other realities could snap those bonds instantly.

There's an evident explanation for why Michael was confounded by Kay's confronting him. She was not of Italian heritage. Roman women did likewise, before the constrictions of Christian-inspired chivalry appeared. Claudius (XXIX), under the sway of his mother and wives "played the part, not of a Prince, but of a servant." They determined "the command of armies, pardons, or punishments . . ." But not all emperors abided overbearing family. Nero (XXXIII) arranged the murder of Claudius (Nero XXXIII) and then confronted his mother. Killing her was not easy. He (XXXIV) tried poisoning her three times, burying her in her bed under a collapsed ceiling, drowning her, and only later succeededby having her brutally attacked by soldiers.

The real power of family is demonstrated not in lighter moments, but in the harsh glare of betrayal. Consider Fredo's betrayal. What's important are his motivations. He is the elder brother passed over by Michael after Sonny's murder. He failed to prove himself whether through military service, as Michael did, or by defending his father against assassins. He can't even control his wife, a fading movie starlet who embarrasses him with her drunken behavior at Anthony's confirmation celebration. Fredo bemoans his fate to his brother: "Mike, you're my kid brother, and *you* (emphasis added) take care of me? Did you ever think of that? Ever once? . . . Send Fredo to take care of that . . . take care of some little unimportant night club here . . . pick somebody up at the airport. Mike, I'm your older brother; I was stepped over!"

Revenge was not Fredo's motive. Like many betrayals, his motivation was personal and petty: "Johnny Ola said there was something good in it for me . . . me on my own." Michael waited until their mother died and only then had Fredo executed, proof he did not play favorites. By contrast, Emperor Titus's (IX) brother continued to plot against him, but "he did not have the heart to put him to death or banish him from court . . ." Titus "begged him with tears and prayers" simply to "return his affection (Latin *ut tandem mutuo erga se animo vellet esse.*)" Although

Michael adopted the more "prudent" solution, like Titus he mourned his brother's actions. Kissing Fredo on the lips, he tearfully declared, "I know it was you, Fredo. You broke my heart."

## Exile and Execution

In Roman tradition, exile is frequently a voluntary act to avoid a worse fate—execution. It also had a benefit: the prospect of return. Rome origins lie with exiles. One of the city's founders, Romulus, gathered in prisoners, slaves, criminals, and exiles. Ovid conceived his great works, the *Tristia* and the *Epistulae ex Ponto,* during his banishment. Seneca, the celebrated philosopher, lived in exile in Corsica and returned only to fall prey to the cruelty of his former pupil, Nero (XXXV).

Exile is at the heart of *The Godfather*. Both main protagonists, Vito, and Michael Corleone, are exiles. Vito, in the opening scenes of *The Godfather II*, escapes the clutches of Don Francesco who is intent on killing the young boy lest he seek revenge for his murdered father. As it happens, Vito's mother dies attempting to assassinate Don Francesco and the orphan, like Moses, is hidden in a basket and escapes to America. Unable to communicate his last name, Andolini, Vito is given the name Corleone, his birthplace, and a reminder of his exile in the New World. As a young man, Vito confronts Don Fanucci, the padrone and extortionist of Little Italy. He kills the "black hand" and eventually emerges as boss and benefactor to the poor and downtrodden. But to close the circle, Vito must return to Corleone. There, in an apparent act of homage, he presents Don Francesco with a tin of the Genco company's olive oil only to stab him in revenge—"My father's name was Antonio Andolini . . . and this is for you!"

Michael's exile parallels his father's, but in reverse. To avoid death—either because of revenge or a court sentence—after the assassination at Louis's restaurant, he flees to Sicily. There, under the protection of Don Tommasino, he makes a life for himself. He marries Apollonia, only to face the ongoing consequences of his actions in New York—death and betrayal. When he finally returns from exile, it's under a veil of secrecy.

For both Vito and Michael, exile brought new lives and success. For Vito, escape from poverty and the chance to create a strong family; for Michael, the opportunity to connect with his family's roots, and to ponder how to make the family legitimate. Legitimacy always hangs like a pall over the family. As Michael vows to Kay, "In five years the Corleone family is going to be completely legitimate." Exile engenders a "new birth" Cicero maintains. The Greek word embodying that idea, "paliggenesia," eventually took on a theological bent in the New Testament.

## Religion

In the Gospel of Matthew, Jesus admonishes his followers to: "Render unto Caesar the things that are Caesar's, and to God the things that are God's." As polytheists, Romans attended to the needs of their gods, although they did not necessarily connect personal moral conduct with their fate in this and the afterworld. Nevertheless, the gods were demanding. As Suetonius, explains, religious duties fell within the emperor's scope of responsibilities. Of Claudius (XXII), he notes, "He revived some old customs or even established new ones in matters touching religious ceremonies and civil and military customs . . ." The gods certainly needed to be appeased for fear they might suddenly intervene in your life.

There's a certain pagan view implicit in Michael's attitude towards religion. Although he seems to abide by Jesus's dictum, for him, religion seems little more than a ritual. Indeed, he is really only intent on appeasing God in the fashion of a pagan god.

Two important scenes stand out in *The Godfather* series. First is the final scene of *The Godfather* where Michael is fulfilling his responsibility as godfather to Connie's child. At that very moment, he is also cementing his role as Godfather of the Corleone family. As Michael's hitmen go about their business, the movie cuts back and forth between bloody murder and divine invocations (implicitly "the blood of Christ"), as Michael confirms his belief in "God, the Father Almighty" and "the Holy Ghost," something he intones with a perfunctory, almost anemic, "I do." Clearly, Michael has not renounced Satan and abides evil, consciously and with a clear mind. He does not recognize the dichotomy between his formal faith and actions. After all, "lived religion," especially in the southern Italian Catholic tradition, is above all a matter of religious practices, not beliefs. Consequently, Michael is more than capable of living with personal religious dissonance.

Similarly, Michael and his family celebrate the first communion of his son Anthony at Lake Tahoe in *The Godfather II*. That it is a sacrament of initiation for the Church seems to elude Michael. It's fitting that instead of Anthony receiving a blessing, Michael obtains the official blessing of the Nevada Senator Pat Geary who accepts an endowment check on behalf of the university. Ironically, minutes later that blessing turns to contempt when the Senator tries to extort Michael in return for a gaming license and taunts him, "I'm going to squeeze you, Corleone, because I don't like you; I don't like the kind of man you are. I despise your masquerade, and the dishonest way you pose yourself and your fucking family." Powerful affirmation that religion is just part and parcel of the "masquerade" and Michael's doomed effort to turn legitimate.

## Demeanor, Lust, and Madness

Well before *Dress for Success* was published in the 1970s, Romans and Christians pondered whether a person's dress and demeanor were a window on the soul. The color red was a favorite among Romans. It spoke of martial prowess and blood. Presaging America's own despotic president, the book suggested red ties were integral to "power dressing." Christian lore, by contrast cautioned against appearances, the well-known medieval dictum being "The habit doesn't make the monk" (Latin: *cucullus monachum non facit.*)

For Suetonius, physical appearance was a mirror of character. He considered Julius Caesar (XLV), the father of the despot's combover, to be vain: "Because of his baldness, he used to comb forward his scanty locks from the crown of his head, and enjoyed . . . the privilege of wearing a laurel wreath at all times." Likewise, Caligula's appearance spoke to his perverse character: "He was very tall and extremely pale, with an unshapely body his hair entirely gone on the top of his head, though his body was hairy."

Vito, and Michael offer stark contrasts in style. Vito, although dressed in formal attire when we first meet him is anything but a clothes horse—although he doesn't hesitate to dispense with prize horses. In a critical meeting with Sollozzo, Vito wears a scruffy gray jacket, a bland tie, and a greenish shirt. The Don still dresses like a Sicilian villager whose Sunday best can't match that of his urban counterparts.

Michael, by contrast, wears what Sonny calls an "Ivy-league suit" and as he transforms into a Don, he adopts more conservative clothes. His attire, and the imposing limousine that trails him during his meeting with Kay, signal Michael's determination to be a conventional businessman, down to the homburg hat. In his meeting with Senator Geary, we are reminded, however, that he is still a slick criminal as his shiny sharkskin suit testifies. Italians, and other swarthy undesirables whom Senator Geary reviled, often wore such suits as Lucette Lagnado recounts in her childhood memoir *The Man in the White Sharkskin Suit.*

As for lust and madness, they are, by Suetonius's telling, responsible for the demise of the republic and the turmoil of the Empire. Time and again, he recounts plots, assassinations, and debauchery. And although his language is modest, he nevertheless conveys his horror. Tiberius (XLIV), we learn, had a predilection for little boys who nibbled on his member as he swam naked (the emperor termed them his "little fishes," Latin *pisciculi*). For Suetonius, of such "depravities . . . one can hardly bear to tell or be told, let alone believe." But not all depravity or madness stemmed from sexual deviancy. For sure, we're told Caligula slept with his sisters, although the classicist Mary Beard doubts these accusations. Cruelty was another matter. "When a Roman knight on being thrown to the wild beasts loudly protested his innocence, he [Caligula, XXVII,] took him out, cut off his tongue, and put him back again." Why cruelty? As Caligula (XXX) explained "Let them hate me as long as they fear me (Latin*"Oderint, dum metuant")*."

The Corleone family hardly indulges in sexual depravity. Sure, Sonny has dalliances at weddings or trysts as his bodyguards wait. Fredo may be, as Moe Green says, "banging cocktail waitresses" or indulges in watching sex acts in Cuban cabarets—the moment he inadvertently revels his betrayal to Michael—but that's far from the debauchery pictured in Suetonius.

What about madness? For Suetonius, Caligula's madness is attributable to his poor education and isolation after his rise to power. His limited education resulted from his being "an army brat," brought up on the Empire's frontiers. As his nickname suggests, soldiers teased him because his mother dressed him in military garb—"caligula" being the diminutive of "caliga," the legionnaires' sandal. More to the point, because of his isolation Caligula's (LV) "partiality became madness when it came to those to whom he was devoted." Such statements raise a valid question about Michael Corleone: was he mad?

Like many Roman emperors, Michael lived in isolation. Although well educated, hints of Michael's isolation abound. Most striking is the final moment of *The Godfather* when one of Michael's henchmen closes the door on Kay.

Isolation progressively brings on obsession. And it's debatable whether Michael's effort to expose Hyman Roth's plot against his family drives him to madness, and to plotting the murder of his own brother, Fredo. As suggested earlier, this may just be prudence. Conversely, given Michael's singular devotion to his family, he may have slipped into madness. The final scene of *The Godfather II* has him gazing out at Lake Tahoe. He stares longingly into the gray scenery perhaps to capture a glimpse of a happier past, of his days as a war hero before joining the family business. Those moments of regret and reflection may point to the unresolved contradictions of Michael's being. He is a calculating killer but a man who bemoans a life ill spent. Yet, looking back in anger, as John Osborne suggests, engenders more pain, and perhaps represses madness.

## Angelic and Monstrous

Suetonius's *The Twelve Caesars* and the *Godfather* movies may be seen as holding up a mirror to our angelic and monstrous qualities. We have seen the use and abuse of rites of loyalty, prudence, family, religion, the endurance of exile, and more. Angelic virtues may be thin in comparison to the monstrous when it comes to the Caesars and the crime families in *The Godfather*. If so, they may motivate us to consider the more humble paths of Socrates and Musonius. Both eschewed the pursuit of powerful domination, enduring instead the harsh treatment of imposing state power (Socrates being executed by the city-state of Athens and Musonius being banished from Rome under emperor Nero). Both sought to demonstrate the love of wisdom (the literal meaning of 'philosophy') through dialogue, the power of reason, and the renunciation of selfish ambition.

The lives and deaths of the Godfathers and most of the Caesars give us reason to consider the warnings of Socrates, Musonius, and those who follow their example today, of the danger of falling prey to the temptation of worldly power.

# 19
# From Friend to Monster

FR. THEODORE VITALI, CP

Viewing the entire *Godfather* trilogy, we can see an evolution, or perhaps better, a devolution from Aristotle's theory of Friendship to Hobbes's theory of Nature, the Natural State of War.

The devolution occurs from the beginning scenes of *The Godfather Part II,* taking place in Corleone, Sicily, where young Vito's father is being buried, and his brother and mother are murdered by the Mafia, or Black Hand. Vito escapes through family friends to America, where he begins a peaceful, "normal" life among friends, and his growing family. In these early scenes in America, Vito depicts the essence of Aristotle's theory of virtue and friendship. He is loyal, faithful, honest, and deeply loving towards his family and his friends, even though he had emerged and escaped from a purely Hobbesian world of terror and violence. Vito is virtuously happy. But Vito is never very far from the Hobbesian world, either.

The head of the Mob in his neighborhood extorts from Vito's friends and eventually costs him his job. He is thereafter forced to enter that Hobbesian world out of necessity and choice: to care for his family, whom he loves, and to survive in this Hobbesian world of nature, everyone against everyone else. In so doing, he begins to see that he must enter that world, at least in part. The key scene is when his neighbor, Clemenza, tosses him a bundle through the side window for his safe keeping. It is a bundle of revolvers. Vito opens the bundle, hides them from his wife, thus excluding her from the ensuing business, and then joins Clemenza in the stealing of a rug.

He enters the criminal world at the margins, with his family at a distance and separate. The revolvers symbolize the violent world of crime, murder, and deceit. He does not reject that symbol. Eventually, he will kill the tyrant of the neighborhood and assume the role of Don, Leader. While retaining his "Aristotelian" relationship to his wife and family, he now fully enters the Hobbesian World. Vito becomes the Don, the Leviathan.

At the opening scene of *The Godfather*, Vito is the supreme Don, the supreme Leviathan. But, as supreme as he may be, he is cautious and concerned about a visit from Sollozzo; The Turk was known for his role in the narcotics business. In the following scene, while visiting with the Turk, Vito rejects the Turk's offer to join him in his narcotics enterprise. But, at that very moment, Sonny interrupts and with a slip of the tongue indicates to both the Turk and Don Vito, the vulnerability of the Leviathan: one flaw, one disagreement within the family, and the superpower comes apart and a state of war will ensue . . . and it does! The Leviathan is powerful but fragile and vulnerable. His power is not absolute. The Leviathan Family begins to collapse.

## Michael, The Hobbesian Aristotelian

Michael, the youngest son, is outside the Criminal Family. He is a decorated war veteran and a man in love with Kay, a non-Italian New England woman. Kay is not part of the Hobbesian world. Michael is not either . . . almost! But, after the attempt on the Don's life, Michael realizes that he has to engage the enemy of his family to save his family, his father. And so he murders the Turk and McCluskey, the police captain. But just before he murders the Turk and the police captain, he sends Kay back to New Hampshire, a place of innocence and safety. He is still the faithful son and loving partner to Kay. His Aristotelian virtues transcend his commitment and engagement in the Hobbesian world of violence. He has heroic virtues of fidelity to his family and friends, the same virtues that made him a war hero. But, he has compromised the highest of virtues, justice.

Michael escapes to Sicily, where his father grew up. While there, he goes on a walk with his bodyguards. While sauntering around the countryside, he sees and becomes enthralled with Apolonia, the beautiful young woman of the village. He falls in love with her and courts her appropriately. After marrying Apolonia, he lives in the village under the constant care of bodyguards. Michael and Apolonia are living within the bonds of Aristotelian friendship. They are happy together in a loving friendship. But Michael and Apolonia are not safe. Upon learning of his brother's murder, he knows he is no longer safe and plans to move to a safer place, leaving

Apolonia with her father and family. But, in an attempt to kill him, his betrayer kills Apolonia instead. There is no escape from the Hobbesian World.

The end of Aristotle's world comes with Apolonia's death. Michael returns to America a pure Hobbesian. Two years later, when he seeks to marry Kay, he does so on purely Hobbesian terms telling her that "he 'needs' her" rather than "he loves her.' His marriage is contractual à la Hobbes, not à la Aristotle. And so it continues.

## Michael, the Hobbesian

In each stage of *The Godfather Part I and II*, Michael descends from Aristotelian Hero to Hobbesian Monster, trusting no one, not even his own family. He kills his brother-in-law, Carlo, and then, in *Part II*, his brother Fredo, even though Fredo was no longer a threat. He continues to close out Kay from his life. One can barely feel or see any affection or love between Michael and Kay, or even Michael and his children. There's one tender moment with his son Anthony, right after Anthony's first Communion, but we can also see that the business of Hobbesian survival transcends all other values. And so the story ensues.

Michael descends even deeper into the Hell of the Hobbesian World. When Michael is away in Cuba, Kay tries to escape his Hobbesian world by aborting their unborn son in a horrific moment to end this "thing of yours." Michael drives her away. There is never again a sign of any Aristotelian friendship, anywhere or with anyone. Every relationship is strategic and contractual, guarded by self-interested survival à la Hobbes.

In *Part III*, Michael seeks his redemption, now twenty-five years later. He even attempts a renewed relationship with Kay. But, his son, Anthony, will not join him in his enterprises. Only his daughter, Mary, is with him, though in a legitimate enterprise, a charitable institution founded by Michael in an attempt to make peace with his own conscience and life.

Michael seeks redemption in society and in the Church. He even goes to confession, trying to be forgiven for having killed his brother. He is absolved but never gets the redemption he desperately seeks. In the very last scenes of the movie, while again taking place in Sicily, an attempt is made on his life. In the process, the assassin misses his target, Michael, and kills Mary instead. The penultimate punishment for Michael in his Hobbesian world is the death of his beloved Mary, the only person left he loves in the Aristotelian mode. He truly loves her.

But he could not keep her free or safe from the Hobbesian World he created and managed. His punishment was twofold: Mary's death because of him, and his final isolation and death in Sicily, the last scene of the trilogy.

As an old, sick man, he sits alone in a rocker in the garden of the house in Italy where his father was born. He is back to the beginning. He sits alone with a little dog as his companion. He keels over and dies. The dog walks away. He did not even have the affection of the dog. He died a pure Hobbesian death: alone, unloved, ignored! The Hellish death of the Tyrant, the Leviathan.

Aristotle believed that for human flourishing, it was necessary that individuals develop and sustain those precise virtues that "humanize" the person leading them to be "good citizens" in a moral and life-sustaining community. Friendship was the highest culminating virtue, the virtue that fostered and sustained personal and communitarian life. Hobbes, on the other hand, saw the key virtue as the constant, careful, and calculating pursuit of your survival in a world of war, everyone against everyone else. But, Hobbes, like Aristotle, knew you could not 'do it alone'. Community or social structure is necessary.

For Aristotle, community arises out of the virtues of friendship. For Hobbes, communities form by contract initiated out of self-interest. To foster the latter, it was and remains necessary that there be a supreme ruler, the Leviathan, powerful but equally fragile. For Hobbes, self-interest transcends all other values. Hence, if a person can successfully "beat the system," they are obliged by their "self-interest" to "beat the system." Hence, even the power of the Leviathan is as fragile as the self-interests of his society. Clearly, in the *Godfather* series, the virtues of friendship, though present, are fleeting in the corrupting world of the mob; Hobbes trumps Aristotle. And so, loneliness, isolation, distrust, and violence ensue. In the end, the Leviathan dies alone without even the friendship of a dog. The *Godfather* trilogy leaves the audience with a choice: friendship or war, Aristotle or Hobbes: take your pick. Michael and his father made that pick. Michael dies alone!

## What My Mother Taught Me

"Do 'em favors, don't ask for a favor"

"Shady character"

"Keep your nose clean"

"Don't interfere."

"See, but don't notice"

Mario Puzo, who wrote all three versions of the *Godfather* Trilogy, grew up in New York, at the very epicenter of the Mob World. Though never a part of that world, he knew this world within the immediacy of the culture in which he lived.

The Italian culture Puzo grew up in is one I am also familiar with, growing up in New Haven, Connecticut, a densely Italian populated community of three generations of Italians. Within that community, there is the logic of the culture, both beautiful and cultural, familial and inimical; Aristotle within Catholic piety: Hobbes with Aristotle. I recall quite vividly, though we were never part of the Sicilian culture and, derivative thereof, the Mob Culture, I recall my mother, a first-generation Italian and an educated schoolteacher, telling my brother and me some basic truths. One of which, displayed throughout the Godfather Trilogy, was this: "Do 'em favors, never ask for a favor."

Recall the very opening scene of *Part I* when the Undertaker asks the Don for a favor, to take revenge on the two boys who assaulted his daughter. The Don willingly obliges but reminds him that "one day, and that day may never come, I will ask you for a favor. But for now, take this favor as a gift on behalf of my daughter's wedding." We knew, growing up, that we did not go to these "shady" people for a favor.

One other remark shared among our community: "Keep your nose clean". Don't stick your nose in anyone else's business. Don't ask! This is especially true if you were aware of or suspected that the persons involved or who drew your attention are or were "connected." How many times among my family and others, the word "connected" would come up in conversation about someone. Sometimes, it was innocently used, depicting someone who had political or social connections. Someone who could help you in need or otherwise help.

I often use that word, myself, when describing my relationship to someone who might help someone else. I also warn folks, especially my students, about bullying or abusing weak and timid people, classmates, or anyone. In *Part II*, you saw vividly what happens when a bully mistakenly abuses the old widow throwing her out of her apartment, and then, when asked by the Don for leniency towards her, let her stay with her dog, he, the landlord, fails to recognize with whom he is speaking. He plays the bully foolishly. He did not know that the old widow was "connected" to Don Vito's wife. He learned, quickly enough, the potential fatality of such a mistake. He returns to beg Don Vito's forgiveness for being the bully-coward he was. The moral principle, be careful whom you bully, she or he or they may be "connected." Then, if so "connected," the Hobbesian world you chose to live and play in will be the world that will bury you! I teach that to my students. Don't bully anyone. Not just because it's immoral or unchristian, but because it may cost you dearly. You never know who that person may be "connected" to.

Finally, "be a friend." Don't make enemies out of friends or potential friends, or even acquaintances or strangers. Friendship always gives rise or can give rise to companionship or at least minimal hostility, even in a Hobbesian World. At least, be a friend. The bully or person who forgets to be a friend, tends to create the Hobbesian world of enemies. How often this is true! Bullies end up bulling someone who could have been a friend, an ally, or at least someone neutral. Instead, by their actions they create a world of people who owe them only enmity in return for their bullying. In such a Hobbesian World, the Leviathans never last.

The *Godfather* trilogy is not only a masterpiece in theatric art, it is a supreme moral drama, an artistic portrayal of the moral life, guiding the viewer through a moral descent from Aristotle to Hobbes, virtue to belligerence, friendship to isolated loneliness, and its consequences. I have no doubt Puzo and Coppola had this in mind as they wrote, produced, and directed this moral masterpiece, right to that final conclusion wherein Michael dies alone without even the friendship of a dog. Choose to live the Hobbesian life, and you will die alone. And you will be slowly dying scene after scene in your life. Just ask the dying Michael.

# V

---

*"Forgive. Forget. Life is full of misfortunes."*

# 20
# With Friends Like These, Who Needs Justice?

ALEX VRABELY

In the opening scene of *The Godfather*, Don Vito Corleone meets with Bonasera, a local undertaker. Bonasera explains that his daughter Maria was assaulted, then beaten by her boyfriend and another man, badly enough to be hospitalized and have her jaw wired shut.

A believer in the American ideals of freedom and justice, Bonasera is shocked when Maria's attackers, who are politically connected, are given a suspended sentence by the judge—they walked free that day. After being failed by the system, he now turns to Don Corleone for Justice. Barely whispering, Bonasera requests that Maria's attackers be killed.

Vito refuses—killing them wouldn't be justice, since Maria is still alive. And what's more, Vito takes offense at Bonasera's business-like attitude. Bonasera has distanced himself from the Corleone family, despite their long acquaintance and the fact that Carmela Corleone, Vito's wife, is Maria's godmother. Don Corleone chastises Bonasera for using him as a last resort, and points out that if Bonasera had been more willing to be Vito's friend in the past, then Maria's attackers would already have been dealt with. Bonasera gets the hint, and asks Don Corleone for his friendship. Vito accepts, reminding Bonasera that from then on, friendship and favors go both ways. For now, though, Bonasera can consider Vito's justice against Maria's attackers a gift.

This scene gives us great insight into Don Vito's character, and raises two interesting sets of questions. First, what is the relationship between friendship and justice? Is justice different for a friend rather than someone else? Second, and maybe more importantly, is Don Vito really even talking about justice? He says that killing Maria's attackers would be over-stepping the bounds of justice, but then offers to carry out a vigilante beating for his new friend only minutes later. These questions, hinted at in the opening scene, reappear through-out the course of the movies, and the different attitudes that characters have towards them directly affect the story and the characters' fates.

    *The Godfather* isn't the first work of fiction to deal with these questions. Almost twenty-five hundred years before Mario Puzo penned the novel that would inspire Coppola's film trilogy, another writer asked similar questions about justice. In the *Republic*, the Greek philosopher Plato has Socrates investigate the nature of justice. Socrates is notorious for never giving straight answers, but over the course of the *Republic*, much like *The Godfather*, we get an idea of some important characteristics of justice, and how things can go wrong if the bounds of justice are ignored or exceeded. And the images of justice presented by these three, separated by more than two millennia, are not all that different from one another.

## Keep Your Friends Close

In the first book of the *Republic*, Socrates is visiting and chatting with some friends when the topic turns to justice. Polemarchus, Socrates's friend, says that justice is simple—justice means giving people what they're owed. Not a bad start, Socrates replies. On the other hand, he asks, wouldn't it be unjust to give your friend something you owed them if you knew that it would do more harm than good? Isn't it wrong to help your friends if it would end up hurting them in the long run? Especially if your friend was someone with a quick temper. Someone, for example, like Sonny Corleone.

    When Sonny takes over as head of the Corleone family in *The Godfather*, it's no cause for celebration. His father Vito has been targeted twice by drug kingpin Sollozzo and narrowly survived both times. Michael, who isn't even supposed to be a part of the "family business," finds himself roughed up by Sollozzo's corrupt police captain after he foils the second attempt on Vito's life. Sonny is out for blood, and wants to demand that the other Mafia families turn over Sollozzo or face all-out war.

    But Sonny's adopted brother and family consigliere Tom Hagen warns Sonny against issuing an ultimatum. If the other families refuse, the Corleones could find themselves cut out entirely, regardless of whether or not Sonny is justified in seeking revenge. An angry Sonny replies, "Just help me win, alright?" But Tom is just as committed to preventing further harm to the family as he is to helping Sonny get his rightful vengeance.

It's not until Michael comes up with a bold plan to personally murder both Sollozzo and the police captain that Tom begins to come around. When Michael first pitches the idea of killing Sollozzo and the captain, Tom is dumbfounded—until now, no family has gone so far as to order a targeted hit on a police officer. Tom starts to come around, though, as Michael and others work through the details of carrying out a hit on the two men. By the end of the scene, Tom is fully on board. He hadn't been opposed to helping Michael and Sonny towards their goal of revenge, but he did want to make sure that neither took any moves that exposed the family to worse danger.

Later, Sonny again loses his temper when his sister Connie calls to tell him that her husband Carlo is beating her. Sonny wants to personally go help Connie, since he had warned Carlo about beating her before. Tom warns Sonny against going himself, since the Corleones are now engaged in an all-out gang war with the other Mafia families. But this time, Sonny can't be talked down. He ignores Tom's warnings, and on his way to Connie's home, Sonny is ambushed and killed by hitmen from a rival family.

Socrates might not have approved of all the gritty details of the Corleone family business, or the specific reasons that Tom Hagen had for looking out for the Corleone family's best interests. But a friend like Tom, who not only helps you get what you're owed but also makes sure you don't harm yourself in the process, seems to be what Socrates has in mind when he says that justice can't be just giving people what they're owed.

## But Your Enemies Closer

Polemarchus admits that Socrates has a point, and that justice must involve only helping friends, and not harming them. But Socrates isn't satisfied. If justice means helping friends, he asks, then what does it mean for enemies? Easy enough, replies Polemarchus. If justice means helping your friends, then obviously it must involve harming enemies. Again, Socrates thinks Polemarchus might be onto something—but there's another problem. Don't people make mistakes in judging people to be friends or enemies? If we're wrong about someone being an enemy, and hurt them somehow, then we would really be hurting our friends. And that, we already decided, isn't justice at all. And what if someone seems like a friend, only to be secretly taking advantage of you?

Polemarchus recognizes the conundrum. Telling the difference between a true friend and a flatterer can be no easy task. But for Plato, being able to tell the difference between something real and an imitation is one of the most important skills a person can develop. In Book VII's Myth of the Cave, Plato describes the difficult process of coming to see the world as it really is, free of illusions. If a person had been held captive in a dark cave for their entire life, they might mistake shadows on the cave walls for real things. But if someone were to try and investigate these shadowy illusions, they might find themselves on a path out of the cave and into the sunlight– free of illusions and seeing clearly. And once they know the way out of the cave, that person can return to the gloom and help others find the way out as well.

Don Vito Corleone has an uncanny ability to see through illusions and false friends, and it benefits him greatly in his dealings with the other mafia families. When Michael kills Sollozzo, a mob war erupts between the Corleone family and Sollozzo's local backers, the Tattaglia family. After Sonny is killed, Vito calls a peace meeting with Tattaglia and the other family heads. At that meeting, a truce is reached which will allow Michael to safely return to the United States from Sicily, having sheltered there with friends after killing Sollozzo. But ensuring Michael's safe return isn't the only thing that Vito accomplishes at the meeting.

Vito suspected that the rival Tattaglias had support during the war from another family, but he had doubts about who it might have been. At the peace meeting, Vito notices that Don Barzini, head of another powerful family, does most of the talking for Tattaglia, and makes demands for peace conditions on Tattaglia's behalf. Vito takes notice of Barzini's behavior and deduces that Barzini has been supporting Tattaglia in the war against the Corleone family. After leaving the meeting, Vito tells Tom, "Tattaglia never could have outfought Santino. But I didn't know until this day that it was Barzini all along."

But finding the way out of the Cave is only half the battle for Plato. It would be better, he says, if those that learn the way out returned into the Cave to help others who can't yet see well enough to find their own way out. After Sonny's death, it becomes clear that Michael will have to take over as head of the Corleone family's criminal enterprise. Towards the end of *Part I*, Vito tells Michael that Barzini is secretly working against them. Once Michael becomes Don, Vito expects Barzini will try to assassinate Michael by convincing someone Michael trusts to betray him. Above all, Vito stresses to Michael that he can't afford to be careless—if Michael doesn't take care in discerning peoples' true motives, it will have deadly conse—quences for him. At Vito's funeral, Michael is approached by longtime friend Tessio, who falsely offers to broker peace just as Vito had predicted.

Michael's a quick study, and displays his own skill at un-covering the true motives of those around him. In a final *Part I* scene, Michael confronts Carlo over Sonny's killing. Everyone in the Corleone family knew that Carlo was abusive towards Connie. But Michael accuses Carlo of beating Connie with the intention of luring Sonny out to be killed. Eventually, Carlo breaks down and admits Michael is right–Carlo had secretly been working against the Corleones and was instrumental in Sonny's death.

## Hit 'Em While You Got the Muscle

Back in ancient Greece, Socrates and Polemarchus are start-ing to get somewhere in their investigation into justice. Polemarchus is confident that justice involves helping your friends and harming your enemies, so long as you're certain who your friends and enemies really are. But Socrates still isn't convinced. He asks Polemarchus whether it's possible for harm to come from something good, and Polemarchus replies that it's not. But everyone knows, Socrates continues, that justice is something good, and so a just person would be a good person. And if a just person is a good person, and harm can't come from something good, then it must be the case that a just person never harms anyone, friend or foe. Polemarchus agrees, but Socrates points out that this means that justice has to be something different from helping friends and harming enemies.

Just as Polemarchus and Socrates are about to renew their investigation into justice, they are interrupted by Thra-symachus, who had been listening to the discussion alongside others. Thrasymachus chastises Socrates for asking questions and talking in circles while not being willing to give an answer himself. But Thrasymachus thinks he can give Socrates a definition he can't refute. Justice is simple, he says—it's merely the advantage of the stronger. For Thrasymachus, might makes right, and any subversion of that order is unnatural and therefore unjust. According to Thrasymachus, Fredo had no right to be upset when Michael was chosen to replace Vito as

Don of the Corleone empire. Even though Michael is younger, he is far more equipped to handle the dangers of Mafia life.

But Thrasymachus's definition that justice is decided by the strong falls apart quicker than Carlo did under Michael's questioning. Socrates makes the same point that he did against Polemarchus. No matter how strong someone is, it's possible for them to make a mistake. So, even if the strongest person thought they were acting in their own interest, they might actually be creating problems for themselves, whether it be in the short or long term. In the third movie, Michael is haunted by his decision to have Fredo killed. His brother had presented a threat, driven by resentment and insecurity, and Michael utilized the full extent of his power to make sure that threat was eliminated forever. But doing so ends up being Michael's biggest regret, and he suffers internally for it.

## Actions Speak Louder than Words

But where does this leave us with respect to the questions we asked at the beginning? Let's assume that Socrates is right about what Polemarchus and Thrasymachus have said, and that neither of them has adequately captured justice. Does that mean that Vito is simply dressing up violence and revenge in pretty words when he offers Bonasera justice for his daughter's attackers? Maybe—but maybe not entirely. There are hints throughout the *Godfather* movies that Vito Corleone might understand a critical aspect inherent in a just character, despite his willingness to cause harm to his enemies.

Continuing their discussion of justice, Socrates and Thrasymachus move away from strict definitions. Instead, they contrast the ethical character of a just person with that of an unjust person by considering the types of actions that each would take part in. Socrates's central question to Thrasymachus is whether or not a just person would "go beyond" another just person, or if such behavior is exclusive to unjust people. But what exactly does Socrates mean by "go beyond"? And what's the connection to justice?

In the original Greek, the word that's translated into English as "go beyond" is *pleonexia*. At face value, pleonexia simply means "to have a lot." But there is also an ethical dimension to pleonexia that's included when it's translated as "go beyond." Because of this ethical dimension, a literal translation is difficult—in different versions of the Republic, pleonexia might be translated into English as "go beyond," "outdo," or "overreach."

But pleonexia is more insidious than greed—it's a pathological impulse towards accumulation of ever-increasing material goods or power. So, when Socrates asks Thrasymachus if a just person would try to go beyond another, what he's really asking is whether or not a just person could display such pathological character traits. The two agree that a just person would not exhibit pleonexia. The just person would recognize the appropriate bounds of justice and not try to claim more than they're entitled to. On the other hand, unjust people believe like Thrasymachus that might makes right. They try to secure everything they can to improve their own position, with no thought to others save how they can be exploited.

## Father-Son Dynamic

But again—what's all this got to do with Vito? Despite the fact that Vito Corleone runs a criminal enterprise, despite the fact that he has people killed, and despite the fact that he involves his own children in that same criminal life, Vito consistently avoids the trappings of pleonexia. Even if Vito doesn't quite make the cut as a fully just person, there's evidence that he abides by a personal code of honor that Thrasymachus would call restrictive.

Recall the opening scene in *Part I*, where Vito chastises Bonasera when Bonasera asks to have his daughter's attackers killed. Vito's reasoning centers on the fact that Maria is still alive, and so having the two men killed would be overstepping the bounds of an appropriate reaction. After Vito agrees to have the men roughed up and hands the task over to Tom, he emphasizes that he wants this job done by people who won't get carried away and accidentally kill them. "We're not murderers," he says.

And when we see young Vito's rise to power in *Part II*, it's clear that he makes it a priority to distinguish himself from others who have exploited the local community. He's even willing to personally cover six months' rent of a widow with no place else to go, negotiating on her behalf with a landlord who's trying to evict her. Sure, he returns Vito's money when he learns more about who he is, but the point is that Vito had been willing to let him keep it. Again, this is something that Thrasymachus would find naive. Why not be done with pretentious formalities and just intimidate the landlord into getting what you want in the first place? Surely Vito could have done just that, given the fear the landlord displays of Vito in their second meeting. But this is not the way that Vito operates.

Vito stands in stark contrast to Michael, who time and again takes actions that reveal the extent of his own pleonexia. Even before taking over as head of the Corleone family, Michael shows us that he is relentless in pursuing his ambitions, and is almost always willing to go further than his enemies expect to achieve his goals. After he's attacked by the corrupt police captain who serves as Sollozzo's guard, Michael offers to personally assassinate both men. When Tom mentions that nobody in any family has killed a member of the police before, Michael persists. When he eventually does kill the two men, his actions kick off the war that ultimately leads to Sonny's death and Michael's ascension to the head of the Corleone Family business.

Michael's pleonexia comes into even sharper focus in *Part II*. Of course, there's the aforementioned fratricide, something that even Thrasymachus would condemn as abominable. But Michael takes other actions that speak to his pleonexia. When Michael's rival Hyman Roth is facing arrest after being denied international asylum, Michael arranges a hit to kill Roth as he's taken into police custody. Tom Hagen tries to reign Michael in, only to have his loyalty questioned by Michael. It's the only time that we see Tom personally offended. By clinging to his demand to have a personal hand in the demise of his enemies, Michael is now actively alienating friends and questioning his staunchest longtime ally.

The only opportunity to get at Roth is to strike as he's being arrested upon returning to the US. But with officers waiting, it's a veritable suicide mission. Michael sends a hitman anyway—and not just anyone, but one that had become one of his most trusted capos. Roth is killed, but the hitman is also shot and killed by police. By the end of *Part II*, Michael is all about harming his enemies, never mind helping his friends, or even trying to keep them out of harm's way.

## Final Moments

Don Vito Corleone seems to be the embodiment of Polemarchus's idea of justice—help your friends, harm your enemies, and make sure you can tell the difference between the two. If we believe Socrates's arguments, then Vito isn't discussing true justice with Bonasera—even if he avoids pleonexia and uncontrollable lust for power. But if we take into account the connection between pleonexia and injustice, then Socrates might have to admit that Vito isn't a fully unjust person either.

Michael, though, is a different story. Time and again, we're shown that Michael will stop at nothing to secure his own position. His pleonexia is so severe that the most heinous and excessive actions are justifiable. He kills his sister's husband. He becomes paranoid, alienating friends by publicly questioning their loyalty. He beats his wife Kay, after deceiving her for years about his criminal activity. He kills his brother, his mother's son, his father's son. When Michael finally confesses at the Vatican in *Part III*, the cardinal's reply may as well have been spoken by Socrates—"Your sins are terrible. It is just that you suffer. Your life could be redeemed, but I know you don't believe that. You will not change."

A final nod to this difference between Vito and Michael comes in depicting their final moments. Michael dies alone, wracked with guilt and regret, Vito at home, surrounded by family and enjoying time with his grandchild. We might not get a picture of a fully just person in *The Godfather*, but we do see the dangers of a psyche mired in pleonexia. And though separated from Plato's *Republic* by more than two thousand years, the success of Puzo's and Coppola's *Godfather* shows we're still dealing with the same questions of what it means to live a just life.

# 21

# The Evolution of Relentless Badassery

CORY CLARK AND BO WINEGARD

> I'm a superstitious man, and if some unlucky accident should befall Michael—if he is to be shot in the head by a police officer, or be found hung dead in a jail cell . . . or if he should be struck by a bolt of lightning, then I'm going to blame some of the people in this room; and then I do not forgive.
>
> —DON VITO CORLEONE

His eldest son assassinated and his second son dimwitted and gullible, Vito's top priority is to save his youngest and most promising son, Michael. In a meeting with the heads of the Five Families, Vito announces that he will retaliate if any injury should befall Michael, even if the misfortunate were apparently as random as a lightning bolt. The point, of course, is to deter his rivals from harming Michael by explicitly declaring his bias will be to blame others no matter the circumstances surrounding any injury.

Few of us have established sufficient enemies—not to mention sufficient importance—to worry our sons might be targeted for assassination, but here, *The Godfather* is displaying a natural human tendency to ascribe excessive responsibility to harmful behaviors. For many decades, philosophers and psychologists have puzzled over consistently replicated asymmetries in judgments of responsibility for helpful and harmful actions such that people more readily hold people responsible for harmful, transgressive behaviors than they do for helpful, charitable behaviors.

## The Crime Should Fit the Punishment

Perhaps the most well-known demonstration of this tendency in the experimental philosophy literature is referred to as the Side-effect Effect or the Knobe Effect (after philosopher, Joshua Knobe, who discovered the puzzling asymmetry). Imagine the following scenario:

- The vice president of a company went to the chairman of the board and said, "We are thinking of starting a new program. It will help us increase profits, but it will also harm the environment."

- The chairman of the board answered, "I don't care at all about harming the environment. I just want to make as much profit as I can. Let's start the new program."

- They started the new program. Sure enough, the environment was harmed.

- Now ask yourself, did the chairman intentionally harm the environment?

If you are like most people, you answered this question in the affirmative. But it turns out, when people are presented with the *exact same scenario* except that the side effect helped rather than harmed the environment, most people say the chairman did *not* intentionally help the environment. So, people ascribe more intentionality to harmful side effects than to helpful ones that result from otherwise identical behaviors.

Dozens of psychology and experimental philosophy studies have replicated similar patterns—people attribute more responsibility to people who cause harmful outcomes than to people who cause helpful or neutral ones, even when the actor behaved in virtually identical ways. (The most important of these studies are listed in the Bibliography to this book.) For example, people report that an actor was more culpable for causing a car accident when his reasons for speeding were criminal or nefarious (rushing home to hide a vial of cocaine) than when his reasons were virtuous (rushing home to hide an anniversary present). Recently, scholars have termed this pro-blame bias *The Don Corleone Principle*. Rather than dispassionately evaluating the intentions and conditions behind a harmful outcome and assigning the appropriate amount of punishment, people feel the desire to punish and then assume there was an ill-intentioned culpable agent.

Moral intuitionism is the view that our moral judgments often work this way. People believe that they form their moral judgments through careful, rational consideration. But often, moral judgments are based on gut-level feelings or *intuitions* about what is right and wrong, and only after we have reached a verdict (and when probed by others to explain our judgments) do we start to search for explicit reasons to justify our moral assessments. When people experience intuitive desires to punish others for their harmful behaviors, they feel compelled to justify their desires to punish by asserting that the harm doer purposefully and intentionally caused the harm and so *deserves* to be punished.

Nietzsche contended (*Twilight of the Idols*) and psychology research has confirmed, that pro-blame biases may even contribute to the human belief in free will. When people desire to punish another person, they report higher beliefs in human free will and are more skeptical of science that challenges it. And so, the very belief that fellow human beings *deserve* to be held morally responsible for their actions may be motivated, in part, by the *desire* to hold people morally responsible.

Throughout *The Godfather*, Vito is portrayed as the kind of person who assumes there is an intentional malevolent agent behind any mishap. As Michael describes his father's attitude,

> Tom, don't let anybody kid you. It's all personal, every bit of business. Every piece of shit every man has to eat every day of his life is personal. They call it business. Okay. But it's personal as hell. You know where I learned that from? The Don. My old man. The Godfather. If a bolt of lightning hit a friend of his, the old man would take it personal . . . And you know something? Accidents don't happen to people who take accidents as a personal insult.

Here, Michael perfectly identifies the benefit of being the sort of person who is quick to blame—other people will work *diligently* to avoid crossing you. The Don is so quick to take offense that not even *accidents* can happen to him.

Vito is aware of the reputational benefits of his vindictiveness as well. In one conversation he declares, "if by some chance an honest man like yourself made enemies, they would become my enemies. And then, they would fear you." Being known as a reliable retaliator not only provides protection for Vito, but also his friends and family.

## They're All Dead from Vendettas

Throughout *The Godfather*, we see that Vito's relentless badassery has earned him deference and respect, but it also cost him his first son and nearly his own life. Although being vengeful may intimidate some potential enemies, it also might cause retribution, especially if the vengeance appears unwarranted or disproportionate in relation to the original offense. Thus, even though people evolved a pro-blame bias, people also evolved primarily to blame and punish others when the blame and punishment can appear justifiable and reasonable to other people. Indeed, Vito and the other heads of the Five Families repeatedly profess to one another that they are reasonable men (after all, they are not communists).

According to moral intuitionism, explicit moral reasoning often occurs *after* we arrive at a moral judgment and primarily serves the function of justifying our moral judgments to others so as to persuade others of our own reasonableness and righteousness. The analogy often used is that we reason more like lawyers, searching for evidence to support our already determined conclusions than like detectives carefully evaluating the evidence to determine which conclusion is correct. Although it is evolutionarily useful to have a reputation as a relentless badass, it is also evolutionarily useful to maintain a reputation as a reasonable and morally upstanding individual. And so, people work hard to justify their judgments and behaviors to others.

Both Vito and Michael justify their behavior as unfortunate but necessary, a way to protect their family and loved ones from the threats and encroachments of rivals. And when explaining to Kay that he is working for his father, Michael explicitly compares it to the behavior of "any other powerful man—any man who is responsible for other people, like a senator or president." When Kay protests that Michael is being naïve, Michael asks, "Why?" Kay responds, "Senators and presidents don't have men killed." And Michael retorts, "Oh, who's being naïve, Kay?" Even as Michael descends into cold vindictiveness and relentless competition against his rivals, he continues to contend that his actions are necessary to protect the family—even as they require the ultimate violence against his own brother. At the end of the second movie, we see Michael, aged and alone, against an autumn background, and we imagine that whatever regrets he has, he is thoroughly convinced that he always strived to defend the interests of the family.

This evolved impulse to appear reasonable explains why biases in human judgment, including pro-blame bias, are observed more frequently in *ambiguous* situations. In the case of the Side-effect Effect mentioned earlier, one cannot know all the desires and intentions of the Chairman when he makes the decision and harms the environment, so it can appear reasonable to ascribe intentionality to him. The only way experimental philosophers were able to detect that people have double standards when side-effects are harmful vs. helpful was by randomly assigning some people to read about the helpful side-effect and other people to read about the harmful side-effect. If people were presented with both stories, they would likely anchor their second judgment to their first to disguise their own double standards. Blatant biases and unfairness can injure a person's reputation and social status, and so people aim to disguise or justify these tendencies to appear reasonable to others and avoid retaliation.

After Sonny is killed, Vito realizes his vengeful reputation has started to harm himself and his family, and he calls off the vengeance, "This war stops now." Instead, he arranges a meeting with the heads of the Five Families and assures them he will not avenge his son's death so long as Michael is able to return to the United States unharmed and live safely. However, he makes this offer while also asserting that he *will* exact revenge should anything—anything at all—happen to Michael, perfectly navigating the balance of relentless badassery with appearing reasonable and trustworthy.

## Khartoum Had It Coming

Evolutionary psychologists contend that pro-blame bias, or *The Don Corleone Principle*, evolved in human psychology because of the asymmetric costs of false positive and false negative blame judgments. If Person A deliberately harms or takes advantage of Person B, and Person B assumes it was an accident and is quick to forgive, Person B signals to their community that they are easily exploitable and thus puts a target on their back for others who might want to take advantage. In contrast, if Person A unintentionally offends Person B, and Person B retaliates by decapitating Person A's champion racehorse and placing the severed head in bed with Person A while he sleeps, Person B signals to their community that they are not to be fucked with. And so, people evolved to err on the side of assuming harm doers are culpable.

Error management is a general principle of evolutionary psychology—when the costs of false positive and false negative errors were asymmetric throughout human evolution, human cognition should display *biases* in favor of the less costly error. This is why, for example, when we are lying in bed at night and hear creaks down the hallway, we assume an armed burglar is in the house. Most of the time we are wrong, but it is costlier to assume incorrectly that the creaks are just regular house sounds and get slaughtered in bed by an armed robber (a false negative error) than it is to assume there is a murderer in the house and unnecessarily grab a bat and tiptoe down the hall (a false positive error).

It may seem puzzling that humans would have evolved a tendency to be systematically incorrect in certain judgments. But many decision-making environments are ambiguous—or at least, one cannot be one hundred percent certain of another's intentions or plans, and so perfect accuracy is impossible. And it is often advantageous to make assumptions about others' bad intentions. We can see the benefits of assuming the worst in other people in the final scene between Vito and his favorite son, Michael.

Before disclosing his newly found appreciation for wine, Vito warns Michael, "Barzini will move against you first. He'll set up a meeting with someone that you absolutely trust, guaranteeing your safety. And at that meeting, you'll be assassinated." When there was an invitation to meet, even though Michael could not know for certain he was being set up for assassination, he assumed the worst and was able to preempt his own murder by assassinating the heads of the other five families while baptizing his first Godson. Had Michael assumed the families were looking for a truce, he might have been killed. Just as people evolved a bias toward blaming others, so too people evolved a hypervigilance toward potential dangers.

After Michael successfully unleashes his vengeance against the heads of the other five families and against the traitors of his family, Tessio and Carlo (his sister's husband!), he earns the full respect, a respect compelled by both admiration and fear, that his father achieved after assassinating the gaudy gangster, Fanucci. Rocco, Clemenza, and Neri enter Michael's office and kiss his hand, signaling the elevation of Michael to revered and feared leader.

Michael becomes a ruthless and vindicative Godfather, a man whose goal is to eliminate all viable competitors, and who is so comfortable with hypocrisy that he renounces Satan in a church while his bloody plans unfold. In other words, Michael evolves into a relentless badass.

# 22

# The Corleones and Ronald Coase

F.E. GUERRA-PUJOL

The Corleone Family wants to buy *me* out? No, I buy *you* out. You don't buy me out!

—MOE GREENE

One of my favorite scenes in *The Godfather* series is the confrontation between Michael Corleone and Morris "Moe" Greene in Sin City. The role of Moe Greene is played by Alex Rocco, and Greene's character is loosely based on the real-life Benjamin "Bugsy" Siegel, a Jewish mobster who played a pivotal role in the development of Las Vegas as a gambling and entertainment destination (a story told in Larry Gragg's book about Siegel).

When Michael Corleone decides to relocate the family's center of operations from New York to Nevada, he arranges a meeting in Las Vegas with his business partner, Moe Greene. Michael wants to buy out Greene's entire interest in his hotel and casino operations. Moe Greene, however, wants to keep his business: "*The Corleone Family wants to buy* me *out? No, I buy* you *out. You don't buy me out!*" (*The Godfather Screenplay*, p. 144). If anyone's getting bought out, it's going to be the Corleone family, not Moe Greene. Worse yet, when Michael implies that his business partner has been "skimmin off the top," Moe Greene explodes in anger: "*You goddamn dagos. I do you a favor . . . when you're having a bad time, and then you try and push me out!*" (p. 145).

Although we can feel some sympathy for Moe Greene (after all, Michael wants to freeze Moe out of his own business), at the same time Greene's plight is a self-induced one. The

**209**

Corleone family has been bankrolling his Las Vegas operation, but Greene did not have to go into business with the Corleone family in the first place. Moreover, the dispute between Moe and Michael illustrates a larger pattern in *The Godfather*.

Consider, for example, the opening scene in *The Godfather*. According to an old-world custom, no Sicilian can refuse a request on his daughter's wedding day. As it happens, Don Vito Corleone, the powerful and respected head of the Corleone crime syndicate, receives two such requests on the fateful day of his daughter Connie's wedding—one from a fellow Italian-American immigrant, the undertaker Amerigo Bonasera, the other from his own godson, the suave singer Johnny Fontane. In brief, both supplicants have been harmed by others; they thus come to Don Vito on the day of his daughter's wedding for his help. As it happens, one of the bedrock concepts of philosophy is the harm principle—the idea that mere dislike of a person's actions isn't enough to justify the use of force or coercion unless such actions actually harm or pose a significant threat to someone else's interests (Mill, *On Liberty*). But what if all harms are reciprocal in nature? In other words, what if victims are just as responsible as wrongdoers for their plight?

## Amerigo Bonasera's Plea for Justice

One of the most memorable moments in *The Godfather* is the opening exchange between the Italian undertaker, Amerigo Bonasera, and mob boss Vito Corleone about the meaning of justice. The backstory involves Bonasera's unnamed teenage daughter, who was brutally assaulted by two men as they attempted to rape her, leaving her physically and emotional scarred for life. Alas, the perpetrators came from wealthy and well-connected families. They gamed the legal system, so neither man ended up receiving any jail time.

Since the courts have let Bonasera down, he is turning to Don Vito as a last resort. Bonasera is even willing to pay any amount of money to vindicate his family honor: "How much shall I pay you?" he asks the Godfather. In reply, Vito Corleone delivers one of my favorite lines in the entire *Godfather* franchise, placing the blame for the Italian undertaker's unfortunate plight squarely on Bonasera himself:

> You never armed yourself with true friends. You thought it was enough to be an American. After all, the police guarded you, there were courts of Law. You could come to no harm; you had no need for friends like

me. But now you come to me and you say "Don Corleone give me justice." And you don't ask with respect; you don't offer friendship; you
don't call me Godfather. (*The Godfather Screenplay*, p. 3)

We could also argue that it was Bonasera himself who put his
daughter's safety and his family honor in jeopardy in the first
place by allowing her to date a non-Italian and stay out late,
but at the same time, if Bonasera had not given her this freedom, had he not allowed his daughter to date whom she
pleased, it is the daughter who would have been harmed. (Why
is this the case? Because restricting someone's liberty, even
when it is done for their own protection, is itself a harm!)

## Fontane versus Woltz

Johnny Fontane wants a part in a new Hollywood production,
a role that could relaunch his career and bring him further
fame and fortune. The problem is that Jack Woltz, the head of
the studio that owns the rights to the movie, refuses to cast
Johnny for the part. Given this impasse, Fontane turns to the
Godfather for help; he cries and whimpers and pleads: "I don't
know anymore. Godfather, what the hell can I do . . . ?" (p. 16).
After chastising his godson for crying like a woman, Don Vito
reassures him that he will, in fact, take care of the problem; he
will send his trusted consigliere Tom Hagen to Hollywood to
make Woltz an offer he can't refuse.

Woltz's intransigence, however, provides another textbook
illustration of reciprocal harms. On the one hand, Fontane
would be perfect for the lead role in Woltz's new movie; even
Woltz himself is willing to admit as much. Woltz is thus harming Fontane's career prospects by refusing to cast him in his
new movie, but at the same time, if Woltz were to give Fontane
the role, it is Woltz's reputation that will take a hit. To the
point, Woltz will be made to look, in his own word, ridiculous.
As Woltz himself explains to Tom Hagen:

Johnny Fontane will never get that part, [even though] he's perfect for
it. It would make him a great star. But . . . I'm gonna run him out of
the movies. And I'll tell you why. He ruined one of my most valuable
proteges. . . . That girl was beautiful and young and innocent and she
was the greatest piece of ass I ever had and I've had them all over
the world. Then Johnny comes along with that olive oil voice and
guinea charm and she runs off. She threw it all away to make me look
ridiculous. A man in my position can't afford to be made to look ridiculous. (*Screenplay*, p. 26)

Simply put, Fontane himself, the man who stole the amorous object of Woltz's costly affections, is equally responsible for his sorry predicament.

## The Sonny Corleone Incident

Amid these two special wedding-day requests—Amerigo Bonasera's anguished plea for justice and Johnny Fontane's forlorn desire to land the lead role in Woltz's new production—another memorable incident involving reciprocal harms occurs in real time.

In summary, some strangers are loitering outside the Corleone compound, and one of them is taking photographs of the automobiles belonging to the wedding guests of the Corleone family. Sonny, Vito Corleone's volatile and hot-tempered eldest son, charges out into the driveway and confronts the uninvited guests, yelling "Come on!" multiple times and roughing up the photographer. When one of the strangers flashes his FBI badge, Sonny figures out what is going on. The Feds must have sent in a surveillance team to gather information about the Corleone family's wedding guests, since some of them have ties to the mob. Furious, Sonny grabs the man's camera, hurls it to the ground, and smashes it to pieces. Next, he pulls out some crumpled bills from his pants pocket, tosses them on the ground, and walks away.

By compensating the uninvited photographer for his broken camera, Sonny recognizes that he has committed a harm. This harm, however, is a purely reciprocal one. On the one hand, Sonny has no doubt harmed the photographer by pushing him around and smashing his camera, but on the other, you could argue that the photographer has harmed Sonny's wedding guests—and, by extension, Sonny himself—by showing up uninvited and attempting to invade their privacy. Although you could also argue that the wedding guests don't have a reasonable expectation of privacy if they parked their cars on a public street, at the same time they did not consent to the police taking photographs of their license plates. Also, some of the cars were parked on private property, the driveway of the Corleone compound.

## The Common Thread: Reciprocal Harms

Harms can thus come in many different shapes and sizes: physical, reputational, lost chances, and invasions of privacy, just to name a few. But however the concept of harm is defined, and however the line between justification and excuse is drawn, *The Godfather* offers a strong rebuttal to the harm principle: the possibility that harms are actually reciprocal in nature.

Bonasera would have received justice sooner had he not refused the Godfather's friendship. Johnny would not have been black-listed by Woltz had he not run off with Woltz's prized protege. Sonny would not have smashed the policeman's camera had the photographer not showed up uninvited.

Alas, we often neglect the reciprocal nature of harms by invoking formulaic incantations like "your liberty to swing your arm ends where my nose begins" or John Stuart Mill's influential argument in political philosophy that coercion is justified only to prevent harm to others (*On Liberty*). Although these rhetorical strategies are superficially appealing, they overlook a key point: *Restrictions on liberty are themselves harms.* This notion of reciprocal harms can be traced back to a pair of twentieth-century papers—one published in 1959 ("The Federal Communications Commission"); the other in 1960 ("The Problem of Social Cost")—authored by one Ronald Coase, at that time an obscure British economist, later a Nobel Prize winner.

## The Coasean Analysis of Harms

Ronald Coase's papers deal primarily with the problem of harmful effects in the context of tort law, an area of the common law that imposes legal liability for wrongful acts. Coase's work explores a wide variety of harms, such as air pollution, cattle trespass, noise and vibrations, railway sparks, and radio signal interference. Among other things, Coase noticed that not all harms generate legal liability.

Furthermore, in one remarkable passage of his work, Coase strikes a fatal blow against the harm principal. Because of its eloquent simplicity and flawless logic, it is well worth quoting Coase's piercing passage in its entirety:

> The traditional approach has tended to obscure the nature of the choice that has to be made [between A, the wrongdoer or the person causing the harm, and B, the victim of the putative harm]. The question is commonly thought of as one in which A inflicts harm on B and what has to be decided is, How should we restrain A? But this is wrong. We are dealing with a problem of a reciprocal nature. The real question that has to be decided is, Should A be allowed to harm B or should B be allowed to harm A? The [correct solution] is to avoid the more serious harm. ("The Problem of Social Cost," p. 2)

In other words, one side will suffer harmful effects no matter what we do or fail to do. For instance, to take Coase's original example, if we permit the owner of a factory to emit smoke, the downwind neighbors will be harmed. If, however, we prohibit the factory from polluting the air, then it is the owner of the factory who will be harmed. (In fact, it is not just the owner of the factory who will be harmed but also all consumers who wish to purchase the products produced by the factory.) Likewise, to say that the owner of the factory has a moral or legal right to use the factors of production free from government intervention is not dispositive because we could argue that the neighbors have a moral or legal right to clean air or to good health. However we frame the problem—as one involving property rights in the factors of production or rights to good health—the problem remains reciprocal. One of the parties will suffer harmful effects no matter how we respond to this situation.

Similarly, *The Godfather* contains a treasure trove of reciprocal harms. Who, for example, can forget Amerigo Bonasera's anguished plea for justice or Sonny Corleone's volatile confrontation with a police photographer or Johnny Fontane's desperate desire to reboot his acting career? Among other things, these compelling characters and memorable plot devices share an additional feature in common: they have all been harmed or injured in one way or another. The harm that has befallen Amerigo Bonasera is reputational. His family honor was stained when two men attempted to rape his teenage daughter and then gamed the legal system to avoid jail time. For Johnny Fontane, the harm consists of a lost opportunity. A big-shot Hollywood producer refuses to cast him in a new movie. And in Sonny Corleone's case, the harm is an invasion of privacy. But if we try to stop Sonny in his tracks, or compel Woltz to cast Fontane in his new movie, or berate Bonasera for his decision to raise his daughter in the American fashion, allowing her to go on dates and stay out late without a chaperone, we are now creating a new set of harms.

So, what is to be done? Does the freedom to take photographs override the privacy of Don Vito's wedding guests? Is Jack Woltz's injured pride more important than Johnny Fontane's movie career? Should formal law take precedence over Amerigo Bosanera's family honor and appetite for revenge? If there is no philosophically principled or "foolproof" way of answering these difficult questions, perhaps we are better off acknowledging the reciprocal nature of harms.

Instead of trying to draw impossible lines between victims and wrongdoers, between justified harms and unjust ones, we should consider doing something else entirely, something more pragmatic and sensible. We should strive to do what Vito Corleone would do: we should do our best to avoid the greater harm.

# 23

# Is the Godfather Just? Maybe . . .

Eric J. Silverman and Colin Bunn

What is justice?—a question as old as philosophy itself.

It might seem that Vito Corleone—"The original Godfather" —is obviously a corrupt, vicious, evil man. After all, he regularly violates the law, commits violence, and behaves dishonestly. Yet, this quick dismissal of the Godfather's Mafia ethics relies on current popular views of justice. There are alternative views where we might view the Godfather as a just or virtuous person.

## Accept This Justice as a Gift . . .

One definition of justice in Plato's *Republic* has much in common with Vito Corleone's views. Socrates is arguing about the nature of justice with a rich, young heir named Polemarchus. Like Vito Corleone, Polemarchus claims that the essence of justice is "to help your friends and to harm your enemies." His idea of justice is based on the principle of reciprocity. We should treat others as they treat us. No better and no worse. Therefore, justice is to help your friends and to harm your enemies.

Polemarchus's principle of reciprocity is precisely the view of justice undergirding the Godfather's decision making. Both Polemarchus and the Godfather view justice as demanding that we help our friends. Corleone will "do you a favor" if you are his friend and are willing to grant him a reciprocal favor in return. That's what friends do—they help one another. To be unwilling to help those close to us is to fail at our most important relationships. As Vito claims, "Friendship is everything." Yet, the principle of reciprocity works in both directions: the Godfather does not seek to harm others without reason, but if you choose to become his enemy or stand in the way of his goals, he will harm you. That is also essential to the God-father's view of justice.

We see this view of justice in the opening scene of the original Godfather movie. Amerigo Bonasera has had a family tragedy as two men assaulted, injured, and attempted to rape his daughter. He was failed by the American judicial system, which punished the assailants with a trivial suspended sentence. A mere "slap on the wrist" to the criminals and a "slap in the face" to an idealistic immigrant who believed in the goodness of America.

Amerigo comes to Corleone to hire him to murder his daughter's assailants. But, Corleone believes in real justice, the justice of reciprocity. Unlike the American judicial system, he isn't going to let the assailants go with a trivial penalty simply because they hired a good lawyer. To his mind that's what weak or corrupt men do. Yet, he makes it clear that there are two problems with Bonasera's request.

First, the request itself is unjust because it is too severe. It is unequal and not truly reciprocal. Murdering someone for merely assaulting Bonasera's daughter is a disproportionately severe punishment and is therefore unjust. The request goes against Corleone's commitment to a kind of equal, reciprocal justice. While he does not actually cite the traditional principle of "an eye for an eye" to explain his view, some account of reciprocity and equality is implicit in Corleone's code. In his turn as Godfather, Michael follows a similar code saying, "I don't feel I have to wipe everyone out, . . . just my enemies." There is a rationale, a rhyme, and a reason to the Godfather's violence. From the Godfather's viewpoint, too much violence is a form of injustice.

There's a second problem with Bonasera's request. Vito is outrightly insulted by the assumption that he is merely someone who arranges "muscle" for hire. Everyone in the room visibly recoils at Bonasera's offensive assumption that he can simply purchase Corleone's services. The Godfather does not offer his aid like a transaction at some impersonal business. He doesn't want money. He's not a thug. Instead, like Polemarchus, he values reciprocal loyal friendship and relationship. When Bonasera asks him to be his friend rather than offering him money, Corleone offers to help as an act of justice and friendship. It's a gift that cannot be purchased. However, in return he expects loyal friendship and the potential for a favor in the future.

Years later Bonasera is called upon to repay this favor, but he is not expected to do anything inappropriate or illegal. Instead, Corleone calls upon him to perform the completely legal task of embalming Vito's dead son Sonny to make him presentable for an open casket service. It is better that a trusted friend does an act of such intimate importance rather than a hired stranger. This favor is the sort of thing friends do for one another. As Polemarchus suggests, Corleone's view of justice is to help your friends. It displays the just man's excellence by demonstrating his strength and his loyalty to those close to him. In doing so, he becomes even stronger by creating a small army of loyal friends with open ended indebtedness to him.

Of course, Polemarchus's view of justice also includes a willingness to "harm your enemies." Accordingly, the Corleones treat enemies with reciprocal animosity and are willing to harm them. When Virgil Sollozzo attempts to kill Vito for refusing to get involved with his heroin operations, he becomes a clear enemy of the Corleone family. Therefore, Michael does not hesitate to retaliate against him when given the opportunity even though it meant also killing Captain McCluskey who was acting as Sollozzo's bodyguard, and going into exile in Sicily for years. This is how the Mafia's code of justice works. A harm from an enemy must be avenged. To fail to do so would express weakness, vulnerability, and lack of commitment to the family. The justice of reciprocal violence must be also upheld. To do otherwise would be unjust, foolish, and invite further aggression.

## The Godfather as Übermensch

Great Men Are Not Born Great. They Grow Great.

—Vito Corleone

Polemarchus is not alone in advocating mafia-like justice. Another philosophical view that portrays the Godfather as virtuous can be found in the writings of Friedrich Nietzsche. He was a German existentialist, which is a school of philosophy focusing on the individual within the world and the agency that each person naturally possesses over their existence. Nietzsche offers a series of criticisms of traditional morality and altruistic views of virtue. In his *On the Genealogy of Morality* (1887) Nietzsche describes two patterns he observed in moral sensibilities, patterns he calls: Master Morality and Slave Morality. The Master view of morality is similar to what we see depicted in the Godfather, while the Slave view is the more widely held conventional morality of the lower classes.

Nietzsche's moral framework revolves around his understanding of the *Übermensch*, literally translated as the "overman." Nietzsche discusses this evolved person as one who has broken free of the limitations of slave morality. The slave morality is the conventional, underclass, religious morality typically adopted by common people. It focuses on right and wrong, legal and illegal, or good and evil. When average people think about morality they conceptualize it in terms of what is beneficial to others and the broad community. Lying, stealing, fraud, and murder all harm the community and are forbidden as evil and wrong.

This portrayal of altruistic morality is one where the community, herd, and commoners benefit. The slavish morality of the lower class typically values soft, weak traits like forgiveness, sympathy, kindness, and humility. Such values are encouraged by the lower class, not because they are objectively good, but because the lower class disproportionately benefits from such a system. They cannot compete against the strength of the upper class directly, so they try to create a system of morality which discourages the upper class from effectively using their advantages for themselves.

The overman is above this slave morality and transcends it to embrace a more enlightened view of the world. According to Nietzsche, great men break free from this herd mentality expressed in slave morality. Some of us can transcend everyday morality and live by our own rules. This privileged, upperclass mentality rejects the communal centered morality of the weak and poor. Driven by what Nietzsche calls the Will to Power, the overman shapes the world to their liking. Society and its limited slave morality hold no power over the actions of the overman. Instead, the overman's reality revolves around what's good and bad for *them*. Through these methods the overman rises above the mere herd. Nietzsche considers these people to be a "higher-type" who are greater than those who follow slave morality.

In contrast to the morals of the commoners, the morality of the upper class—Master Morality—values strength, independence, and power. Strong men like Corleone need no help from the legal system or the general altruism of strangers. For a strong person like Corleone, humility is inappropriate. He truly is an accomplished man. Out of his strength and selfsufficiency, he can help you if you need it. In troubled times, you want to turn to a person with Corleone's virtues rather than someone forgiving and kind. Nietzschean Master Morality values these kinds of traits.

Both Slave and Master moralities are products of socio-economic class. Those of the lower or middle classes tend to embrace slave morality. As those outside the upper class, they find themselves at the mercy of those with power. They cannot detach themselves from the expectations of society and their local community. Since they do not have enough power of their own, they benefit by following the model of the altruistic virtuous person, abiding by the rules of society, and living as a member of the herd. It costs them nothing to avoid using power aggressively since they have so little power. So, their morality costs themselves little, but they hope to manipulate the strong into unilateral sacrifice, thus bringing them down to their level of weakness. In contrast, a person from the upper class can and should detach themselves from the herd. Their money, power, and possessions give them the freedom to create their own values. Yet, it is also their mental strength and willingness to violate social convention that distinguishes them from the weakness they see around them.

We see that the Corleone crime family operates in the isolation caused by their own strength and greatness. They live by their own rules and their own code. They acknowledge the similar strength of other Mafia families and offer them respect as a kind of equals, so long as they continue in strength and abide by the jointly acknowledged rules that govern the relationships of the elite class. These rules let each family exercise its strength within their domain.

This emphasis upon strength is one reason for the plot to kill Michael Corleone in *The Godfather*. As Michael inherits control of the family from Vito, who ruled with strength according to the Mafia code of justice, it's unclear to the other families whether Michael will possess similar strength and ruthlessness. This strength isn't merely an issue of how rich, large, or powerful the family is, but also includes a personal strength found in the willingness to break traditional rules of morality to act ruthlessly against any threat. The rival families suspect that Michael doesn't really possess the strength that gives the status of equals within their class of masters.

Yet, we see that Michael Corleone is indeed a strong member of the Master class. He undergoes a transition from slave to master morality over the course of the film. Michael starts the movie with a kinder mentality. He is a war hero and strives for the values put forward by society. He seeks to avoid the violence of mafia life. However, this begins to change after Vito Corleone is almost killed due to his refusal to become involved with heroin trafficking. Michael begins his separation from the values of slave morality.

During his meeting with Sollozzo and McCluskey, we see Michael begin to embrace the Master Morality. Michael hatches the plan to kill his enemies. While he has not yet fully embraced the family business. Yet, he still rejects the peaceful values of broader society and replaces them with the values of the Master class. While the political structures—like McCluskey's legal powers of law enforcement—restrain the herd following slave morality, Michael is not deterred by them.

This decision is not without struggle. As the sound of a train drowns out all audio before Michael murders Sollozzo and McCluskey, Michael wrestles with which morality to embrace. It is an auditory and visual representation of the two moralities clashing with one another. Ultimately, Michael embraces his role as Nietzsche's overman of the Master class by exacting his own justice for Vito's injuries. He was not limited by the conventional morality of the weak, but showed himself strong enough both physically and emotionally to act according to his own morality.

Throughout the story Michael Corleone moves further away from the slave morality which once bound him until the movie's climax. As Michael attends a baptism, he is also "baptized" as he fully embraces his role in the Master Class as Godfather by having his rivals assassinated. In Nietzschean terms, he fully breaks from the old world, rejects the commoner's morality, and becomes the overman. Michael sees the world in terms of strength and benefit to himself, while rejecting society's standards of good or evil.

Justice in the Master Class is found in the code of strength and mutual respect among the strong, but it is inseparable from the self. What is just, good, or right is whatever happens to be valued by the strong individual. Therefore, Michael Corleone's actions might be thought of as just. The attack on Vito, according to Michael, can only be rectified by the shedding of blood. The average person might criticize this action or seek justice in society's courts. But, for Nietzsche and other members of the Master Class, the point is moot. Michael Corleone's physical and moral strength enable him to enforce his own view of justice upon the world without answering to anyone else.

As Vito suggests, there is no reason to trust society to protect you if you are strong. Society—the mass of people adhering to slave morality—is controlled by politicians with no real accomplishment beyond conning voters. The strong individual who can carry out justice himself is more virtuous than those in control of society.

## Doubts about Mafia-style Justice

An eye for an eye will leave the whole world blind.

—MOHANDAS GANDHI

Thus far, we've considered the unusual view that those who live by the Mafia's code might actually be virtuous. Yet, there are good reasons to think that the traditional evaluation of the Mafia is correct: violent criminals—even those who live according to a kind of code—are dangerous and live unhappy lives. They are perfect examples of vice, not virtue, no matter how much we might romanticize them.

While Polemarchus's account of justice might seem superficially persuasive, there are good reasons his view has been rejected by most philosophers from the time of Socrates all the way until today. First, it has "harming others" as a built-in starting goal of its supposedly moral code. Yet, harming others is a goal that is directly against any attractive account of ethics. Many realistic views of ethics accept that as an unfortunate side effect of good goals someone—like an aspiring mass murderer—might need to be harmed. Yet, such unintentional willingness to commit violence is different from Polemarchus's Mafia-like code embedding harm as an explicit, intentional, foundational goal of justice. Justice should be the sort of ideal that aims at helping all, even if it is difficult to succeed in such utopian pursuits in the real world.

Another reason to doubt such a code of justice is that there is an ambiguity when trying to classify people as friends and enemies. Sometimes real friends seem like enemies and real enemies seem like friends. Even the Godfather seems aware of this ambiguity as he says, "Keep your friends close but your enemies closer." Sometimes those close to us are intentionally deceptive. Appearances cannot always be trusted. Other times, people turn out to be more mixed than the simplistic friend-enemy categories allow. Fredo Corleone was Michael's brother, but ultimately betrayed him. People are flawed, mixed, and imperfect as examples of either friends or enemies, and it can be difficult to properly categorize them in time to protect ourselves.

A third problem with the Godfather's view of justice comes from defining friends and enemies in terms of loyalty or the appearance of loyalty. Instead, an ideal like justice should value people who seek the good of all and view them as friends. For the sake of justice, real enemies are not merely those who block—sometimes unintentionally or indirectly—our own personal goals, but rather those who seek ill more generally. Defining friends and enemies in terms of their supposed personal loyalty to us is an unreliable substitute for genuine goodness.

One reason for defining friends in terms of objective goodness rather than subjective personal loyalty might be that the goodness of someone who is genuinely virtuous can be trusted. Yet, trusting that a generally vicious person would still hold to their individual loyalty to you based upon an "honor among thieves" principle is far less reliable. According to some ancient thinkers like Plato and Aristotle, vicious "bad" individuals can't really be reliable friends to anyone. People with deep character flaws—like criminals—will tend to be harmful to anyone close to them. Vicious people are ultimately dangerous to themselves and their closest friends.

A fourth problem is that living by the Godfather's values is psychologically and relationally self-destructive. As Plato suggests, justice includes a kind of harmonious balance in the self. And so the unjust man is inherently out of balance with himself. By embracing the wrong priorities such a person inevitably harms himself. The wise person seeks wisdom, balance, and a virtuous life while the unjust person pursues worldly wealth and power, which cannot fulfill our most important internal needs. Money does not give us inner peace, tranquility, or wisdom. Pursuing such things at the cost of peace, tranquility, and relationships is a foolish choice.

Furthermore, we see that the Godfather's code leads him to live an unnecessarily dangerous life. It is a lonely life where few others can really be trusted. He is in constant danger from the law, from overt enemies, and even from supposed friends. Even family can turn out to be an enemy as Fredo unexpectedly turns out to be a danger to the family when he collaborates with the Roths. Accordingly, the Godfather's life is one of secrets, insecurity, and deceptions. Such a person is hardly flourishing. It is better to enjoy a peaceful life with happy relationships, but less resources rather than the unstable, lonely Mafia life.

There is something within Master Morality that is selfdefeating. It makes you lie to those closest to you. It makes you dehumanize everyone. Everyone is a potential competitor, an asset, a threat, or a liability. It gives you constant reason to distrust others and gives them reason to distrust you. And becoming a coldblooded killer even if it is for retribution or necessary for survival, changes you for the worse. It might be an exaggeration to say that it "makes you less than human" but it does desensitize you, limits your empathy, and damages your self.

Accordingly, we observe the sincere love and warmth within Michael's first marriage to Apollonia, and the contrast of that warm relationship with the distance and deception within his second marriage to Kay Adams. During Michael's time in Sicily with Apollonia, while he was trying to distance himself from meaningful involvement in the day to day life of the mafia he seems happier and more fulfilled than any other time in the trilogy. Of course, this ends as she becomes collateral damage in the Mafia wars, and Michael's past catches up with him. In contrast with the warmth of Michael's first marriage, his marriage to Kay was based on deceit. She didn't even know the true nature of Michael's "business" for much of their time together. And eventually their relationship turns to distrust, domestic violence, divorce, and estrangement.

## Dying by the Sword

Those who live by the sword die by the sword.

—MATTHEW 26:52

We have seen that there are surprising ways that we might portray the Godfather and those who live by the Mafia code as virtuous rather than vicious and unjust. Yet there are reasons mainstream ethicists have long considered such views unsound. The Mafia lifestyle is difficult and dangerous. Their values distance themselves from even their closest relationships. Even if the criminal succeeds by all external measures, they still have to live with themselves. And the unjust values they live by appear to be unfulfilling, isolating, and self-defeating.

Plato warns that it's impossible to avoid the harm brought into the self by embracing injustice. "To go to the world below, having a soul which is like a vessel full of injustice, is the last and worst of all evils."

# VI

---

## *"Don't ever take sides with anyone against the family."*

# 24
# Never Go Against the Family

Casey Rentmeester

While *The Godfather* is full of memorable scenes, perhaps the most climactic is the baptism of Connie's baby at the end of the first movie. Connie's brother, Michael, once explicitly sheltered from the corrupt, evil, and violent actions of his family by his father, is shown standing at the altar serving as the godfather helping to cleanse Connie's child of original sin while simultaneously having ordered a hit on all other New York City dons in his first big decision since becoming the new don of the family upon the deaths of his father Vito and his older brother Sonny.

The sacrosanct context of the church where Michael is publicly avowing his faith in God and renouncing Satan above the austere sound of the church organ is starkly juxtaposed with the shots of Corleone mobsters executing the other dons in cold-blooded, point-blank range at Michael's prior command.

How could a family be so seemingly dedicated to religious sacraments like the wedding that begins the film or the baptism that ends it while concurrently engaging in obviously unethical and downright heinous acts, including arranging for Hollywood bigshot Jack Woltz to wake up to the head of his decapitated prized $6,000 stallion in bed to ensure Vito's family friend, Johnny Fontane, gets a part in a movie, or insisting that Clemenza has Paulie murdered without a shred of remorse despite the fact that the two had been close for decades, as captured so fittingly by the classic line "leave the gun, take the cannoli"?

Is this a matter of the Corleone family operating at a level "beyond good and evil" in the Nietzschean sense of eschewing morality altogether, at least in the sense of it being imposed upon them by an external source, or is there more going on here? While there are times in which the Nietzschean sense that "this world is the will to power—and nothing besides" (*The Will to Power*, §1067) rings true in the movie, insinuating that morality is an unnatural add-on to reality believable only by schmucks, the Corleone family can best be understood from the lens of a pseudo-Aristotelian sort of virtue ethics wherein certain virtues like familial loyalty and respect for social hierarchy take on a sacred status for those within the circle, which leads to both moral and immoral ends from the perspective of a conventional understanding of right and wrong, the perspective that Michael's girlfriend, Kay Adams, seems to embody in the movie.

## You Can Act Like a Man!

What's meant by a conventional understanding of right and wrong? In the introductory wedding scene, Michael shares a story with Kay of his father and hitman Luca Brasi holding a gun to a band leader's head to make sure he released Johnny Fontane from his band contract for a mere $1,000 as opposed to the initial offer of $10,000 with the alternative this time being death. In response to Kay's horror of Vito "making him an offer he couldn't refuse"—in this case his signature on the contract or his brains spilled over it—Michael assures her: "that's my family Kay. It's not me."

The irony is that Michael will come to be the don of the crime family later in the film and turn out to do much more evil deeds than his father, including having his brother Fredo killed in the second movie of the trilogy for betraying the family. As the character of Kay is revealed in the first film, it's clear that she initially has a naive understanding of the way the world works, at least from Michael's perspective, as showcased most vividly in their reuniting in New Hampshire after Michael's exile in Italy upon killing Sollozzo and McCluskey.

Michael explains to Kay that he has joined the family business, arguing that his father's business is no different than the work of senators or presidents who are responsible for other persons, to which Kay replies, "Senators and presidents don't have men killed," a statement Michael finds laughably naive. At this stage, Kay is a schoolteacher who cares for her students and simply wants to live an honest and decent life. In the conventional understanding of morality portrayed by her character, in the least people don't have other people killed and spouses are worthy of honest communication from each other, two simple codes that Michael clearly breaks in the last scene of the first movie.

What, though, *is* the moral code of the Corleone family? First, it seems clear that they agree with Nietzsche that "morality in the traditional sense . . . is something that must be overcome" (*Beyond Good and Evil*, §32) since blind faith in conventional morality "is a stupidity that reflects little honor in us" (§34). This is indicated by Vito's insistence to Michael that he "refused to be a fool dancing on a string held by all of those big shots," a sentiment captured in the iconic image of marionette strings on the movie poster. For the Corleone family, you are either a puppet master or a puppet: there is no in-between. However, even if you climb to the ranks of puppet master, as Vito did, this does not entail operating at a level beyond good and evil: there are still virtues to be upheld and vices to avoid if you're to live well. Vito's insistence to his godson and Sonny that "a man who doesn't spend time with his family can never be a real man" or his claim to Michael that "women and children can be careless, but not men" are signs that he lives by a certain moral code, a code he often ties to masculinity.

How can we make sense of this masculine Corleone code from a philosophical perspective? I think the most obvious starting point lies in Aristotle's virtue ethics as represented in his *Nicomachean Ethics* and *Eudemian Ethics* written roughly 2,500 years ago, since those works contain the first robust ethical system in the Western world and were penned just east of the Corleone family's origins in Italy. In those treatises, Aristotle attempts to answer the question as to how to live well. Upon asking whether the highest human good lies in sensual pleasure, wealth accumulation, or honor, he ultimately argues that living well entails achieving eudaimonia, which he calls "the chief good among the things that fall within the scope of human action" (*Eudemian Ethics*, p. 10). The word "eudaimonia" stems from "eu," meaning "good" or "well," and "daimon," meaning "spirit" or that which gives life. Thus, eudaimonia is best translated as living well. In order to live well, says Aristotle, we need to cultivate *aretes*, that is, virtues, which we can think of as excellent traits of the self, and avoid *kakies*, that is, vices, which we can think of as bad traits of the self. Virtues like courage, temperance, and truthfulness are juxtaposed with vices like cowardliness, self-indulgence, and dishonesty in Aristotle's system of ethics. A good life is one in which a person consistently lives in accordance with the virtues, thus achieving eudaimonia, which is the highest good for which humans can ascend.

While Aristotle thinks persons are born with certain dispositions—some are prone to self-indulgence while others are more temperate—he insists that virtue "is in our own power, and so too vice" (*Nicomachean Ethics*, p. 46). In other words, while your unique make-up lends you to act in certain ways by nature, your character is not set in stone; rather, human characters have an element of plasticity to thcm, meaning that we can choose to mold them through our actions. However, Aristotle is clear that achieving eudaimonia, which entails consistently practicing the virtues "to the right person, to the right extent, at the right time, with the right motive, and in the right way . . . is not for everyone, nor is it easy" (p. 36). Despite the difficulty of living well, Aristotle considers it to be the proper end of a human life and thus worthy of the effort. Indeed, an inability to cultivate the virtues required for eudaimonia can have disastrous consequences, which can be explained through the character of Sonny in the first movie. While Sonny may be naturally prone to anger and thus easily flies off the handle, Aristotle would claim such a lack of temperance is a vice that can be rectified through practice since people become "temperate by doing temperate acts" (p. 23). Sonny's reputation as a hothead who lacks temperance ends up getting him killed, since Sollozzo leverages this fact about him to lure him into the trap at the toll booth: upon hearing of Carlo beating up Connie again, Sonny furiously speeds off only to be massacred by Sollozzo's button men wielding tommy guns.

For Aristotle, that mistake could have been avoided since we have a choice in cultivating the type of character we mold for ourselves, given that "states of character arise out of like activities" (p. 24) that are chosen by ourselves, a belief that Vito clearly shares throughout the movie. For instance, when Sonny angrily runs his mouth to Sollozzo in the attempted narcotics business deal, the mistake that led to his death since it revealed his quick fuse, Vito reprimands him to "never tell anybody outside the family what you're thinking again." Similarly, when Johnny comes to him crying about not getting the role in the movie at his office during Connie's wedding, Vito admonishes him to stop acting like a helpless woman with the stern words: "you can act like a man!"

A real man, for Vito, is a person who reveres certain virtues and values as sacred and lives in accordance with them. Above all else, family loyalty is of the utmost importance in the Corleone code, as seen clearly in Michael's foreshadowed counsel to Fredo in their meeting in Las Vegas when he states, "Don't ever take sides with anyone against the family again. Ever." In the Corleone code, family is first. Period. Fredo's eventual death in the second film was a result of him not heeding that ultimate value. There is also a strong emphasis on the importance of respecting social hierarchy in the Corleone code, as signified so clearly by Vito's insistence on being called "Godfather." Those who demonstrate respect, honor, and deference to the social hierarchy are friends to the family, while those who do not are enemies. Courage also serves as an important virtue in the Corleone code, as showcased most clearly in Michael's character. Already touted as a war hero, Michael showed courage not only in shooting Sollozzo and the crooked cop McCluskey knowing full-well he would be exiled for at least a year, but also in speaking matter-of-factly with Vitelli during that exile about who he was and his intentions regarding his daughter, Apollonia, whom he later marries, after his Italian compatriots unknowingly disrespected her to him. Michael's courage, careful ability to reason through scenarios, respect for truth (at least in certain contexts), and undeniable dedication to the sanctity of family loyalty makes him fit to be the don even though Fredo was chronologically next in line given his age. Fredo's vices of weakness, stupidity, and his penchant for self-indulgence render him unfit even though he is older than Michael since, as Aristotle states, "they should rule who are able to rule best."

## Where Does It Say You Can't Kill a Cop?

Perhaps the most important shift in Michael's eventual rise from do-gooder to don can be seen in the conversation between Sonny, Clemenza, Tom Hagen, and Tessio and him regarding how to respond to Sollozzo's request to meet with Michael after the failed assassination attempt on Vito. In that scene, upon finding proof that McCluskey is on Sollozzo's payroll, Tom makes it clear that "nobody has ever gunned down a New York police captain . . . never," insisting that such an act would lead all five families to turn against the Corleone family. Michael, showcasing his virtues of coolheadedness and calculated precision, concocts the plan to kill Sollozzo and McCluskey, not as a matter of revenge for Sollozzo's attempt on his father's life or as a retribution for McCluskey's punch to Michael's face, but as a matter of protecting the family business.

His dedication to the Corleone code over conventional morality is revealed in his question, "Where does it say you can't kill a cop?" Moreover, his plan of leveraging their contacts with the newspapers to paint McCluskey as a corrupt and greedy cop who got caught up in the drug game not only demonstrated astute intelligence and foresight, but also heeded Aristotle's notion that sometimes it's necessary to "use friends and riches and political power as instruments" (*Nicomachean Ethics*, p. 14). As it turns out, his intuitions end up being spot-on, since the initial headline of "Police Hunt Cop Killer" eventually turns to the headline "Police Captain Linked with Drug Rackets," a sign that they've won public opinion and adeptly maneuvered the figurative puppet strings to their favor, despite the seeming incomprehensibility, among the group at first, of the possibility of gunning down a cop in public.

It's at this point and others, though, where the Corleone code makes a stark departure from Aristotle's virtue ethics *per se*, since Aristotle thought that certain actions like murder "are themselves bad . . . It is not possible, then, ever to be right with regard to them; one must always be wrong" (p. 31). For Aristotle, a virtue works as means between two extremes, which serve as vices. So, for instance, courage is the mean between cowardice and rashness. In order to cultivate the virtue of courage, you determine where you fall on the spectrum in terms of your dispositions and engage in actions that call for courage on a consistent basis until you've formed that virtue into your character, "for it is activities exercised . . . that make the corresponding character" (p. 47). This intentional approach requires you to function outside of your natural comfort zone (the cowardly person needs to act bravely and the rash person needs to tone it down, even when your natural dispositions point otherwise, a lesson Sonny never learned); but once a person becomes comfortable practicing the virtue consistently, then it's a good sign that the virtue has been formed in their character.

For Aristotle, there are certain acts, though, such as murder and adultery, that are bad in and of themselves such that doing them is a sign of a depraved character. Aristotle puts the point the following way: "goodness or badness with regard to such things does not depend on committing adultery with the right woman, at the right time, and in the right way, but simply to do any of them is to go wrong." From a strictly Aristotelian perspective, "adultery in itself is a form of depravity" (p. 21): you cannot live well and simultaneously be an adulterer or a murderer.

This is where the ethics of the Corleone family depart from Aristotle's system. In the Corleone code, there is certainly a sacred sense of the importance of family, but it seems that men are still able to "have their fun" with women and still be a good man. For instance, in discussing whether or not to get into the narcotics game, Vito says that access to women "is something that most people want nowadays" even if it's forbidden by the Church. This is why he turns a bit of a blind eye to Sonny's adultery: it only becomes an issue when it affects Sonny's focus on the family business, as implied by Vito's conjecture to Sonny that "I think your brain is going soft from all that comedy you're playing [foolin' around] with that young girl" after he ran his mouth to Sollozzo. In the Corleone code, men are higher on the social hierarchy than women, which is why not only Luca Brasi wishes to Vito that Connie's child be a son but also why Michael is hopeful for a son with Kay in the second movie, a son that never came due to her opting for abortion, a symbol of the inability to reconcile conventional morality with the ethics found in the Corleone family. Being a man in that family means living up to certain responsibilities, but also being able to have a little fun, which helps to explain why Sonny can simultaneously be a good Corleone and a known adulterer at the same time.

Murder functions differently than adultery in the Corleone code: it is not so much tolerated but rather seen as necessary. In fact, whereas Aristotle thinks that an act of murder is a sign of a depraved character since murder is always wrong, you can clearly climb the social hierarchy of the Corleone family by committing murders, especially if they are done courageously and improve the family's position. Michael's murders of Sollozzo and McCluskey earn him a stronger reputation, not a weaker one, as is obvious upon his return from Italy. Moreover, his bold act of executing the other five dons and Connie's husband Carlo to boot is met with deep respect, as is evident by the way in which Rocco, Clemenza, and Neri embrace him in the very last scene of the movie.

In the Corleone code, you can't simply be the puppet master without engaging in bloodshed. This is where the Corleone code is more Nietzschean than Aristotelian, as the family seems to agree with Nietzsche that "the weak and the botched shall perish . . . And they ought even to be helped to perish" (*The Antichrist*, p. 4). Indeed, these lines almost perfectly capture Fredo's fate.

In the end, the Corleone code is more of a pseudo-Aristotelian virtue ethics with Nietzschean undertones, a code in which the puppet master sometimes needs to make offers that can't be refused and even a brother needs to be killed if he breaks the code.[1]

---

I thank Richard Greene, Josh Heter, Russ Leary, and Cassie Rentmeester for comments on earlier versions of this chapter.

# 25

# Mary and Vincent's Dangerous Romance

CHRISTOPHER M. INNES

Mary and Vincent's romance in *The Godfather Part III* is a passionate affair born out of impulse, but not necessarily a fling doomed to failure. It's a romance that we might normally admire in a young couple as we get the feeling that it very well could have resulted in a healthy, successful relationship. However, before anyone could get too carried away, Michael, Mary's father steps in and knowingly asks Vincent, "What are you doing with my daughter?"

Of course, this almost certainly is because one of the more noteworthy aspects of Mary and Vincent's relationship is that they are cousins. Michael later tells Vincent, "It's too dangerous." Mary's brother echoes this; "It's *really* dangerous." There's a moral tone in Michael's voice when he tells Kay that it's wrong *and* it's dangerous. That said, it's worth asking: why exactly is Michael concerned about Mary and Vincent's romance being *dangerous*?

Vincent and Mary's grandfather, Don Vito consistently embraced the value of being loyal to the family. You put the family first and it's made strong; a family tied together can be a successful family. But incest is taboo, so such a forbidden relationship might work against the good of the family. Vito very likely would have been more heavy-handed in putting a stop to Mary and Vincent's romance. And, such a prohibition is based on the notion of taboo that is deeply ingrained in our values but is difficult to understand. Is this where Michael gets the idea that Mary and Vincent's romance is dangerous? Is his view based on morality, or is it based some other threat?

## Sex and Taboo

Like much of the forbidden, the idea that some acts are dangerous or taboo is deeply ingrained in our understanding of right
and wrong. We have firmly held beliefs about that which is permissible and that which is not. To say that an act is taboo is to
say that the act is not only forbidden, but it is a behavior that
goes against something that is sacred and consecrated.
However, it's an open question whether or not any particular
taboo has such a status for good reason; what is considered a
taboo may very well be arbitrary.

It is generally taboo to commit adultery or interfere in the
marriages of others. These acts are considered to go against the
value system people hold dear. Mama Corleone respects these
taboos, but Michael's brother and Vito's heir, Sonny, does not;
he often interferes in his sister's marriage, and commits adultery with his mistress, Lucy (ultimately resulting in the birth
of Vincent). Such acts typically make us particularly uncomfortable as the transgression of these taken-for-granted values
is offensive to our sense of morality or runs afoul of some type
of social ethic.

That incest is taboo is also so deeply ingrained in our values, so much so that even an attempt at an explanation of it
might be taboo in itself. The Corleones are of course Roman
Catholic, and with their religion comes the belief that incest is
wrong or taboo with specific details about its prohibition.
Parents and their children, brothers and sisters, and first
cousins are not to have sexual intercourse. It is a law of nature
that prescribes these important and reverential family relationships to be incompatible with a sexual romance. Mary is
Michael's daughter and Vincent is the illegitimate son of her
uncle, Sonny. Their sexual romance as cousins will pollute and
make impure their reverential familial relationship.

It could be argued that prohibiting a romantic relationship
between first cousins but not second or third cousins is arbitrary. If so, there would be no problem if Mary and Vincent
were not *first* cousins. That said, the Corleones' Catholic faith
may go a long way to explaining why the relationship may be
seen as a taboo. For Catholics, the practice of incest is seen as
so obscene that its avoided even as a topic of conversation.

That said, can the idea that Mary and Vincent's romance is
dangerous or wrong be ultimately defended? On the one hand,
the romance is consensual with no hint that either has been
coerced into the relationship. They are over the age of consent,
and it appears as if they are equally in love as two responsible
adults. On the other hand, *they are cousins*. And, Mary comes

off as having a youthful crush, while Vincent doesn't seem terribly brokenhearted when he is forced to end their relationship. Nevertheless, the sum total of the case thus far seems to point to their romance as relatively danger-free. We might be uncomfortable with their age difference or their aforementioned family bond, but while Mary and Vincent's incestuous relationship might be taboo, and it might leave us a bit uneasy, what is the case that it is wrong or dangerous?

## The Genetics Argument

One argument against Mary and Vincent having any sort of romance is based on their shared genetics as first cousins. This argument rests on the idea that the physical health and well-being of the family is harmed by the incestuous relationship because any children born from it are far more likely to be born with genetic disorders.

There is some chance of this, but there is a substantial body of research which tells us that the risk is only slight as there is only a moderate, three-percent chance that genetic disorders will result from such a relationship. Genetic disorders increase substantially only after three or four generations of intermarrying. As most of us know, there is a fair amount of folk history of (for instance) royal inbreeding leading to genetic abnormalities, but this is more gossip than fact.

Even if there is a modest increase in Mary and Vincent's potential offspring having genetic abnormalities, does that itself entail that their relationship is wrong or even dangerous enough to warrant its prohibition? Four thousand or more known genetic disorders exist, but people with already diagnosed genetic disorders are not prohibited from having children.

For example, there are a quarter of a million people in the United States suffering from Huntington's Disease; a progressive, inherited disease which causes the nerve endings in the brain to break down, resulting in loss of mental and physical function (and which often substantially shortens its victim's life). A child of a parent with this disorder has a fifty-percent chance of inheriting the gene. However, it is not taboo for those suffering with Huntington's Disease to have children, and most would not try to make a moral argument against it. If relationships between close family members who demonstrate no disorders are prohibited, with little chance of passing on genetic defects to their children, and if those with a much higher chance of passing on a genetic disorder *are* allowed or encouraged to have children, then what exactly is the genetic case to be made for the prohibition of incestuous romances? The genetics argument condemns incestuous relationships because of a presumed likelihood of children being born with genetic deformity. But, those who are much more likely to pass on genetic disorders have no such limits put on their relationships.

In addition, for well over a generation, genetic counseling has been available to those with genetic disorders wanting to have children so they can be advised on the likelihood of passing on a genetic disorder. However, if this counseling is available for those with known genetic disorders, then why not make it available to incestuous couples? This would mean that Mary and Vincent could be advised on any possible genetic disorder their potential future children would have, and they may act accordingly. As luck would have it, the National Society of Genetic Counselors was founded in 1979, the very same year Mary and Vincent begin their romantic relationship. But, the point is this. There is a non-zero chance that their "dangerous romance" will result in their children inheriting a genetic disorder, but that chance is manageable with the help of genetic counseling. And, it is (at the very least) arguable that the risk is reasonable and analogous to the risks taken on by others who might pass down genetic disorders.

## The Family Argument

A second argument that Mary and Vincent's relationship is wrong or dangerous is the family argument. Vito speaks of the family in reverential terms. The family needs to be kept strong to be successful. Incest is seen as immoral because it undermines the family which is the emotional center of each family member, and pursuing sexual activity within the family instead of developing non-romantic, emotional ties with each other goes against the (well-being of the) family. The argument proceeds with under assumptions: 1) incest undermines the family, 2) the family is the emotional center of the person, and 3) it is immoral to undermine this emotional center. And of course, if incest is immoral and Mary and Vincent's relationship is incestuous (as we know that it is), then Mary and Vincent's romance is (dangerous or) wrong.

Again, the first assumption is that incest undermines the family. This sounds intuitive if not correct; there seem to be a fair number of cases in which the stability or well-being of families have been gravely harmed by incest. But, could there be cases in which it leads not to harm but stability?

Typically, incest has as disrupting effect on the emotional dynamic of a family. Cousins should be tied by the simple joy of being related and participating in family activities like going on holiday together. The underlying supposition here is that we should dedicate our attention to emotional family ties and sexual relationships get in the way of this. We know that in mafioso families, romantic relations between family members is prohibited, even in the cases in which there is no blood relationship. If the relationship breaks down, then the family ties break down. This sounds like a sensible reason to avoid such romantic relationships.

But, by the time Mary and Vincent reconnect at the reception celebrating Michael's papal honor, the Corleones as a family unit have largely disintegrated. Mary and Vincent have been raised outside of any meaningful family dynamic. There *is* no substantial family relationships to destabilize. Arguably, the most likely outcome of their romantic union may be to steer the Corleones back towards some form of family stability.

The case could be made even stronger if we imagine that the eight-year-old Mary and fifteen-year-old Vincent never meet (as Mary references when she first approaches Vincent at the reception). Instead, suppose they meet in their thirties, fall in love, get married, and have children. The children are raised in an emotionally secure and healthy environment. After ten years of great family life, they learn that they are first cousins. Upon hearing this news, should they break up their family? If it is a successful, stable family, that would seem at best imprudent as the destabilization of families is the very thing a prohibition of incestuous relationships is aimed at preventing.

The second assumption of the family argument is that the family is the emotional center of the person. The family is seen as a place of solace, comfort, and joy. This is based on the presumption that family is *uniquely* capable of such emotional support, and that it is the only emotional center for the child. However, often families break down, parents divorce, and all too often, they neglect their children, leaving them to find emotional support elsewhere. We see this with Vito on his arrival to America in *The Godfather Part II* as he is forced to find his emotional support in friends he makes on the street. Beyond this, Mary's relationship with her father, Michael seems to be less than ideal despite the fact that she grew up to be seemingly emotionally healthy and secure. As for Vincent, despite being raised without his father, Sonny, he's sure of himself and is able to take Michael's guidance on family matters. It seems that emotional support and the sources by which it is derived are more complex than the second assumption of the family argument presumes and needn't necessarily be found in one's family.

The third and final assumption of the family argument against incestuous relationships is that it is immoral to undermine the emotional center of the family. Simply put, any act that goes against maintaining the emotional center of the family is wrong and any act supporting it good, and sex between family members gets in the way of a family's emotional bond. Of course, there is at least one type of sexual relationship between family members that does not seem to come with any (inherent) harm to a family's emotional bond: the sexual relationship between husband and wife. This is to say that a married couple having sex with each other is neither bad for their marriage in particular or their family in general.

With all this in mind, it seems as if there is a strong case to be made against all three assumptions that underlie the family argument and they give us no special reason to prohibit Mary and Vincent's dangerous romance.

Michael's predilection for the use of reason should lead him to conclude that his moral proclamation to Kay that "It's wrong" is without foundation. To be sure, Michael is not normally bound by moral restraint. He had his brother-in-law, his own brother, and the heads of the five crime families all assassinated. And, he did all of this despite the fact that as godfather to his nephew, he promised to "reject Satan . . . and all his works". In *Part III*, he confesses to Cardinal Lamberto, showing great repentance, but we are still aware of Michael's morally flexible view of the world. Traditional morality does not dictate Michael's choices. Could there then be another (type of) reason he is convinced that Mary and Vincent's romance is wrong (or dangerous)?

## Prudence versus Danger

It seems as if the genetics argument and the family argument make for fairly weak defenses of a prohibition against Mary and Vincent's incestuous relationship. However, perhaps Michael has more prudential reasons in mind for his disapproval of it. A family like the Corleones is focused heavily on protecting its own financial interests. The family considers wealth as a fundamentally important component of their wellbeing. Vito considered himself to be a reasonable man and put business over family sentiment. His view was that family conduct should not get in the way of business. Similarly, Michael (stepping into his father's shoes) assures his brothers and partners that his motives for assassinating Sollozzo and McCluskey are "strictly business." In so doing, he implies that he is acting in the interest of good business and reason unclouded by emotion. Like Vito, he doesn't drink; nor does he have a mistress because both are bad for business.

Could Michael's concern about Mary and Vincent's "dangerous" romance simply be that it is bad for business? If so, could he be right about that? When Michael marries Kay, he knows she will not get in the way of business. Michael met his first wife, Appollonia, in Sicily, and he was instantly attracted to her mysterious beauty. His bodyguards, Calò and Fabrizio, explain to Michael that he's been struck by "the thunderbolt." This is a dangerous longing a man has for a mysterious woman. He doesn't pay attention to reason and instead eventually gets permission from Apollonia's father to marry her. For a number of reasons, this was not a sensible marriage, and it eventually results in Apollonia's death by a car bomb intended for him. As Michael seems to have forgotten, letting your emotions get the better of you leads to being caught off guard.

The memory of his own "dangerous romance" perhaps influences Michael's thoughts about Mary and Vincent's romance. Michael tells Mary about Apollonia and implies that the more Vincent is involved in the Corleone family business, the more danger Mary will be in. Again, the message is that emotions should not get in the way of family business. With this in mind, it may be worth taking a closer look at Michael's thought process via the ethical worldview of one particular, prominent modern philosopher.

## Utility and the Family Business

Not unlike Sonny, Fredo, or Michael, the philosopher John Stuart Mill was destined to join the family business. Mill was a member of a mid-nineteenth-century family made up of a number of philosophers. He was the son of a philosopher and taught by philosopher Jeremy Bentham. He was godfather to Bertrand Russell, perhaps the most important analytic philosopher of the twentieth century, and he even married fellow philosopher Harriet Taylor. Mill is perhaps most well-known for utilitarianism: the ethical worldview that the moral worth of an action should be calculated solely by its outcome. The outcome must be for the greater good. We get a feeling that both Vito and Michael, much of the time, put reason before sentiment and use utilitarianism as a guiding principle.

Mill's utilitarianism can be thought to come in two forms: act-based and rule-based. Which variety does Michael use? The rule-based variety dictates that the right act is based on the *rules* that result in the greatest amount of pleasure. Michael seems to use the rule that emotion must not cloud judgment and that reason must prevail at all times. The idea here is that the right thing to do is to follow a rule which will tend to produce the most amount of (happiness or) pleasure. Since (it would at least seem), following the rule of not allowing emotion to cloud judgment tends to produce the most amount of pleasure (in the long run), acting in according with that rule is the right thing to do, according to the rule-utilitarian.

According to the act-based utilitarian, an action is allowed to be carried out on a one-time basis if it creates more pleasure at that time. The right thing to do is whatever *in fact* produces the most amount of happiness or pleasure. Michael has Carlo and Fredo killed. These were one-off killings. He has lots of people killed, but there was arguably no guiding rule in place that dictated that these actions should be performed. These killings were done on a case-by-case basis, perhaps to increase security or to exact retribution, making it seem that in these circumstances, Michael's guiding moral outlook is act (as opposed to rule) utilitarianism.

If we assume that Michael's guiding compass is some sort of utilitarian reasoning, we get the impression that his declaration that Mary and Vincent's romance is dangerous is based on rule-based utilitarian reasoning that such romances generally lead to trouble. It has nothing to do with abstract eternal moral codes or the teachings of the Church. It would be silly to think Michael is bound by anything other than practical interests after he has Carlo and Fredo killed. He is simply looking after the family business, and as such, it is a pitiful irony that Mary is eventually killed by an assassin's bullet meant for him. This fits the unfortunate pattern of the terrible fate of Apollonia. The need to keep business and emotion separate is demonstrated in the most brutal way, making Mary and Vincent's dangerous romance bad for business.

Michael's reason for thinking of Mary and Vincent's romance as dangerous is possibly based more on his mourning for the unfortunate death of Apollonia. The killing of Mary had nothing to do with her romance with Vincent. And, as we've seen, the genetic and family arguments against incest are not without their weakness.

Michael's prohibition of Mary and Vincent's "dangerous" relationship might be based on utilitarian reasoning and his worry that it will be bad for the family business. It might also only be that Michael is pining for Apollonia. Nevertheless, *all* of these concerns may be unfounded. Perhaps (yet another) cut of *The Godfather Part III* would present Mary and Vincent's romance as relatively safe and acceptable.

# 26
# Is the Godfather Wise?

MATTHEW HAMMERTON

Suppose that Don Vito Corleone was *your* "Godfather." Anytime you faced a difficult life choice, and wanted wise counsel, you could pick up the phone and seek his advice. Would you do so? Is he a source of wisdom that you would tap? Many people would apparently answer in the affirmative.

A quick search online reveals several dozen popular articles, lists, and blogposts with titles like "10 wisest Don Corleone Quotes," "Spiritual Wisdom from *The Godfather*," and "Some Wisdom of Don Corleone." Given the Godfather's reputation for shrewd, discerning judgment, this association with wisdom is unsurprising. Yet, we might wonder whether shrewd judgment alone is enough to be truly wise. Furthermore, we might wonder whether the Godfather's life choices—particularly the decision to pursue criminal enterprise—are consistent with being wise.

## What Is Wisdom?

Wisdom is an exalted ideal. Who wouldn't want to be wise? And short of that, who wouldn't want to have a wise person to consult when making important life decisions? But what exactly is wisdom? Philosophers have had much to say about this topic. This is unsurprising as the word "philosophy" originates from the Greek words for love (philia) and wisdom (sophia), suggesting that philosophers are lovers of wisdom. There is broad consensus among philosophers that knowing how to live well is the key feature of being wise. Therefore, a good working definition of wisdom is "knowing how to live well."

Does Don Corleone know how to live well? Maybe. The answer depends on what this involves. The philosopher Robert Nozick gives the following plausible account:

> What a wise person needs to know and understand constitutes a varied list: the most important goals and values of life—the ultimate goal, if there is one; what means will reach these goals without too great a cost; what kinds of dangers threaten the achieving of these goals; how to recognize and avoid or minimize these dangers; what different types of human beings are like in their actions and motives (as this presents dangers or opportunities); what is not possible or feasible to achieve (or avoid); how to tell what is appropriate when; knowing when certain goals are sufficiently achieved; what limitations are unavoidable and how to accept them; how to improve oneself and one's relationships with others or society; knowing what the true and unapparent value of various things is; when to take a long-term view; knowing the variety and obduracy of facts, institutions, and human nature; understanding what one's real motives are; how to cope and deal with the major tragedies and dilemmas of life, and with the major good things too. (*The Examined Life*, p. 269)

The first item on Nozick's list—knowing the most important goals and values of life—is the one that might cause us the most trouble. We can all agree that this is important for living well. However, when it comes to the question of what the most important goals and values of life are, there is widespread disagreement. So, let's put this question aside for now.

The rest of Nozick's list is an articulation of what philosophers call "instrumental rationality"—the ability to choose the best means for achieving your ends. Don Corleone is a master of this aspect of living well. He has an uncanny ability to find, in any circumstance, the best course of action for getting what he wants. He does this by skillfully calculating what's at stake, what risks are involved, and what outcomes are achievable.

This involves numerous other skills. He's an astute judge of the character and motives of others, which he uses to ascertain when someone will be useful to him and when they pose a threat. He appreciates the value of different kinds of relationships and maintains an inner circle of trusted family and confidants while preserving, as much as possible, good relations with those outside. He understands the inner workings of civic institutions and knows how to make use of them and how to work around them. He is realistic about the limitations he faces and knows how to strategically "play a long game," biding his time until the right moment comes. He is honest with himself about his own strengths and weaknesses, which enables him to learn from his mistakes and to receive frank feedback from his close confidants (rather than be told whatever he wants to hear). Finally, he knows how to deal with the major tragedies of life; how to process setbacks and grieve losses without becoming debilitated by them or swept up in unproductive emotions like vengefulness.

We see these skills in one of *The Godfather*'s early scenes. As the Corleone family hosts their daughter's wedding reception, some men are spotted outside taking down the number plates of the guests' parked cars. The eldest son, Sonny Corleone, aggressively confronts them and is flashed an FBI badge. He then struggles to control himself and, after shouting a few obscenities, makes his way back to the wedding. Meanwhile, we are told that, although the FBI surveillance was perceived as an indignity, the Don was not angry as he had already anticipated that the FBI might do this and so had advised his intimate friends to attend the wedding in automobiles that could not be traced back to them. We are further told that, although the Don disapproved of his son's angry outburst, he immediately recognized that it served a useful purpose. It would cause the FBI agents to wrongly conclude that their surveillance was unexpected and unprepared for (Mario Puzo, *The Godfather*, p. 16).

Here we see the foresight, poise, and strategic nous of Don Corleone. In a situation where many would act sub-optimally, he is able to anticipate, plan ahead, and find the best course of action.

More generally, it is helpful to contrast the Don's skillful instrumental rationality with that of ordinary people. Most of us fail in areas where he excels. We misjudge the motives and character of others, surround ourselves with the wrong people, misunderstand key social and civic institutions, misread available evidence, take a short-term view when we should take a long-term view, mishandle risk, overlook threats, miss opportunities, waste time on futile projects, overestimate our strengths and underestimate our weaknesses, repeat our mistakes, disregard feedback we don't like, and deal poorly with the setbacks and tragedies of life. By being flawed in these ways, we fall short of wisdom.

## The Ultimate Goal of Life

Clearly, many people are unwise because they are instrumentally irrational. However, as Nozick makes clear, having outstanding instrumental rationality is not enough for wisdom. You must also know what ultimately matters in life. It is only when you know both these things—the ends of life and the means to obtain them—that you know how to live well.

So, what ultimately matters in life? There are many answers, each with its own appeal. One answer—hedonism—focuses on pleasure. Perhaps what matters most most in life is experiencing pleasure and avoiding pain and everything else matters only insofar as it contributes to this.

Another answer—preferentialism—focuses on satisfying your preferences. Perhaps what matters most in life is that you get what you want, even when that is different from what gives you most pleasure. To live well is to have your desires and the world match up as much as possible.

Many find these answers too permissive because they imply that *anything* you want or take pleasure in is valuable for you. Imagine someone who strongly desires, and gets immense pleasure from, cavorting in the pigsty with pigs, or being in a heroin induced stupor, or torturing kittens. Would a life filled with these depraved activities really be a good life? Many will say "No."

This leads to a third answer, which we can call the "reflective endorsement view." Perhaps to live well is to live in accordance with the values that you would endorse upon sustained, sober reflection. Suppose that such reflection leads *you* to most value creativity, community, and spirituality, but leads *me* to most value knowledge, self-autonomy, and achievement. In that case, each of us does best to pursue these divergent values for ourselves, even when their pursuit does not correspond with what we want or find most pleasurable. Thus, although a heroin addict might get a desired buzz of pleasure from their next hit, this activity may, nonetheless, be bad for them because they wouldn't reflectively endorse it. This shows how the "reflective endorsement view" can do better than hedonism and preferentialism when it comes to depraved tastes. However, it is not entirely convincing. Couldn't someone deeply committed to sadism find that, even after sober reflection, they still endorse the thrill of torturing kittens?

Philosophers classify the above answers (hedonism, preferentialism, and reflective endorsement) as types of "subjectivism" because they each make what has value in our lives depend on the subjective *thoughts* and *feelings* we have. The problem of depraved tastes pushes us towards a different kind of answer that philosophers call "objectivism."

Perhaps some things are objectively valuable in *all* lives regardless of what anyone thinks or feels. For example, perhaps friendship is essential to living well and thus a hermit is living poorly even if he finds solace in his isolation and would prefer to keep it that way. Other potential objective goods include love, knowledge, health, achievement, the appreciation of beauty, moral virtue, self-autonomy, having and raising children, creative activity, intellectual activity, and spirituality. Whatever the correct list of objective goods is, other things can only matter in our lives by contributing to these goods.

Almost everyone will find some of the goods listed above appealing. However, objectivists believe that there is a single correct list of the goods that matter, and yet cannot agree on what that list is. This naturally raises the concern of what could justify and ground such a list. What makes it the case that friendship is good for its own sake, even for those who don't care for it? Can appealing to fundamental facts about human nature justify this claim? Is there a realm of normative truths that we have intuitive access to? Philosophical defenders of objectivism have attempted to provide answers. However, many remain unconvinced and are driven back to subjectivism.

## The Godfather's Values

How does the Godfather fare by these philosophical standards of what has value in life? If the best thinkers on this topic can't agree on what has ultimate value in life, then it is unlikely that others can come to know these truths. Thus, basing your life on a single, contested, view of what has value seems risky and unwise. A better strategy, given our normative uncertainty, is to look for ways of living that do reasonably well by all the leading accounts of what is good in life. In other words, we should seek lives that are pleasurable, give us what we want, can be reflectively endorsed, and are filled with the kinds of goods proposed by objectivists. In practice, this is not easy to do. However, techniques like cultivating your pleasures and preferences to better match what you reflectively endorse can help.

Does Don Corleone do reasonably well by all accounts of what has value in life? At first glance he does. He has genuine loving relationships with his family members, significant friendships, a thorough knowledge of the world he inhabits, substantial achievements, reasonably good health (although his line of work sometimes puts this in jeopardy), self-direction, and creative flair and intellectual acumen for his line of business. He also potentially has spirituality (his family are devoted Catholics) and a refined appreciation of beauty (his home and office display some fine pieces of art). However, it is unclear whether these are the product of genuine spiritual and aesthetic sensibilities or are merely a calculated form of image management. Finally, he seems to want these things in his life, take pleasure in them, and reflectively endorse them.

However, missing from this picture, is one of the most commonly proposed objective goods—moral virtue. And, it is here that serious questions can be raised about Don Corleone's knowledge of what has value in life. By the standards of conventional morality (not to mention, almost all philosophical ethical theories) Don Corleone is a bad person. His willingness to kill, maim, bribe, threaten, and intimidate to get his way makes him highly unethical. Insofar as being a morally good person is part of living well, the Don fundamentally fails, in this respect, to live a good life.

Not everyone will be convinced by this argument. If you are a subjectivist who thinks that what ultimately matters in life is pleasure, or satisfying preferences, or reflectively endorsing your values, then moral virtue is unnecessary for living well. In your view, if the Don's unethical conduct serves his subjective ends, it enhances rather than diminishes the quality of his life.

In any case, you might argue that Don Corleone has a kind of moral virtue, just not the kind that is recognized or appreciated in the circles that most of us inhabit. After all, he is *not* an archetypal villain driven by malice and egomania. Instead, he is guided by a moral code that prizes honor, loyalty, accomplishment, and restraint. For the Don, his family and his honor come first and would never be sold out for money or power. His long-term goal is to "legitimize" his family business and, although he has no qualms employing strategic violence, he is against its indiscriminate, disproportionate, or reckless use. Even though we reject his moral code, we may respect that he is a man of principle and even find ourselves, as viewers, sympathizing with his character. Film critics often cite this switch (to a protagonist who is less repulsive and more relatable) as the main way *The Godfather* broke with earlier Hollywood gangster films and reinvigorated the genre.

Most moral philosophers reject the idea that someone like Don Corleone, who draws his ethics from an Old-World patriarchal honor culture, could be genuinely virtuous. They argue that some forms of conduct are objectively wrong, even if they are accepted in certain cultures and traditions (after all, isn't slavery objectively wrong even though many historical cultures permitted it?) Nonetheless, "moral relativism" remains popular in the broader culture, and if you are drawn to it then it is natural to think of Don Corleone as virtuous because the moral code he has inherited condones his conduct.

Where does this leave us? Well, the Godfather clearly exhibits *most* of the traits needed for wisdom. If you are willing to accept moral relativism, or subjectivism about living well then you can go further and say that he knows *everything* a wise person needs to know. Otherwise, you must hold that he falls short of wisdom because of the dubious moral code he follows.

## The Wheel of Virtue

Suppose that your verdict, after thinking through the various arguments, is that Don Corleone is wise. In fact, you see him as an exemplar of wisdom within his world. It can then be instructive to compare his wisdom to the abilities, knowledge, and temperament of his four sons. Each son, as a potential successor, seeks to emulate his father's wisdom. Yet, each seems to fall short in his own way.

Sonny Corleone, the Don's eldest son, is hotheaded and impulsive. Although his confidence and chutzpah make him a natural leader and win him several battles, his rashness and strategic ineptness eventually cause his downfall.

The second son, Fredo Corleone, is foolish, clumsy, and neurotic. These traits cause him to mishandle the low-key assignments he is given, enter an ill-advised marriage, and eventually ruin his life by stupidly betraying his family. When it comes to wisdom, he is the antithesis of his father.

The third son, Michael Corleone, unlike his elder brothers, approximates the instrumental rationality of his father. He is shrewd, cunning, and strategically adept. However, he fails to be the principled man that his father is and his pursuit of power and dominance eventually overrides everything, including family and honor. Even by relative standards, he is not virtuous. Indeed, the bitterness and guilt that we occasionally glimpse is proof that he cannot reflectively endorse the values he has lived by. In this respect, he fails to be wise.

It is the family's adopted son, Tom Hagen, who best approximates the wisdom of Don Corleone. Like Michael, he is sharp, calculating, and strategically adept. However, unlike Michael, he stays moored to the value system of Don Corleone and puts family and honor above power and money. Perhaps he would have been the best successor as "Godfather." However, instead, as Michael takes charge of the family, Tom is removed as consigliere. The reasons for this are somewhat opaque. One possibility is that, as Michael says, Tom is "not a wartime consigliere" and lacks the audacity and grit that the family needs in that moment. Alternatively, perhaps as a non-Sicilian, he will always be an outsider in the world of the five families. Tom's failure to grasp fully his standing in the family appears to reflect a limitation of his own wisdom.

The contrasts that we see among these characters are an example of, what the philosopher Noël Carroll calls, "the wheel of virtue." According to Carroll, narrative art (novels, films, and plays) typically contain

> a studied array of characters who both correspond and contrast with each other along the dimension of a certain virtue or package of virtues—where some of the characters possess the virtue in question, or nearly so, or part of it, while others possess the virtue, but only defectively, or not at all, even to such an extent that their lack of the virtue in question amounts to the vice that corresponds to the virtue.

And this makes narrative art morally instructive because it

> prompts the audience to apply concepts of virtue and vice to the characters, thus exercising and sharpening their ability to recognize instances of these otherwise often vaguely defined or highly abstract concepts. ("The Wheel of Virtue," pp. 12–14)

In *The Godfather*, the virtue of wisdom is the best candidate for a virtue that plays this thematic role. However, unlike classic literature, where a wholesome hero models the relevant virtue for us, *The Godfather* leaves us with an uneasy feeling as we struggle to square the putative wisdom of Don Corleone with his role as the head of a criminal enterprise.

## The Last Word

Earlier, we praised Don Corleone's insight into his own character and motives. Possessing the virtue of self-awareness is surely one aspect of being wise. Yet, Mark Winegardner, who was selected to write a third "Godfather" novel (*The Godfather Returns*) after Mario Puzo's death, interprets the Godfather as falling short on this aspect of wisdom. He writes:

> Vito Corleone often said that every man has but one destiny. His own life was a powerful contradiction of his own cherished aphorism. Yes, he fled Sicily when men came to kill him. Yes, when a young neighborhood tough named Pete Clemenza asked him to hide a cache of guns, Vito had little choice but to comply. And, yes, when Vito committed his first crime in America, the theft of an expensive rug, he

thought at the time that he was just helping Clemenza move it. All of these things had found him. This is not unusual. Bad things find everyone. Some might call this destiny. Others might call it chance. Tomato, tomahto. But Vito's involvement in his next crimes "hijacking trucks along with Clemenza and another young tough from Hell's Kitchen by the name of Tessio" had been a willful act. When they invited Vito to join their band of thieves, he could have said no. Saying yes, choosing to become a predatory criminal, sent him down one path. Saying no would have sent him down another, perhaps a family business his three sons would have been able to join without first becoming murderers. Vito was a skillful, intuitive mathematician, a brilliant assessor of probability, and a man of vision. Believing in something as irrational and unimaginative as destiny was out of character. It was beneath him. Still, what human being is above rationalizing the worst thing he ever did? Who among us, if directly and indirectly responsible for the killing of hundreds of people, including one of his own children, might not tell himself a lie, *something* that, unexamined, might even seem profound? (*The Godfather Returns*, pp. 21–22)

On Winegardner's retelling, Don Corleone is not as principled as we thought. Deep down, he knows that his conduct is immoral (and thus has the moral knowledge needed for wisdom). However, rather than acknowledging this uncomfortable truth, he has succumbed to a major self-delusion and rationalized away the unethical aspects of his life. This, in turn, diminishes his instrumental rationality (self-delusions impede rational decision-making) and ultimately his wisdom.

However, you don't have to buy Winegardner's version of events. Maybe Don Corleone has *not* swallowed some self-serving drivel about destiny, and he only expounds it to others because he has calculated that doing so best serves his ends. Furthermore, maybe his choices were starker than Winegardner presents them. Maybe it was hijack trucks or go back to being an impoverished member of the immigrant underclass. And maybe, once modest success came his way, getting out of the crime business was too dangerous as associates and rivals, concerned about his insider knowledge, would have quietly eliminated him as soon as his stepped away. Or, maybe not. As with the best narrative art, there's much room for interpretation here. The last word, as reader, viewer, and fan, is yours.

# 27
# Connie's Nietzschean Transformations

RAYMOND ANGELO BELLIOTTI

Throughout the *Godfather* trilogy, Constanzia ("Connie") Corleone transforms from an innocent bride (in the opening of *The Godfather*) to a promiscuous, prodigal daughter (in *The Godfather Part II*) to a family conciliator (later in *The Godfather Part II*) to the iron surrogate leader of the family (in *The Godfather Part III*).

At first blush, Connie's radical conversions seem inexplicably capricious or desperately contrived for theatrical effect. Who undergoes such transformations in the real world or even within the confines of three movies covering only a few decades? As is the case with numerous seemingly arbitrary or artificial phenomena, however, the work of master psychologist and philosopher Friedrich Nietzsche (1844–1900) can help us explain, understand, and analyze Connie's sweeping dispositional changes.

## Nietzsche's Three Metamorphoses and Quest for Perfection

Nietzsche's philosophy pertains most closely to Connie's biographical arc in its depictions of the human quest for perfection and the process of the "three metamorphoses" defining human self-creation.

Nietzsche is clear that "all great things bring about their own destruction through an act of self-overcoming; thus, the law of life will have it, the law of the necessity of 'self-overcoming' in the nature of life" (*Genealogy of Morals*, III, sec. 27). Nietzsche is not a perfectionist in the sense that he believes that human nature is perfectible, that most human beings will maximize their higher potentials, or that there is one final goal to which all human beings should aspire or even that human beings can attain a final goal or constitute a finished product; but he is a perfectionist in a more modest sense.

Nietzsche's perfectionism is individualistic and aristocratic. As such, he does not intend that his normative message be embraced by everyone. In fact, he speaks only to the few who have the potential to understand fully the tragic nature of life yet affirm life in all its dimensions.

The crucial ingredients that define higher human beings, for Nietzsche, are the capability of enduring great suffering and turning it to practical advantage; the impulse to exert high energy and enthusiasm into projects requiring uncommon creativity; and full participation in the ongoing process of personal construction, deconstruction, re-imagination, and re-creation. For the greatest among us, our paramount artistic project is crafting a grand self. This ongoing process marks the progress of those brandishing what I call a robust will to power (*Jesus or Nietzsche*, pp. 126–131). To prepare to even approximate a higher human type, we must pass through three metamorphoses of discipline, defiance, and creation.

The disciplined human spirit, like a camel, flees into the desert to bear enormous burdens (the process of social construction); the defiant spirit, like a lion, must transform itself into a master, a conqueror who releases its own freedom by destroying traditional prohibitions (the process of deconstruction of and liberation from the past); but the lion cannot create new values, so the spirit must transform itself into a creative child, whose playful innocence, ability to forget, and enthusiasm for challenging games signals the spirit's willing its own will (the processes of re-imagination and recreation) (Nietzsche, *Thus Spoke Zarathustra*, Part I, "On the Three Metamorphoses"). This describes the full process of Nietzschean becoming—recurrent personal construction, deconstruction, re-imagination, and re-creation—the virtues of the grand striver who embodies a staunch will to power.

Distinguishing healthy self-overcoming from unhealthy self-destruction is critical to understanding Nietzsche's pro- ject. Self-destruction arises from psychological neurosis and grave insecurities, self-contempt, and repressed hostilities. Such unworthy motivations contaminate the later stages of re-imagination and re-creation. On the contrary, according to Nietzsche, self-overcoming arises from worthy motivations and is required for self-aggrandizement, not self-destruction. Nature and life are dialectical forces, and the value of the self lies primarily in its ability to transcend itself in tacit recognition of the contingency of the world of Becoming. Because the world is in a continuous state of flux, truculent adherence to a fixed self-understanding will interfere with the fundamental project of human life.

But no project, however successful, can complete the self once and forever. Our lives, instructs Nietzsche, are processes that end only with death or from that moment when we lose the basic human capabilities required for self-making. Until then, we should view ourselves as elegant artists whose greatest creations are the selves we continue to refine. Thus, growth, expansion, and accumulation—the increased power we realize as will to power engages us with life—animates Nietzsche's perfectionist ideal. Unlike Sisyphus, who was condemned to endure a tedious, stagnant task, human beings fueled by will to power can realize increased strength, process values, and undeniable progress in their quest toward self-perfection.

The three metamorphoses are most keenly experienced by those embodying a robust will to power, those who strive grandly along the path of self-perfection. Most human beings remain comfortably within the orderly confines of relatively static self-understandings. For example, one of Nietzsche's foils is the "last man," whom he describes as the most contemptible and despicable type of human being. Last men exert themselves minimally and avoid suffering to the greatest possible extent. They are shallow, narrow egalitarians, who pursue a superficial happiness that extinguishes their possibilities for intense love, creation, longing, striving, and excellence. The highest ambitions of last men are contentment and security. They are the extreme case of the herd mentality: habit, custom, indolence, egalitarianism, self-preservation, and muted will to power prevail. Last men embody none of the inner tensions and conflicts that spur transformative action: they take no risks, lack convictions, avoid experimentation, and seek only bland survival. The terms "last man" and "three metamorphoses" enter the same sentence only to signal contrast. But the last man lives the longest. He is as eradicable as the "flea beetle." For Nietzsche, this is feeble consolation.

## Connie's Nietzschean Journey

During the movie trilogy, Connie Corleone demonstrates amplified will to power as she undertakes a nonlinear adventure in self-creation rendered comprehensible by Nietzsche's three metamorphoses.

In *Part I*, Connie, the pampered, youngest Corleone sibling, is physically and emotionally abused by her opportunistic husband, Carlo Rizzi. When Michael orders Carlo's death because of his role in the murder of Santino ("Sonny"), Connie is the hysterical, betrayed sister riling at Michael's violence. Connie confronts her brother accusatorily. Convinced Michael has ordered the murder of her husband, Connie's outrage is palpable through her tears. Michael, at once condescending and consoling, neither confirms nor denies her allegations. Instead, he coolly embraces his sister, and then dispatches her to see a physician. The film invites the impression that Connie is irreparably alienated from Michael.

The novel concludes differently. There Connie, within a week, reconciles with Michael after apologizing to him for her accusations and assuring Kay that they were unfounded. No explanation is offered for why Connie changes course so rapidly. Surely, she still recognizes that Michael had given the order to kill Carlo. More likely, she concludes that Carlo's death was justified or at least excusable given his role in Santino's murder, as well as his abuse of her. In any event, in the novel, Connie remarries in less than a year to an Italian American graduate of a prestigious business school (Puzo, *The Godfather*, pp. 441–42). Readers are left with the impression that Connie has reconfigured her life, accepted reality, and discovered domestic tranquility, an impression that the movie trilogy obliterates.

Our introduction to Connie locates her as a Nietzschean camel: bearing heavy burdens as a dutiful daughter and compliant wife, family orientations moderating conflicts between a nineteenth-century tribal Sicilian ethos and twentieth- century American individualism (Belliotti, *The Godfather and Sicily*, 39–49). Shrouded from vibrant public enterprises, Connie is fully immersed in the private sphere of kinship. Her complacent socialization is shattered by Carlo's abuse, Sonny's violent reaction, Sonny's murder, and Michael's revenge on Carlo. Connie's comfortable certitude in established social roles dissolves, as this series of events undermines the security of the uneasy truce between the Sicilian ethos and American individualism. The Sicilian ethos decrees that family members must not connive against, much less murder, their relatives. Connie's value system, hitherto a source of order, crumbles. She becomes radically alienated from her family and from her social role. Moreover, she yearns to retaliate against Michael, whom she regards as the architect of her distress.

Unfortunately, Connie does not deconstruct her self-understanding in the spirit of a Nietzschean lion. Instead, she spirals into self-destruction. Irrationally striving to hurt Michael by harming herself—after all, the Sicilian ethos elevated family identity not solely individual attainments—and mired in self-contempt and disdain for old ways, Connie plummets into a counter-productive caricature of hedonist living from which no honor or salutary power results.

Worse, she seemingly abandons her children. Predictably, from a Nietzschean standpoint, Connie's self-destruction poisons her attempts at personal re-creation. Although her suffering fosters rebellions against her past socialization, promotes declarations of independence, and spurs repudiations of familial obligations and values, Connie's self-destructive frenzy arises from unworthy, counterproductive motivations: resentment, hostility, and contempt of self and others. Rather than artfully fashioning practical advantage from grievous suffering, Constanzia Corleone circles into an existential abyss.

Later in *Part II*, Connie's pivotal moment of self-discovery — her epiphany—appears to be the death of her mother. Both of her parents are now dead; she has stepped up in the turnstile of mortality; her own death is no longer an abstraction from which she can bracket her concern; Michael's marriage is asunder; he and Fredo are divided; Connie's sense of loss and lack of sustaining intimacy intensify. Most important, she recalls the strength and love of her father. Connie is jarred back to her past. If she is to reconnect to the security, order, and affection that once nourished her, Connie must reaffirm the family. From a Nietzschean perspective, Connie, severed by calamitous family events from her previously unworthy motivations, attempts to re-create her self-understanding by refining the nineteenth-century tribal Sicilian ethos.

Still confined to the private sphere, Connie undertakes a project of familial reconciliation. She counsels Kay, whose marriage to Michael has disintegrated, and conspires with Kay, behind Michael's back, to visit the estranged couple's children. After the death of her mother, Carmela, Connie reconciles with Michael, forgives him, and appreciates the obligations he has incurred as family patriarch. She offers to care for Michael and his children after his divorce from Kay, and beseeches him to forgive their bumbling, traitorous brother, Fredo. Connie meanders back to her roots, older and wiser. The result, however, bears mixed tidings: Michael freezes Kay out of his life, orders the murder of his brother, while welcoming Connie back into his fond graces.

*Part III* opens with Connie presiding over the celebration of Michael's induction ceremony in the (fictionized) order of St. Sebastian. Connie orchestrates communal vocalizing of "Eh, Cumpari!," Julius LaRosa's adaption in 1953 of an Italian folk song. Her efforts are coarsely interrupted by the menacing presence of Joey Zasa and his henchman, Anthony ("The Ant") Squigliaro. Viewers soon learn that Connie's presence, however, extends far beyond that of matriarchal overseer of family festivities. She champions the interests of her nephew, Vincenzo Mancini; she boldly advises and evaluates Michael's judgments and actions; and operates generally as an unofficial *consigliere*. She has not merely reaffirmed family values, but also transformed her role within its structure. Nietzschean re-creation has occurred.

Tom Hagan, Sonny, and Fredo have all died. B.J. Harrison is little more than a financial and legal advisor, and Al Neri, who has risen from soldier to chief of security to *caporegime* and, possibly, to underboss, cannot fulfill two crucial positions. Thus, an official *consigliere* is absent. Michael is deeply ambivalent, often indecisive, suffering from diabetes, and flirting with a redemption that he can never realize (pp. 115–163). Although not fully in public view, Connie is now operating in the public arena, scheming against the family's perceived enemies, making decisions while Michael is incapacitated by a diabetic stroke, repeating the falsehood that Fredo drowned accidentally, and exerting, yes, robust will to power. She has attained the mindset that distinguished her father: guiltless embrace of necessity and celebration of destiny.

In *Part III*, Connie's transformation is striking. She becomes the iron surrogate leader of the family. Plagued by self-doubt and guilt, Michael seeks redemption. Connie perceives Vincenzo Mancini, Sonny's illegitimate son, as the future leader of the clan. As Michael struggles with illness, uncertainty, and heightened vulnerability, Connie orders Vincent to slay the obnoxious Joey Zasa and hatches future murderous schemes. In the end, Connie is much less conflicted than Michael. Connie becomes the camouflaged head of the family who orchestrates the passing of power to her nephew, Vincent. She rebukes Michael when she learns he has confessed his sins to Cardinal Lamberto and peddles the fiction that Fredo died from an accidental drowning. Creating comforting illusions and alternate realties as a reverse form of gaslighting, however, provides Michael no succor. She confides to Vincent Mancini that he is "the only one left in this family with my father's strength." Connie's transformation as a shadow don may well be the most surprising aspect of *Part III*.

Old-world subordination has morphed into new-world female empowerment. Connie even fashions a plan to kill her godfather, the treacherous Don Altobello, by poisoning her birthday gift to him—cannolis, of course—which the aged patriarch consumes during the opera in Palermo. Constanzia Corleone, beginning as a symbol of new-world ethnic princess, ends as perhaps the most ruthless, cold-blooded killer and conniver in the Corleone family. Connie's will to power sparkles as she fashions herself as an even fiercer offshoot of her father (pp. 159–161).

What spawned this Nietzschean transformation? The film trilogy does not spell out the answer, but several vectors are suggested. First, the transformations within Michael, from gelid racketeer to wavering, aging, ill patriarch demand a response from those closest to him. Second, Connie longs for the clarity, security, and affection, all wrapped in understated power, brandished by their deceased father. Michael can no longer trigger that recipe. Third, Michael's profound guilt and stunning vacillations generate a power void. The likes of Zasa, Altobello, and Italian *pezzonovante*, Licio Lucchesi all sense the vacuum and connive to fill it. Fourth, Connie is older, more experienced in the ways of the world, and stronger than in her earlier years. She exemplifies the Italian adage that generously predates Nietzsche: *Ciò che non mi distrugge mi rende più forte* ("What does not destroy me makes me stronger").

The Corleone family requires a savior. Connie steps forward, employing Vincent as her instrument of vengeance and restoration. In Nietzschean fashion, Connie has, finally, deconstructed her self-image and value system, and reimagined and re-created herself as a late-twentieth century version of her father. She acts as a parent to Vincent Mancini and even to Michael in certain respects, scolding him for confessing his transgressions to a stranger and defending her decision to order Vincent to whack Joey Zasa. Connie reminds Michael of the value of being feared, to which he responds, "Maybe, they should fear *you!*" Of course, they should.

Connie has reinvented herself: returning to *la via vecchia* ("the old way") but in an entirely new role. Her will to power glistens. We must imagine Nietzsche approving, at least insofar as we focus only on Connie's will to power. She manifests a strong visceral connection to and a maximally affirmative attitude toward life. Connie has swallowed all doubts and misgivings, evincing the dispositions of a guiltless grand striver. Her creative energies have returned, her ability to command has emerged, and her resolve has steeled.

Still, the family business remains disreputable and countless of Connie's first-order desires are immoral. This illustrates that possessing and exerting a robust will to power is, at most, only a necessary but far from a sufficient condition of living a fulfilling human life.

## Nietzschean Happiness and Connie's Future

Surprisingly, in *Part III*, Connie Corleone, at least prior to the final scenes, achieves a distinctively Nietzschean version of happiness. To understand that connection, we must distinguish Nietzschean happiness from a more common understanding.

For Nietzsche, popular notions of happiness, grounded in attaining a predominately positive state of mind, are mistaken in that they aspire to eliminate or minimize resistance and suffering, both of which are required for increased power and strength which are in turn required for higher human beings to make progress toward Nietzsche's perfectionist ideal. Robust will to power does not will the overcoming of all resistance or the attainment of a fixed, final serenity. An enduring contentment in which nothing remains to be desired would, at best, generate suffocating boredom and, at worst, prefigure the last gasps of will to power. For Nietzsche, the ongoing desire to engage in challenging activity defines a robust will to power. The difficulty of satisfying a first-order desire adds to its value.

Accordingly, overcoming grave obstacles and defeating stiff resistances are critical to "the feeling that power is growing." More power, greater proficiency, and accelerated self-revision are the hallmarks of Nietzschean happiness. As such, worthwhile happiness is not the attainment of a particular state or enduring condition; instead, it is experienced and deepened in the exercise of will to power. Thus, suffering greatly while confronting and overcoming major obstacles and resistances is critical to worthwhile happiness. Nietzschean happiness is not a particular state or condition to be achieved, but an ongoing activity distinguished by increased power that is accompanied by the feeling that power is growing. In this manner, the feelings of happiness are connected to value because they arise from the continual activity of salutary exertions of will to power.

All such features inform Connie's transformation in *Part III*. Thus, although Connie does not attain the common understanding of happiness as a predominantly positive state of mind (for example, enduring peace, abiding contentment, final self-satisfaction, or prevailing pleasure), she exercises robust will to power while encountering daunting challenges, thereby experiencing increased power and strength. We must imagine Nietzsche smiling.

Still, life remains tragic: its greatest value is in the process of participating in a grand serious of contests; in sculpting one's soul; in waging a glorious struggle in full knowledge that final, fixed success is unattainable; and, ultimately, in perishing in service to one's highest values. In Nietzsche's view, the greatest among us will not only endure all of this but love it. This captures Nietzsche's highest value, *amor fati* ("love of fate"), a maximally affirmative attitude toward life in all its dimensions (*Ecce Homo*, "Why I Am So Clever," section 10; *The Gay Science*, section 276.

Nietzsche insists that the three metamorphoses are recurrent. At the conclusion of *Part III*, Connie has not attained final serenity or a fixed self-understanding. How might she deconstruct, re-imagine, and re-make her identity in the future?

The attempted murder of Michael and slaying of Mary on the steps of Teatro Massimo in Palermo should generate self- interrogation and self-evaluation. Might Connie feel guilty over her role in the escalating violence? Might she recognize the venality of her past and seek redemption in like fashion to Michael? Or might the treachery of enemies to the Corleone family deepen her resolve and lure her further into criminal enterprises? After all, Vincent survives, and he has been anything but ambivalent about restoring the family's preeminence.

Or might Connie craft a third way between apology and remorse for past transgressions, and thorough immersion in criminality? Unless *The Godfather Part IV* materializes, the answers to such questions must forever remain a mystery.

# 28
# Silkroad Traditions and American Tragedy

Matthew Crippen and Iris Hiu Man Yeung

Pretty much all of us have argued with our elders. This amounts to a kind of culture clash because our conventions are rarely the same as our parents'. Going back to the Medieval era and farther, philosophers have likewise engaged in intergenerational and intercultural exchanges, for example, with St. Thomas Aquinas debating and building on older ideas from the Islamic world. *The Godfather* movies get at something close to this, exploring divergences between individuals born in different centuries on opposite sides of the Atlantic.

Based primarily on Mario Puzo's 1969 novel, the first two movies revolve around father and son, Vito and Michael Corleone. Vito—who likes to be called Godfather—spent his early years in Sicily, fleeing a vendetta as a child and relocating to the US at the very beginning of the twentieth century. There, he wed Carmela, also of Sicilian stock, having four children, including his last-born son Michael, who is destined to head the family. While retaining some of Vito's Old-World ways, Michael is Americanized. He marries Kay, a New Hampshire woman. His management style is more corporate than his father's, and the Corleone family enters increasingly into the American world of big business, for instance, acquiring Las Vegas casino holdings.

The *Godfather* movies accordingly supply an elegy to the decay of older Sicilian ideologies as they're supplanted by the customs of a brash young America. But Sicily itself has a complex history. It was Arabized under Muslim rule in the Middle Ages. In this same period, it was part of a larger political jurisdiction that included North Africa. Going back to ancient Rome, moreover, Sicily was a hub on Silkroad routes through places like Iran, India, and China, not to mention Africa. These regions not only traded goods, but likely ideas as well. Consequently, it's unsurprising that the values advanced by Old-World characters like Vito converge with philosophies that developed along the Silkroad.

Silkroad mindsets tend to stress interconnectivity, whereas mainstream American attitudes lay heavier weight on individualism. The first movie opens during the wedding of Vito's daughter, thereby emphasizing family. On this day, Vito grants favors to people in the larger Italian community on the provision that they may be asked for a small service in the future, showing that he regards social and business relations as tightly knotted.

Concern for family also leads his youngest son into crime, but Michael's purpose rapidly orients towards building individual power within the underworld kingdom he inherits from his father, all at the expense of family. This condemns him to loneliness. Michael tries to resuscitate relations with estranged loved-ones in the last movie, but too late since the final scene shows him in Sicily reminiscing about family members sacrificed to business, just before he dies of old-age in solitude in the land of his father.

## Greco-Italian-American Tragedies

Obviously, no *Godfather* character gets close to what any reasonable ethicist would applaud. But Vito's code at least retains some moral orthodoxy because it's geared towards providing for his family. To the extent that a worthy personality trait provokes his fall into crime, the *Godfather* movies mirror the tragic literature of ancient Greece, which was geographically and culturally close to Sicily.

As with many others, Vito's fundamental morality derives from his mother. But unlike most of us, he's centrally shaped by one catastrophic event: his mom's death. The scenario is that the local Mafia chieftain, Don Ciccio, had her husband and eldest son murdered, leading her to go and beg for Vito's life. The Don refuses, saying the boy will grow up to seek revenge, prompting Vito's mother to threaten the man with a knife while screaming for her son to run. She takes a shotgun blast to her chest, which Vito witnesses. Her sacrifice for family impresses itself upon him, as does a second lesson: the importance of respect, which is what allows Don Ciccio to get men to do his bidding.

Vito takes the first lesson—protecting family—to heart. After the ordeal with his mother, he flees across the Atlantic to

New York City, making it his new home, eventually marrying Carmela and starting a family. Initially supporting them with a job at a grocery shop, he rapidly learns it's difficult to earn a living without social status, more so because the police and courts do not protect the Italian community. This is what allows Don Fanucci—a preening extortionist—to compel the shopkeeper to surrender Vito's job to another. Rather than getting angry, Vito respectfully thanks his tearful boss for being a father figure, saying he won't forget it.

Out of this extremity, Vito falls somewhat reluctantly into burglary with Peter Clemenza and Sal Tessio, only to have Fanucci try to extort money from the three. This is when Vito, after careful planning, kills Fanucci, immediately returning home and telling baby Michael that he loves him, reinforcing that the murder was committed for his family.

Vito is consequently a tragic figure in the vein of the ancient Greek character Oedipus. This is insofar as conventional virtues—love in Vito's case, truth seeking in Oedipus's—instigate the downfall of both. Vito in fact sometimes places family above business and his public status. This happens when he enters a business arrangement he disagrees with and relinquishes vengeance for the murder of his first-born son, Santino ("Sonny") to ensure the safe return of Michael, who's hiding in Sicily.

At a glance, Michael's fall looks similar because he's initially kept from his family's criminal activities, only stooping to murder to stop enemies from finishing off his father, who's recovering from bullet wounds. Soon, however, Michael seeks power at almost any cost. This supplants his wish to protect family, so that he diverges from Greek characters, who typically get in trouble because of good impulses, not bad ones.

The first movie in the trilogy accents the contrast between father and son by starting with Vito presiding at his daughter's wedding and concluding with Michael having her husband killed. As the new head of the family, Michael rules over an almost spiritless age, something reinforced by the rarity with which people call him Godfather. At least until the last movie, Michael would rather be feared than loved, as he topples his father's traditions for the sake of business, a fact emphasized in the concluding scene when the door closes to cut him off from his wife, whom he'll divorce in years to come.

## Sicilians Bearing Gifts

Virgil's *Aeneid* is an epic poem that warns us to beware of Greeks bearing gifts, but its author was actually Roman, dying in the southern part of the Italian peninsula not too far from Sicily. The adage is made in reference to the Trojan Horse that had Greek warriors hidden inside, set to attack after the gift was taken behind enemy walls. The proverb can be construed as a caution against accepting kindnesses from those with ulterior motives. Applied to Vito, however, the meaning is more nuanced. On the one hand, he seems to act with concern when aiding supplicants from the Italian-American community. On the other, he often sees favors as a future investment—a sort of emergency "cache," as Michael says in the novel—that he may call upon in the future. So people should beware of accepting gifts from him.

Gift giving is familiar to almost everyone. But older hospitality-oriented civilizations engage in the practice as an informal mode of economic exchange, which is less common in mainstream America. It's appropriate, then that the movie begins with the fittingly named Amerigo Bonasera, who doesn't comprehend the etiquette of favor-for-favor arrangements. Amerigo laments that he believes in America, which made his fortune, yet failed his family by not punishing men who assaulted his daughter, Maria. He offers money for the slaying of the attackers.

Vito finds this request offensive. One reason is that cash isn't the currency he trades in with supplicants. Another is that he isn't in the murder-for-hire business. A third is that Amerigo doesn't even think to call him Godfather until reminded. He grumbles that Amerigo never sought his advice or friendship in the years they've known one another, despite the fact that his wife is Maria's godmother. In his role as adjudicator and patriarch, Vito expounds temperance, saying that since Amerigo's daughter survived, death is unjust. But Vito agrees to make the attackers suffer after Amerigo pleads, "Be my friend, Godfather," also kissing his hand.

This scene shows that Vito wants to be loved, not just feared. He enjoys small gifts as tokens of respect, like a few free oranges from a street vender, though money is no object. While Vito expects to be able to call upon those he has helped, as when requiring Amerigo to deploy all his skills as a mortician to make the bullet-riddled body of Sonny presentable for the funeral, he demanded this service to avoid further traumatizing his wife, Carmela. So love for others also motivates Vito, who collects this small debt out of tenderness and not for business.

Though we may doubt that Amerigo really sees Vito as a friend, others are genuinely devoted. One such individual is Enzo, who Vito prevented from being deported at the request of the young man's father in-law. Enzo arrives at the hospital with flowers for the recovering Don, who's had his protection detail removed at the command of a corrupt police captain. Michael expects an assassination attempt, urging Enzo to go so that he's not caught in the crossfire. Enzo, despite obvious fear, insists on staying, and with Michael, pretends to be an armed bodyguard, scaring away the would-be attackers. This kind of relationship is key to Vito's way of organizing things and his role as patriarch and adjudicator, which relies on an older currency: genuine bonds.

## Family Ties and Continental Drift

Although favor-for-favor stances may have been indigenous to Sicily, this form of social comportment additionally infuses largely Muslim areas in Western Asia and North Africa. Here, it's worth remembering that Sicily was Arabized under Muslim rule, also connecting to easterly territories like Persia and India via Silkroad trade routes. Though we should be wary of equating views from different parts of the globe, more than one tradition along the Silkroad agreed that we find meaning in things beyond ourselves, a theme echoed by the *Godfather* movies.

The *Bhagavad Gita* is perhaps the most famous text to come out of India and is in the Hindu lineage. The poet Rumi is a widely read Sufi Muslim from Persia, or what is modern-day Iran. Despite their religious differences, both concur that we become more enlightened if we engage in just actions without concern for our personal desires. One reason is that this breaks down boundaries between ourselves and others and ultimately is said to help us merge with the divine, which is equivalent to the cosmos in the *Gita*.

Though Vito's life falls short of the ethical standards of ancient religious texts, his purpose and identity is at least grounded in his commitment to something beyond himself, namely, family. It's appropriate, then, that the setup for the *Gita* and *The Godfather* are similar. The first movie starts with dancing, singing and other wedding festivities. The *Gita's* lead-in (found in a larger book of which it is a part) is similarly a community event with games and a princess selecting husbands. As with *The Godfather*, the *Gita* stresses the importance of social roles, the duties of spouses being a case in point.

India was an intellectual capital and a place where many different religions emerged or met. Persia was likewise a philosophical and scientific powerhouse during the Middle Ages. Persia abutted Arabic- and Turkic-speaking regions. It was also sandwiched between the Indian subcontinent, Europe and

Africa (the latter a center of learning with the world's first two universities). All this was reflected in Rumi's poems, which were written in Persian, Arabic, Turkish, and Greek. Vito likewise is spread between places. After all, he bridges North America and Europe, and Sicily was specifically a place where cultures converged. Together, this suggests a second way of living a cosmic existence: being "cosmopolitan," a word with Greek roots that connotes a citizen of the universe or world.

Drifting farther to the south, Vito's family orientation also resonates with an African tradition, "ubuntu," which is a word, concept and philosophical outlook that stresses metaphysical and moral interconnectedness of humans. Ubuntu additionally emphasizes place, which is key to *The Godfather*, with the Corleones named after Vito's home village in Sicily, albeit due to a misunderstanding with a US border agent. Though unquestionably Sub-Saharan, a few scholars speculate that ubuntu has partial origins in North Africa, which in any case adopts compatible social practices. Among these is the idea that we develop importantly human qualities like language, cooking and religion in group contexts and that it's contradictory to pursue individual wellbeing at the expense of the community since the two entwine.

Ubuntu strongly emphasizes an etiquette of receiving guests, a social grace Vito exhibits at the beginning of *The Godfather*. Vito's home in America was in a residential neighborhood, and there are many scenes—typically set in warmer months—with family members gathering and children playing on the grounds, also in line with ubuntu ideals.

Michael, by contrast, was born and raised in North America and drifts towards isolationist values. His estate is in a remote compound in the country. Family gatherings are rare. This is punctuated by the camera resting on an empty dining room table at one point. Numerous scenes in the second movie, which shows Michael at the height of his power, are also set in cooler months, as if to highlight his lack of warmth. As compared to his father, Michael lives like an elite CEO, segregated from his community.

## Cannoli Crime and Chinese Punishment

The Silkroad went from Mediterranean Europe through India and into China. Ancient Chinese philosophy customarily divides into three major traditions: Confucianism, Daoism and Legalism. This is in addition to a fourth perspective—Buddhism—which percolated into the region from India.

Legalism is the most aggressive of these outlooks, also the most obviously connected to Mafia social structures.

Legalism refers to Chinese political philosophies that came to fruition during the Warring States period, a time of military conflict and governmental consolidation that began around 500 B.C.E. A core idea of Legalism was that people can be made to do anything through reward and punishment, a tactic Tom Hagen illustrates. He does so first by offering favors to the movie director Jack Woltz in exchange for casting Vito's Godson, Johnny Fontane. When this fails, men decapitate Woltz's prize racehorse, so that he awakes with its bloody head in his bed as a gruesome punishment and simultaneously a threat that ends up motivating the behavior the Corleone family wants.

Vito took a similar tack years earlier when trying to get a big band leader to release Johnny Fontane from an unfavorable music contract. He first offered $10,000. After this failed, Vito returned with the notorious Luca Brasi, and got the release for $1000 by assuring the band leader that "either his brains—or his signature—would be on the contract."

Legalists preferred public punishment, regarding it as a lesson to the community. The Corleones sometimes employ the same principle, as when Peter Clemenza and Rocco Lampone forgo the usual practice of disposing of a corpse, instead leaving Paulie's body to be found as a message to other would-be traitors. This scene has the famous line: "Leave the gun. Take the cannoli."

Legalist scholars also advocated that leaders should command inferiors, who then dictate to lower-rank individuals, continuing in this top-down way through the hierarchical chain. This is a further feature that pervades many social structures, including mafia syndicates. Legalists additionally stipulated that penalties for disobedience should be harsh and immediate. Indeed, one ancient text—attributed to Han Fei—suggested that even a hardened criminal will not pick up molten gold because the instantaneous result is severe scalding. Han Fei argued that bad behavior similarly warrants swift pain, and the prompt killing of Paulie mirrors this sentiment.

In some ways, Michael adheres more to Legalist tenets than his father, particularly strictures demanding total obedience, the idea being nobody under the ruler is above the law. Michael acts on this when he has his brother killed for violating his expectations, even though the breach was not fully intentional. By contrast, Vito's commitments get a little closer to an approach advanced by the Chinese thinker, Mozi, who lived during the heyday of Legalism and taught that we can avoid fighting by making it unprofitable for enemies. Father and son, to be sure, both employ violence in ways that would have appalled Mozi. But Michael does so with greater frequency and brutality. By comparison, his father regularly got results without murder.

So, rather than killing or even causing physical injury to Woltz, the horse's head communicates that further resistance will be costly. Likewise, Vito sues for peace in order to bring his son home, but with the thinly veiled threat that any harm to Michael will be severely injurious to the rival crime families. Sometimes no threats are needed. In one instance, Vito merely approaches a greedy landlord in a placating way, asking him not to evict a widow and her son, even offering to pay additional rent on the woman's behalf. However, upon asking around, the landlord discovers Vito isn't to be trifled with, and obsequiously reduces the rent.

## Far Eastern Dons

Confucius's ideas were collected by students into the *Analects* after his death around 479 B.C.E. Confucius stressed hierarchy and piety to parents or elders, something obviously seen in the *Godfather* movies. Yet Confucius moved more towards meritocracy than was standard in his day because he insisted advisers should be chosen on the basis of ability, not birth. In *The Godfather*, Tom Haggen is an example. He's not Italian, nor is he related by blood to the Corleones. Yet he's the consigliere because of his loyalty, sagacity and legal training. He also gets shuffled out of the role at a time of heightened aggression because he's "not a wartime consigliere," meaning again that the role is assigned based on merit.

While stressing merit, Confucius simultaneously advocated a harmonious social order where people know their place. He said a father should take care of his sons, and rulers their people, just as sons and citizens should show deference to their superiors. Punishments can also be avoided by a skilled leader, who inspires admiration, devotion and therewith loyal behavior, as Vito in fact does with Enzo, Clemenza, and others.

For all this, subordinates should respectfully raise questions if their superiors are making mistakes, which is in the interest of harmony and the collective good. So, a leader following Confucian ideals will at times voice decisions only after hashing ideas out with subordinates, trying to reach agreement, thereby benefiting from collective wisdom and promoting harmony.

To be sure, Vito's criminal activity deviates from the upright proclivities of Confucianism (not to mention Buddhism and Daoism). But aside from this, the Corleone family structure runs pretty close to the great sage's ideal for society. There's deference to authority inasmuch as people honor Vito (and later Michael) as a wise elder. Simultaneously, subordinates such as Sonny and Tom advise and occasionally disagree with Vito, although recognizing he has final say. Vito's primarily interest is preserving his family, understood conventionally and also more broadly to include everyone under his care. This means he's after a kind of social harmony.

As compared to Confucianism, Daoist and Buddhist practices lean towards separation from society (for example, in monasteries) to cultivate personal enlightenment. Yet all these traditions esteem harmony as a central virtue. Despite arising outside of China, Buddhism shares a second feature with Daoism: an emphasis on relationality. Daoism emblemizes this with the symbol of Yin and Yang, which indicates that the cosmos consists of harmonies of contraries that mutually produce and support one another. As the *Dao De Jing* asserts, plentitude and absence generate each other, and difficulty and ease are mutually revealing, just as parents and children only *are* in virtue of one another, to put it in the terms of *The Godfather*. Buddhist teachings similarly hold that things rely upon one another for their existence. So, to give an example from physics, an object has no length in isolation since its dimensions vary according to the relative velocity at which it's encountered. A further point Buddhists stress is that everything is changing—in effect, always dying and being reborn.

On these grounds, Buddhists reject the idea that humans even have a self since anything identifiable as such is here now and gone an instant later. Buddhists add that the distinction between "me" and "not-me" doesn't make sense since individuals and their worlds are mutually defining. This view gets close to Daoist ideas. It's also not far from Confucianism. But this isn't because Confucius denied that the self exists. It's because he stressed relationality, believing the self is formed from hierarchal layers with family members, friends and the broader social-political community, and if we strip all this away, there's nothing left. Michael's lonely life attests to this since, by the end of the film, he's a hollow shell of a man precisely because he has no family relations. Vito likewise reinforces Confucian concepts of self since social bonds are everything to him. These ties literally make him who he is: the Godfather.

Vito's management style sometimes also conforms to a Daoist principle called *wu-wei*, meaning "effortless action." The idea here is that one can win by doing nothing. A leader acting within these precepts might take a hands-off approach when subordinates are functioning fine, and let them do their own thing, only interfering when underlings are way off course. This isn't exactly Vito's way, yet he exhibits something close to *wu-wei* when he offers to pay additional rent that the greedy landlord will get from another family on the condition that the widow be allowed to stay with her son and dog, which was the provocation for her eviction. Not only does the landlord let her stay upon learning who Vito is. He keeps lowering the rent as Vito sits with a passive smile. So, Vito's strategy here is to more or less do nothing until he gets the desired result.

Vito's motivations for aiding the widow are also illuminating. He probably would have just given her a little money to assist with a move had his wife not been present during the discussion as the woman's advocate. Since it's doubtful that Vito had much to gain from helping the widow, aside from slightly fortifying his reputation as patriarch, we have to conclude that while he has mild sympathy for her, his loving devotion to his wife is the main motivator.

This returns us to where we began. Vito descends into crime because he loves his family more than anything. Michael falls for the same reason, but comes to sacrifice what he was trying to protect. Acknowledging that "times are changing" and tacitly that he was born in a different land than his father, when his mother says "You can never lose your family," Michael relinquishes just that for personal power.

# 29

# Is Michael Fredo's Keeper?

WALTER BARTA AND GRAHAM LEE

Is killing your brother worse than killing a stranger? In other words, do we have more obligation towards some people than to others? In *The Godfather* trilogy we see Michael Corleone struggle with such questions as he navigates the complicated web of relationships that comprises the Corleone mafia family.

Like the Corleones, many philosophers have believed in the importance of *special obligations*: obligations towards a particular person or subset of people. These contrast with general obligations: obligations towards all people. To these philosophers, we are individuals with specific relationships with other individuals that provide special significance. Thus, our actions should be in some sense agent-relative: dependent upon who we are. Nineteenth-century philosopher Henry Sidgwick describes these as the obligations "appropriate to special relations and circumstances" (p. 312). Contemporary moral philosophers Thomas Nagel and Derek Parfit elaborate on these obligations as those that we have towards families, friends, colleagues, and those closest to us.

As an example of such a special obligation, consider the following: "No Sicilian will refuse a request on his daughter's wedding day." This is an obligation inasmuch as it prescribes a course of action: one will not refuse a request. However, it is also a *special* obligation in at least three ways: 1. it is only made by a *Sicilian*, 2. it is only made on a Sicilian *wedding day*, and 3. more specifically only for a Sicilian *daughter's* wedding day. In other words, it is special inasmuch as it specifies the persons to whom, by whom, for whom, where and when it is obliged. Although we may not all be Sicilian fathers on our daughter's wedding day, similar such special obligations are ubiquitous in our lives:

whether we are picking up oranges from the local grocery for our wife, babysitting our grandson in the vegetable garden, or delivering a cannoli. These specific duties for specific people seem to factor into our commonsense conceptions of what we ought to do on a day-to-day basis.

According to some philosophers (such as Immanuel Kant), there are no special obligations but universal ones. Others, like Sidgwick, believe these special obligations derive from more general ones. Some contemporary philosophers, like Samuel Scheffler and Alan John Simmons, believe that special obligations arise from agent-centered or positional duties. And yet, some, like Nagel and Parfit, worry that special obligations may undermine the impartiality, objectivity, and self-consistency of ethics.

Notably, throughout *The Godfather* trilogy, considerations regarding special obligations are paramount: a Godfather seems to be obliged and defined by his own specific set of duties. Furthermore, violating these special obligations seems to be Michael's ultimate unforgivable sin: the first death in the Bible, fratricide, the murder of brother by brother. At the end of the first part, Michael has murdered his brother-in-law Carlo Rizzi, husband to his sister and father to his godson; and worse still, at the end of the second part, he has murdered his blood brother Fredo. Even with all the murders under Michael's belt, the murder of a brother by brother seems *especially* bad. But how can we explain this special obligation and its special transgression? Is Michael Fredo's keeper?

## Universal Obligations

Firstly, some philosophers have argued that special obligations do not exist; rather, all ethical obligations are universal. In such a universalizing philosophy, special obligations are just a subset of the more general set of obligations. For example, Michael's obligation to his family would just be a small part of his general obligation to all of humanity. No matter who they are, a brother or a stranger, we owe them the same. We are all good Samaritans who owe kindness to strangers and in turn are owed kindness by strangers. In the terms of Christian doctrine, of which the Corleones, as good Catholic Italians, are supporters, this is the "Greatest Commandment": "love your neighbor as yourself."

The most famous philosopher to articulate universal obligations was Immanuel Kant, who believed that the only moral actions were "universalizable": correct for all persons in all circumstances. In Sidgwick's terms, these are "the more indefinite obligations which . . . correspond to the goodwill which we think ought to exist among all members of the human family." To Nagel, these are "neutral reasons and impersonal values" (p. 165). Some philosophers, notably Parfit, further believe that personal identity should not matter at all, from which the natural conclusion is that the only valid obligations are impersonal and universal. If true, special obligations can only be conceived in terms of and collapsed into these more general obligations. We are all neighbors in kind and our actions should thus be agent-neutral: independent of who we are.

For example, early on Michael serves in the military, even though his father wants him home running the family business. Presumably, Michael feels an obligation to something higher than his family or even his motherland of Italy, towards humanity in general, to serve in World War II against fascism. Michael's father chides him about this: "You would risk your life for strangers? . . . Anyone not in your family, is a stranger." However, others shower him with praise. His father's capo, Peter Clemenza, even says, "You know, Mike, we was all proud of you—being a hero and all. Your father, too."

Even the police let their guard down with Michael because of his selfless history; the corrupt police captain, Mark McCluskey, is assured by one of his fellow officers, "The kid's clean, Captain . . . He's a war hero, and he's never been mixed up in the rackets." Furthermore, Michael distances himself from his family, even telling his future wife, "That's my family, Kay. That's not me." In all this, Michael starts off universalizing about his obligations. His family is just one small part of the larger whole to which he has universal duty. For one who universalizes in this way, there is nothing special about brotherly obligation. Thus, Michael's murder of Fredo is bad, not because Fredo is a brother, but because Fredo is a person.

But universal obligations seem to pose a question: do universal duties ultimately supersede special duties? Sidgwick reframes the question: if marooned on an island with my own child and an abandoned orphan, am I obligated to care for both of them the same? (pp. 346–47). As Sidgwick frames it, treating the orphan differently seems intuitively wrong: duties seem owed to both children equally. The Corleones seem to apply such universal duties when they adopt Tom Hagen, a neighborhood orphan, and raise him as their own. But then, why do we so often feel justified treating our own children specially? After all, the Corleones never give Tom their last name, specially reserving that for their children by blood. So, if all obligations are universal, why does it seem as if some are special?

## Derivative Obligations

Some philosophers, like Sidgwick, believe that special obligations are merely "derivative obligations," derived from universal obligations due to the specific circumstances of persons. In
other words, the agent is the cause of an action and thus the
center of its area of effect, which decreases with distance. As
such, we may have a general obligation to all people, but we are
especially suited to help ourselves, due to our own special
knowledge of and access to ourselves (pp. 84, 439). Furthermore, because of our specific time and place and causal influence in the world, we may have more obligation to the specific
people around us. The family itself might simply be one local
extension of these derivative duties. Parents may be uniquely
positioned to care for their children when young and helpless;
and children may be uniquely positioned to care for their parents when old and infirm.

Certain people may be especially qualified for some actions.
Because of its unique Mediterranean climate, Sicily is especially good at producing olive oil; and because of its growing
melting-pot markets for international cuisine, America is especially good at consuming olive oil. And, because he is a native
Sicilian and an American immigrant, knowing both Italian and
English, Michael's father, Vito Corleone, is uniquely qualified
to become an importer of Italian goods. Thus, even though the
world is a better place when people have affordable access to
goods *generally*, Vito has a special qualification for importing
olive oil *specifically*.

Similarly, most persons are uniquely qualified to benefit the
people directly in their lives, to help people they know, specifically because they know them, being imparted with specific
knowledge about how in fact to benefit them: what they need,
want, and deserve. To use another example, if we are at the
market and see a man being shot, we have a specific obligation
to help because our proximity to him renders us uniquely capable of assistance in ways that a person across town is not. As a
bystander standing next to him, we might be able to apply
pressure and stop the blood flow, at least long enough for professional assistance to arrive. A person across town cannot render such aid: arriving at the scene for them might take longer
than it takes for him to bleed out. Thus, our special spatial
position and scope of causal influence lends derivative special
obligations. By this reasoning, the murder of Fredo is especially bad because Fredo is a person whom Michael specifically
has the ability to protect.

However, derivative obligations may not fully explain our obligations to our family. Derivative obligations only explain obligations to family members as long as we are uniquely qualified to help them, but they do not explain cases in which we are not. Michael is derivatively obligated to protect his father so long as he is at the side of his hospital bed, but not when he is on the other side of town. Similarly, when Michael flees to Italy and his family is less able to immediately provide protection for him, they seem to have no derivative obligation to do so. But these conclusions seem contrary to intuition because we often believe that we're obliged to family members even when we're not qualified to help them. Michael seems to feel obligated to protect his father and brothers, even when doing so would be inconvenient.

## Agent-Centered Obligations

Other philosophers have justified these special obligations with self-interested reasoning. For example, Samuel Scheffler suggests that, in order to be properly motivated, obligations are always self-interested (p. 14). Scheffler describes this as "agent-centered": "each agent would have the prerogative to devote energy and attention to his projects and commitments out of proportion to their weight in the impersonal calculus." Sidgwick seems to agree with a version of this point, suggesting that we "do not hold the reasonableness of aiming at happiness generally with any stronger conviction than we do that of aiming at one's own." Although it's reasonable to be an altruist, it's just as reasonable to be an egoist. The agent, as the person beholden to the action, is the center of motivating factors, which radiate outward into their various relationships. Although Michael has general duties to all people, those duties can be stronger when more important to him personally. Michael has a special obligation to brothers and sisters, as his immediate family members; after that, Michael has obligations to his cousins, uncles, and aunts; after that to his second cousins, third cousins, etc. The extent of Michael's duties may depend upon the interpersonal distance between himself and those to whom he is dutiful. Thus, we can easily derive a family-first philosophy. Michael is still obligated to strangers, but only in a more distant, tangential, and secondhand way than to his family.

So, according to this model, Michael can justify his special regard for his loved ones. When Michael says that he is merely protecting his family, and then proceeds to murder four other mafia families, a case can be made that he is justified according to an agent-centered view. Namely, Michael is specially obligated to protect his immediate family, and universally obligated to protect others; but when others threaten his immediate family, his special obligation can supersede his general obligation. So, by the agent-centered view, the murder of Fredo is especially bad because Fredo as *his* brother is especially important to Michael personally.

However, as some have noted, this form of special obligation seems at odds with universal obligations, not supplementary to them. We can see that agent-centered action is precisely contrary to agent-neutral action in many cases. Indeed, taking agent-centered action to its logical extreme, the strongest obligation of all seems to be a person's obligation to himself. Indeed, in certain ways, Michael's actions often seem self-serving. As he says himself, "I command this family, right or wrong! It was *not* what I *wanted!*" He frames the family in terms of himself, centered on himself. For example, when he divorces his wife, Kay, he insists on taking his children to raise as his own. In a case like this, being raised by Kay, away from the mafia business, may genuinely be the safer course of action for his children; however, raising his children himself seems to be the course of action that will bring Michael the most personal satisfaction. Indeed, if the family is defined in terms of Michael himself, then Michael can simply dismiss members from the family, as he does with Fredo, saying, "Fredo, you're nothing to me now. You're not a brother, you're not a friend. I don't want to know you or what you." In other words, agent-centered obligations may bottom out in mere selfishness, which seems contrary to what special obligations should be.

## Positional Obligations

However, some philosophers have argued for positional obligations: ethical obligations grounded in positional relationships. According to such a model, we may have special obligations to family members, due to their positional status as our blood relations, as well as to people in other social positions—such as employers, employees, neighbors, citizens, law officials. In other words, we are family members and community members with specific, complex relationships. In Christian terms, these take the form of "honor thy mother and father" and being "my brother's keeper," which the Catholic Corleones would abide by.

In philosophical terms, Sidgwick explains that many philosophers "consider man in his social relations—as father, son, neighbor, citizen—and endeavor to determine the 'natural' rights and obligations that attach to such relations" (p. 82). Contemporary philosopher A.J. Simmons defines them: "positional duties are requirements which must be met in order to fill some position successfully" (p. 13). Different positions have different duties. Families have family values: honoring each other's bonds of kinship. Similarly, professionals, like doctors and lawyers, have professional values: taking the Hippocratic oath and treating patients, upholding the law and defending their clients. Likewise, the position of Godfather might come with its own positional duties.

Indeed, Michael's entrance into the Mafia begins and ends with the duty he feels as a family member. Michael is in the position of being his father's son. For example, when corrupt police arrive at the hospital to assassinate his father, Michael chooses his familial duty to his father over his more general duty to following the law. From then on, Michael frames most of his choices around his position as Godfather in protecting his family. The Corleones insist on this family-first attitude. Michael's father claims that "a man who doesn't spend time with his family can never be a real man" and Michael himself claims, "I spent my life protecting my son. I spent my life protecting my *family!*" The Corleones certainly seem to define themselves in terms of these positional relations. Indeed, Michael's father, Vito, declines to have Carlo, his son-in-law, murdered, due to his position as Godfather; and, likewise, while Michael's mother is alive, she declines to have Fredo, her son by blood, murdered. Even though Carlo and Fredo have betrayed the family, Michael's parents' parental duties towards their sons are too strong. So, when Michael indeed does the deed, the murders are especially bad because Carlo is a brother-in-law and Fredo is a brother, each bearing their special positional relations to Michael.

However, the existence of positional obligation seems difficult to justify and uncomfortable in consequence. Firstly, it is not clear that a natural fact like brotherhood should bring any new ethical obligation to bear or justify it in any way. Perhaps we believe that blood-relation is a natural criterion of moral duty, as some sociobiologists perhaps believe. Or, perhaps a shared upbringing and ongoing relationship bears special moral purchase because of the experiences, emotions, and histories—what Sidgwick might call duties of the "the stronger affections" (p. 312).

Contemporary philosopher Harry Frankfurt has described these further as "the reasons of love." Or, perhaps brotherly guardianship has specific contractual ramifications, like a promise made that is legally or morally binding. But, while these considerations certainly bear biological, emotional, and legal resonance, it is less clear why they should bear moral resonance. Secondly, brotherhood can lead to bad consequences as often as not. For example, during World War II, the very enemy that Michael fought against, the army of Germany under Hitler, was motivated towards genocide by an ethic of positional duties: those of German nationalism and blood-relation: pro-Aryan and anti-Semitic. The logical extremes of these positional obligations do not seem to have pretty consequences.

## Conflicting Obligations

Furthermore, regardless of their justifications, special obligations seem to involve inevitable conflicts. Parfit develops this idea into what he calls the "Parent's Dilemma": if everyone takes special care of their own children, then they may neglect the children of others and their children may be neglected by others, which undermines the purpose of the special care in the first place (pp. 95–98). In other words, if everyone adopts their own set of special obligations, then these special obligations lose specialness. Parfit believes this dilemma disqualifies special obligations from universal adoption because they are self-defeating.

This problem only multiplies as we add more obligations. If the Corleones have a special obligation to their family, and the Barzinis have a special obligation to their family, then in any case of conflict between families their purposes will be irreconcilable. But, worse still, if there are five families there will be as many special obligations: five special obligations. It follows that each may conflict with each, so there may be a square of that many conflicts of special obligations: $5^2 = 5 \times 5 = 25$ conflicts (for example: Corleone vs. Barzini, Corleone vs. Tattaglia, Corleone vs. Cuneo, Corleone vs. Stracci, and even Corleone vs. Corleone; and so on for each of the other families.) There will also be a factorial of 5 ways of ordering the priorities of the special obligations: $5! \times 4 \times 3 \times 2 \times 1 = 120$ orderings (Corleone first, Barzini second, Tattaglia third, Cuneo fourth, Stracci fifth; and so on). The more duties the more complex the situation gets: no wonder the five families couldn't get along!

Seemingly all special obligations are put to the test in this manner, for even a single special obligation may conflict with itself. For instance, in honoring his obligation to his family, Michael finds himself forced to choose between various family members, all of whom he owes familial obligation, but none of whom he owes exclusive familial obligation. Competing with fellow brothers, both Carlo and Fredo, and yet obliged to both as brothers, Michael is unavoidably conflicted and compromised. Michael's conflict with Carlo begins when Carlo beats up Michael's sister Connie and ends when Carlo betrays the Corleones for a rival family, for which Michael has him murdered, much to Connie's dismay. Michael's conflict with Fredo begins when he chastises Fredo for siding with Moe Greene, "Fredo you're my older brother, and I love you. But don't you ever go against the family again. Ever." Then it is brought to a head when Fredo betrays Michael for Hyman Roth, leading to Michael's wife and kids being almost murdered by machine gun fire. Michael has Fredo murdered as well, even though Fredo is arguably the closest relation that Michael has left. Carlo's and Fredo's betrayals place them outside of the family, outside of the sphere of special obligations, because they conflict with the interests of other family members, especially Michael's. Accordingly, the murder of Carlo and then Fredo is a necessary evil, because Michael has become embroiled in a zero-sum game of conflicting special obligations, forcing him to choose between non-ideal outcomes.

## Conclusive Obligations?

No matter how we characterize it, through the murder of his brothers, Carlo and Fredo, Michael rejects numerous special and general obligations. Michael removes his brothers from universal, agent-centered, positional, and interpersonal consideration. For all his pains, it's hard to imagine a person like Michael happy. As Sidgwick puts it, "the tyrant, who is represented as necessarily suspicious of those nearest him, even of the members of his own family, we feel prepared to admit that such a life must involve the extreme of unhappiness" (p. 166). From Sidgwick's point of view, Michael becomes a moral monster, digging his own grave of familial betrayal, ethically and personally.

As *The Godfather* story teaches, many special obligations come with our relationships, but these bring special moral challenges. A Godfather's duty to his brother may conflict with his duties to his other family members, which themselves may conflict with his duty to others. Balancing these various obligations is part of the complexity of the human condition, as complicated beings living in expansive worlds with sometimes conflicting values.

# Bibliography

Alicke, M.D. 1992. Culpable Causation. *Journal of Personality and Social Psychology*. 63:3.

Aristotle. 1943. *Politics*. Random House.

———. 2009. *Nicomachean Ethics*. Oxford University Press.

———. 2011. *Eudemian Ethics*. Oxford University Press.

Asmis, Elizabeth, Shadi Bartsch, and Martha C. Nussbaum. 2012. Seneca and His World. In Robert A. Kaster and Martha C. Nussbaum, eds. *Seneca: Anger, Mercy, Revenge*. University of Chicago Press.

Cicero. 1987. *De Finibus*. In A.A. Long and D. Sedley, eds., *The Hellenistic Philosophers*. Volume I. Cambridge University Press.

Seneca, Lucius Annaeus. 1969. *Letters from a Stoic*. Penguin.

Barkun, Michael. 2003. *A Culture of Conspiracy: Apocalyptic Visions in Contemporary America*. University of California Press.

Baumeister, R.F., E. Bratslavsky, C. Finkenauer, and K.D. Vohs. 2001. Bad Is Stronger than Good. *Review of General Psychology* 5:4.

Belliotti. Raymond Angelo. 2013. *Jesus or Nietzsche: How Should We Live Our Lives?* Rodopi.

———. 2016. *Power: Oppression, Subservience, and Resistance*. State University of New York Press.

———. 2021. *The Godfather and Sicily: Power, Honor, Family, and Evil*. State University of New York Press.

———. 2022. *Heroism and Wisdom, Italian Style: From Roman Imperialists to Sicilian Magistrates*. Fairleigh Dickinson University Press.

Butter, Michael. 2020. *The Nature of Conspiracy Theories*. Polity.

Caplan, Bryan. 2013. Some Wisdom of Don Corleone. Econlib <www.econlib.org/archives/2013/02/some_wisdom_of.html>.

Carrol, Noel. 2003. The Wheel of Virtue: Art, Literature, and Moral Knowledge. *Journal of Aesthetics and Art Criticism.*

Cheeda, Saim. 2019. The Godfather: 10 Wisest Don Corleone Quotes. Screenrant. <https://screenrant.com/the-godfather-don-corleone-wise-best-quotes>.

Citron, Marcia J. 2004. Operatic Style and Structure in Coppola's "Godfather Trilogy." *Musical Quarterly* 87:3 (Autumn).

Clark, C.J. 2022. The Blame Efficiency Hypothesis: An Evolutionary Framework to Resolve Rationalist and Intuitionist Theories of Moral Condemnation. In T. Nadelhoffer and A. Monroe, eds., *Advances in Experimental Philosophy of Free Will and Responsibility.* Bloomsbury.

Clark, C.J., R.F. Baumeister, and P.H. Ditto. 2017. Making Punishment Palatable: Belief in Free Will Alleviates Punitive Distress. *Consciousness and Cognition* 51.

Clark, C.J. Luguri, J.B., Ditto, P.H. Knobe, J., A.F. Shariff, and R.F. Baumeister. 2014. Free to Punish: A Motivated Account of Free Will Belief. *Journal of Personality and Social Psychology* 106.

Clark, C.J., A. Shniderman, J.B. Luguri, R.F. Baumeister, and P.H. Ditto. 2018. Are Morally Good Actions Ever Free?. *Consciousness and Cognition* 63.

Coase, R.H. 1959. The Federal Communications Commission. *Journal of Law and Economics* 2 (October) <www.jstor.org/stable/724927>.

———. 1960. The Problem of Social Cost. *Journal of Law and Economics* 3 (October) <www.jstor.org/stable/724810>.

Coppola, Francis Ford, director. 1972. *The Godfather.* Paramount Pictures.

———. 1972. *The Godfather Deleted Scene: Going to Portella Delle Ginestre* (Paramount Pictures, 1972), <https://www.youtube.com/watch?v=t7HjHWYbyEQ>.

———. 1974. *The Godfather Part II.* Paramount.

———. 1990. *The Godfather Part III.* Paramount.

———. 2020. *The Godfather Coda: The Death of Michael Corleone.* Paramount.

Empire. 2020. The 100 Greatest Movie Characters <https://www.empireonline.com/movies/features/100-greatest-movie-characters>.

Frankfurt, Harry G. 2006. *Taking Ourselves Seriously and Getting It Right.* Stanford University Press.

———. 2019 [2004]. *The Reasons of Love.* Princeton University Press.

Gragg, Larry D. 2015. *Benjamin "Bugsy" Siegel: The Gangster, the Flamingo, and Making of Modern Las Vegas.* Praeger.

Gramsci, Antonio. 2000. Some Aspects of the Southern Question. In David Forgacs, ed., *The Gramsci Reader: Selected Writings 1916–1935.* New York University Press.

Greene, Richard, and Rachel Robison-Greene, eds. 2020. *Conspiracy Theories: Philosophers Connect the Dots*. Open Court.

Griswold, Charles. 2007. *Forgiveness: A Philosophical Exploration*. Cambridge University Press.

Haidt, Jonathan. 2001. The Emotional Dog and Its Rational Tail: A Social Intuitionist Approach to Moral Judgment. *Psychological Review*.

Hall, Edith. 2020 [2018]. *Aristotle's Way: How Ancient Wisdom Can Change Your Life*. Penguin.

Hobbes, Thomas. 2017 [1651]. *Leviathan*. Penguin.

Hooker, Brad. 2015. The Elements of Well-Being. *Journal of Practical Ethics*.

Huston, Mark. 2020. The Greatest Conspiracy Theory Movies. In Richard Greene and Rachel Robison-Greene, eds., *Conspiracy Theories: Philosophers Connect the Dots*. Open Court.

Kant, Immanuel, 2020. *Groundwork of the Metaphysics of Morals*. Oxford University Press.

Kekes, John. 1983. Wisdom. *American Philosophical Quarterly* 20.

Knobe, J. 2003. Intentional Action and Side Effects in Ordinary Language. *Analysis* 63:3.

Kopko, K.C., S.M. Bryner, J. Budziak, C.J. Devine, and S.P. Nawara. 2011. In the Eye of the Beholder? Motivated Reasoning in Disputed Elections. *Political Behavior* 33:2.

Lavine, T.Z. 1984. *From Socrates to Sartre: The Philosophic Quest*. Bantam.

Lindemann, Hilde. 2016 [2014]. *Holding and Letting Go: The Social Practice of Personal Identities*. Oxford University Press.

Machiavelli, Niccolò. 2003. *The Prince*. Penguin.

McFarland, Ian A. et al., eds. 2011. *The Cambridge Dictionary of Christian Theology*. Cambridge University Press.

MacKinnon, Catharine. 1991. *Toward a Feminist Theory of the State*. Harvard University Press.

Manne, Kate. 2017. *Down Girl: The Logic of Misogyny*. Oxford University Press.

Marx, Karl, and Friedrich Engels. 1992 [1848]. *The Communist Manifesto*. Bantam.

Mill, John Stuart. 1978 [1859]. *On Liberty*. Hackett.

Nagel, Thomas. 1985. *The View from Nowhere*. Oxford University Press.

Nietzsche, Friedrich. 1954 [1889]. *Twilight of the Idols*. Penguin.

———. 1954. Thus Spoke Zarathustra. In Walter Kaufmann, ed., *The Portable Nietzsche*. Viking.

———. 1966. *Beyond Good and Evil: Prelude to a Philosophy of the Future*. Random House.

———. 1967. *The Will to Power*. Random House.

———. 1967. *Ecce Homo*. Random House.

———. 1974. *The Gay Science*. Random House.

———. 2000. *The Antichrist*. Prometheus.

———. 2008. *Beyond Good and Evil: Prelude to a Philosophy for the Future*. Floating Press.

Nozick, Robert. 1989. *The Examined Life*. Touchstone.

Okin, Susan Moller. 1991. *Justice, Gender, and the Family*. Basic Books.

Parfit, Derek. 1984. *Reasons and Persons*. Oxford University Press.

Paul, L.A. 2016 [2014]. *Transformative Experience*. Oxford University Press.

Plato.1997. Republic. In *Plato: Complete Works*. Hackett.

Plato, *The Republic*. Translated by Benjamin Jowett, (Auckland, New Zealand: The Floating Press. 2009), p. 475.

Premiere Magazine. 100 Greatest movie characters of all-time. <www.filmsite.org/100characters4.html>.

Puzo, Mario. 1969. *The Godfather*. Putnam's.

———. 1972. *The Godfather Papers and Other Confessions*. Putnam's.

———. 1979 [1978]. *Fools Die: A Thriller*. Signet.

———. 1997 [1996]. *The Last Don*. Ballantine.

———. 2001. *The Family*. Morrow.

———. 2001 [1984]. *The Sicilian*. Ballantine.

———. 2001 [2000]. *Omertà*. Ballantine.

———. 2004 [1992]. *The Fortunate Pilgrim*. Ballantine.

———. 2019 [1969]. *The Godfather*. 50th Anniversary Edition. Berkley.

Puzo, Mario, and Francis Ford Coppola. 1971. *The Godfather Screenplay*. Paramount Pictures <https://indiegroundfilms.files.wordpress.com/2014/01/godfather-mar-1-79-numbered-2nd.pdf>.

Royce, Josiah. 2005. *The Basic Writing of Josiah Royce, Volume II: Logic, Loyalty, and Community*. Fordham University Press.

Ryan, Richard, and Edward Deci. 2012. Multiple Identities within a Single Self. In Mark Leary and June Tangney, eds., *The Handbook of Self and Identity*. Guilford.

Scheffler, Samuel. 1982. *The Rejection of Consequentialism*. Oxford University Press.

Seal, Mark. 2021. *Leave the Gun, Take the Cannoli: The Epic Story of the Making of The Godfather*. Simon and Schuster.

Shapiro, Ian. 1986. *The Evolution of Rights in Liberal Theory*. Cambridge University Press.

Sidgwick, Henry. 1962. *The Methods of Ethics*. Seventh edition. Palgrave Macmillan.

Simmons, Alan John. 1979. *Moral Principles and Political Obligations*. Princeton University Press.

Souza, Raymond J. de. 2022. Spiritual Wisdom from 'The Godfather'. National Catholic Register

<www.ncregister.com/commentaries/spiritual-wisdom-from-the-godfather>.

Stoljar, Natalie. 2018. Feminist Perspectives on Autonomy. *The Stanford Encyclopedia of Philosophy* <https://plato.stanford.edu/archives/win2018/entries/feminism-autonomy/>.

Strohminger, Nina, Joshua Knobe, and George Newman. 2017. The True Self: A Psychological Concept Distinct from the Self. *Perspectives on Psychological Science*.

Suetonius. 1914. *The Lives of the Caesars*. Two volumes. Loeb Classical Library. Harvard University Press. Roman numeral references in parentheses are to the paragraph number in the life of that particular Caesar.

———. 2007. *The Twelve Caesars*. Penguin.

Swanson, Judith. 1992. *The Public and the Private in Aristotle's Political Philosophy*. Cornell University Press.

Tetlock, P.E. 2002. Social Functionalist Frameworks for Judgment and Choice: Intuitive Politicians, Theologians, and Prosecutors. *Psychological Review* 109:3.

Tiberius, Valerie. 2007. *The Reflective Life: Living Wisely With Our Limits*. Oxford University Press.

Vidal, Gore. 1962 [1959]. Robert Graves and the Twelve Caesars. In Vidal, *Rocking the Boat*. Little, Brown.

Winegard, B.M., C.J. Clark, C.R., and R.F. Baumeister, R.F. In press. Equalitarianism: A Source of Liberal Bias. *Journal of Open Inquiry in Behavioral Science*.

Winegardner, Mark. 2004. *The Godfather Returns*. Random House.

# La Famiglia

**WALTER BARTA** is a research lead studying literary and philosophical topics for the M.D. Anderson Library at the University of Houston and definitely didn't have any fellow academics whacked to get that position.

**JOE BARTZEL** is a postdoctoral fellow in the Program in American Culture Studies at Washington University in St. Louis. He received a PhD in religious studies from Indiana University, with an emphasis on ethics, philosophy, and politics in the study of religion. Joe's research focuses primarily on public practices of reconciliation in the United States, but he never talks business at the dinner table.

**RAYMOND ANGELO BELLIOTTI** is State University of New York Distinguished Teaching Professor of Philosophy Emeritus. He is the author of twenty-six books including *The Godfather and Sicily: Power, Honor, Family, and Evil* (2021). Notably frugal, he still owns the original paperback version of *The Godfather* he bought in 1969.

**ARLENE BHUIYAN KHAN** is an engineer, independent scholar, and mother of two who schemes about taking over the world one philosophy paper at a time.

**COLIN BUNN** plans to graduate with a Bachelor's degree in philosophy from Christopher Newport University in 2023. His research focuses on existentialism and adaptive leadership theory. His greatest strength is that he always makes sure to leave the gun and take the cannoli.

My name is **CORY(LEONE) CLARK**. I am a Visiting Faculty Scholar in the Psychology and Management Departments at University of Pennsylvania. I've always liked to drink wine, but I am drinking more anyway.

**MATTHEW CRIPPEN**'s publications intersect philosophical history, psychology and cross-cultural issues relating to ethics, politics, and aesthetics. He enjoys academic appointments at universities in Korea and Germany, and sometimes proffers his students lessons so that they can't *not* be disabused.

BRUNO ĆURKO PhD is an assistant professor in the Department for teachers in the Faculty of Humanities and Social Sciences, University of Split, founder and secretary of the *Association for supporting non-formal education, critical thinking and philosophy in practice "Petit Philosophy,"* and leader since 2007 of the Croatian delegation to the International Philosophical Olympiad. In short, he tries to teach children and adults to think critically.

TIMOTHY DUNN is an Associate Professor of Philosophy at the University of Wisconsin Milwaukee. Nothing he said about Michael or Vito Corleone in this volume was personal—it was just business.

ERIC FLEURY is an Assistant Professor of Government and International Relations at Connecticut College. His wife never asks him about his business. His son is smarter than he is; he reads the funny papers. And he is raising his daughter in the American fashion.

LANDON FRIM is Associate Professor of Philosophy and Religious Studies at Florida Gulf Coast University. He writes books and popular articles on radical thinkers from Spinoza to Marx. His essay traces the *Godfather* trilogy from Old-World Feudalism, through New-World capitalism, to socialist revolution. He might be an egalitarian commie at heart, but if you ask his kids about him, they'll say, "My father is no different than any powerful man, any man with power, like a president or senator."

RICHARD GREENE is a Professor of Philosophy at Weber State University, where he also directs the Richard Richards Institute for Ethics. He is the author of *Spoiler Alert: It's A Book about the Philosophy of Spoilers* (2019), co-author of *Conspiracy Theories in the Time of Coronavirus* (2022), and the editor or twenty or so books on philosophy and pop culture. He is co-host of the popular podcast I Think, Therefore I Fan. Richard holds office hours on Monday, Tuesday, Thursday, Wednesday, Friday, Sunday, Saturday.

F.E. GUERRA-PUJOL received his JD from Yale Law School. Currently, he is a professor at the University of Central Florida. His research interests include illegal markets and his hobbies involve model trains, chess, and Latin jazz.

MATTHEW HAMMERTON is Assistant Professor of Philosophy at Singapore Management University. He specializes in moral philosophy and has published articles on well-being, meaning in life, consequentialism, and moral reasoning. Despite being a little bit scared of the real Mafia, he likes playing the Mafia role in the social deduction game, Mafia.

**JOSHUA HETER** is an Associate Professor of Philosophy at Jefferson College in Hillsboro, Missouri. He co-edited *Asimov's Foundation and Philosophy* (2023), *Punk Rock and Philosophy* (2022), *Better Call Saul and Philosophy* (2022), *Westworld and Philosophy* (2019), and *The Man in the High Castle and Philosophy* (2017). Each of these volumes took so much time and effort that prior to working on this book, he had planned on taking a good long break from his editing duties. But, just when he thought he was out, *they pulled him back in!*

**ALEXANDER E. HOOKE** is a philosophy professor at Stevenson University. His most recent books are *Alphonso Lingis and Existential Genealogy* (2019) and *Philosophy Sketches: 700 Words at a Time* (second edition, 2018). He has unknowingly practiced Omertà (the law of silence) at innumerable faculty meetings, where everything is personal and business—except that your death is immersed in tedium rather than bloodshed.

**MARK HUSTON** is currently Associate Professor and Chair of Philosophy at Schoolcraft College located in Livonia, Michigan. He has published articles and essays in the journals *Ratio, Film and Philosophy*, *The Journal of Philosophical Research* and in the books *Tennis and Philosophy* (2010) and *Golf and Philosophy* (2010). Mark has given numerous talks on conspiracy theories, both locally and nationally, including the keynote address at the 2015 Forest Park International Festival at St. Louis Community College. His most recent publications include "Medical Conspiracy Theories and Medical Errors" in the *International Journal of Applied Philosophy*, "Beyond *Apocalypse Now*: Just War Theory and Existentialism" in *The Community College Humanities Review*, and "The Greatest Conspiracy Theory Movies" in *Conspiracy Theories: Philosophers Connect the Dots* (2020). Mark currently keeps his funds in the Vatican bank, along with the rest of the Illuminati . . . but don't tell anyone; it's a secret.

**CHRISTOPHER M. INNES** earned his PhD from Goldsmiths College, University of London, where he was made an offer he could not refuse. His PhD in Social and Political Philosophy allows him to explore the many platitudes of a gangster's life. He now teaches philosophy at Boise State University in Idaho, and like any university, he has got to watch his step, keep his mouth shut, and not go against the Department. Unlike Fredo, the word is not out that he has been talking.

My name is **CHRISTOPHER JANAWAY**. I teach philosophy at the University of Southampton in the UK. For years I've spent much of my time reading people like Plato, Nietzsche and Schopenhauer. I don't apologize, that's my life.

**JENNIFER KLING** is an Assistant Professor of Philosophy at the University of Colorado, Colorado Springs, where she teaches social and political philosophy. She writes on war and peace, protest, feminism, and American racism, maintains excellent relationships with her grocers, and never forgets a favor.

ANTONIO KOVAČEVIĆ is a researcher and writer for the NGO "Petit Philosophy," Zadar, Croatia. Don't ask him about his business; he's still trying to figure out what he's doing. Holding an MA in History and Philosophy, his interests cover more topics than he's realistically capable of processing. These include ancient philosophy and history, bioethics and ethics, Socratic dialogue, fantasy, and cinema.

TIMOTHY M. KWIATEK is a philosophy PhD candidate at Cornell University. He works on moral psychology and teaches Buddhist philosophy. He is not under subpoena and his reputation in his own country is impeccable.

GRAHAM LEE holds an MA in Philosophy from the University of Houston. While he enjoys writing about philosophy, he carefully heeds a wise man's advice to never let anyone know what he is thinking.

MICHEL LE GALL is a former Associate Professor of Middle Eastern History at St. Olaf College in Northfield, Minnesota. He received his PhD from Princeton University. His research interests and specializations include the Near East and North Africa. He is the co-editor of, and contributor to, *The Maghrib in Question: History and Historiography* (1997) and also authored several articles on late nineteenth-century Ottoman Libya. A recovering academic, he is currently a senior business writer at a New York-based global consultancy and, with Dr. Charles Taliaferro, has contributed to several volumes in the series *The Philosophy of* ...

ABIGAIL LEVIN is an Associate Professor of Philosophy at Niagara University, in Lewiston, New York. When not teaching social and political philosophy, you can likely find her in her kitchen, attempting to perfect a Clemenza-worthy red sauce.

COLIN J. LEWIS PhD is a Senior Instructor in the Department of Philosophy and Director of the Asian Studies minor at the University of Colorado, Colorado Springs. He is the author of *Confucian Ritual and Moral Education* (2020), and has authored articles in such journals as *Dao*, *Asian Philosophy*, *Journal of Military Ethics*, and *Educational Philosophy and Theory*.

CASEY RENTMEESTER is the Director of Academic Success and Associate Professor of Philosophy at Bellin College in Green Bay, Wisconsin. He is author of *Heidegger and the Environment*, co-editor of *Heidegger and Music*, and has written numerous articles and book chapters on philosophy. He agrees with Vito that a man who doesn't spend time with his family can never be a real man, as he spends most of his free time with his wife and three children in De Pere, Wisconsin.

**ALEXANDRA ROMANYSHYN:** just this one time, she'll let you ask her about her affairs. She is an Assistant Professor of Philosophy at Seattle University, and her research interests include philosophy of psychology, the self, and identity.

**SAMANTHA SEYBOLD** is a graduate student in philosophy at Purdue University. She enjoys teaching and studying feminist philosophy, epistemology, and ethics. Memes and obscure popular culture references abound in her classes, in the hopes that her students see why studying philosophy is something that they can't refuse (because it's so fun!). She's expecting her PhD in 2023.

**ERIC J. SILVERMAN** is Professor of Philosophy at Christopher Newport University. He has interests in ethics, philosophy of religion, and medieval philosophy. He has authored or co-authored thirty articles and book chapters, as well as published five books including *The Ultimate Game of Thrones and Philosophy* (2016). He likes to say that ice cream sundae is a dish best served cold. Strangely, no one ever thinks this is a profound insight.

**EDDIE TAFOYA** is a professor of English at New Mexico Highlands University in Las Vegas, New Mexico, and is the author of the book *The Marxist Revolution: How Chico, Harpo, Groucho, and Zeppo Changed how we Laugh* and the novel *Finding the Buddha: A Dark Story of Genius, Friendship, and Stand-up Comedy* (2015). He lives in Albuquerque, where he studies gangsters, comedy, philosophy, and how to finagle, sneak, bribe, and extort his way into Plato's World of Pure Forms.

**CHARLES TALIAFERRO**, Professor Emeritus of Philosophy, St. Olaf College, godfather of Marcus and Nicholas, is eternally grateful that the brilliant Dr. Sally Engebritson has rescued him from sleeping with the fishes on multiple occasions. With Dr. Michel Le Gall, Charles has contributed to other pop culture and philosophy volumes.

**FR. TED VITALI**, CP PhD is a Catholic priest in the Passionist Congregation, hence the CP after his name. He is also an Associate Professor in the Philosophy Department where he earned his PhD in 1976. After teaching and chairing at Bellarmine College/University in Louisville, he returned to SLU in 1989 to chair the Philosophy Department until 2017. When asked by an incoming Dean of the College what his AOS was, Fr. Vitali replied: "chairing." And so it has been such for the vast amount of his academic career in higher education. Perhaps that is why he has been affectionately called and given the title "The Godfather."

**ALEX VRABELY** is currently expecting a PhD from Purdue University in 2024. His research interests include Ancient Greek philosophy and social ontology as well as metaphysics. As far as he knows, the Mafia doesn't even exist.

**Bo Winegard** has a PhD in social psychology and is an executive editor for *Aporia Magazine*, but he considers thinking about the *Godfather* movies vastly more important than anything he has accomplished in academia. If time allows, he may write a three-volume defense of *The Godfather Part III*, which will be his magnum opus.

**Iris Hiu Man Yeung** is a citizen of Hong Kong and China. Fluent in English, Cantonese, and Mandarin (the language, not the fruit), she's interested in philosophy, psychology, and criminal law. She also likes oranges and has an obsession with baked goods, including cannoli.

# Index

# The Ultimate *Supernatural* and Philosophy

## *Saving People, Killing Things, the Family Business*

VOLUME 3 IN THE OPEN UNIVERSE SERIES,
POP CULTURE AND PHILOSOPHY®

### Edited by Richard Greene

*"This book invites thoughtful fans of the hit TV show to explore heroism, morality, evil, freewill, and, well, the supernatural.* The Ultimate Supernatural and Philosophy *embodies what good philosophy writing should be: deeply reflective yet instantly readable."*

—JACK BOWEN, author of *The Dream Weaver: One Boy's Journey through th Landscape of Reality* (2006)

*"In* The Ultimate Supernatural and Philosophy, *the many layers of* Supernatural *are explored by creative, first-rate philosophers. You should read this book if you want to investigate the show's epic display of demons and angels, evil and good, the merely human and the supernatural."*

—CHARLES TALIAFERRO, author of *Cascade Companion to Evil* (2020)

*"Imagine Job takes a road trip with god and the devil. This is the journey you sign up for in* The Ultimate Supernatural and Philosophy. *Questions of good and evil, our culture, and our identity are some of the sights you'll see. Buckle up!"*

—JAMEY HEIT, author of *Vader, Voldemort, and Other Villains* (2011)

RICHARD GREENE is Professor of Philosophy at Weber State University and co-host, with Rachel Robison-Greene, of the pop culture and philosophy podcast, I Think, Therefore I Fan. He wrote the definitive and much-acclaimed study, *Spoiler Alert! (It's a Book about the Philosophy of Spoilers)* (2019), and co-wrote, with Rachel Robison-Greene, *Conspiracy Theories in the Time of Coronavirus* (2022).

ISBN 978-1-63770-010-5 (paperback)
ISBN 978-1-63770-011-2 (ebook)

**AVAILABLE FROM ALL BOOKSTORES AND ONLINE BOOKSELLERS**

For more information on Open Universe books, visit us at

**www.carusbooks.com**